Angela Lee

Language and Understanding

Language and Understanding

Edited by:
Gillian Brown, Kirsten Malmkjær, Alastair
Pollitt, and John Williams

*Research Centre for English and Applied
Linguistics, University of Cambridge*

Oxford University Press 1994

Oxford University Press
Walton Street, Oxford OX2 6DP

Oxford New York Toronto
Delhi Bombay Calcutta Madras Karachi
Pataling Jaya Singapore Hong Kong Tokyo
Nairobi Dar es Salaam Cape Town
Melbourne Auckland

and associated companies in
Berlin Ibadan

Oxford and *Oxford English* are trade marks of Oxford
University Press

ISBN 0 19 437 191 3

Set in 10/12 pt Sabon.
Typeset by Wyvern Typesetting Ltd, Bristol.
Printed in Hong Kong

Contents

Acknowledgements

The editors and publishers would like to thank the following for permission to reproduce material that falls within their copyright:

Cambridge University Press and the authors for an extract from *Communicative Methodology in Language Teaching* (1984) by C. J. Brumfit; and for two figures from *Dialectology* (1980) by J. K. Chambers and P. Trudgill.

Blackwell and the author for a table from *On Dialect* (1983) by P. Trudgill.

News International for an extract from the *Sun* newspaper, 21 June 1984 © News International.

Every effort has been made to trace the owners of copyright material in this book, but we should be pleased to hear from any copyright holder whom we have been unable to contact.

Preface

In putting together this volume, we have benefited from discussions with the participants in the Summer Institute in English and Applied Linguistics held at Downing College, Cambridge, in July 1991. The participants, young scholars and distinguished academics alike, shared with us and with the contributors to this volume their own insights, drawn from their own varied experience. We have tried to take account of their comments in our introductions to individual contributions, clarifying certain concepts, and drawing out implications for teaching, testing, and research.

We are grateful to the contributors for making their papers available so readily, and for their prompt responses during the editing process; to the Board of Continuing Education, Cambridge University—particularly Dr Richard Mason, Ms Sarah Ormrod, and Ms Julia Wade—for undertaking the administration of the Institute; to The British Council, The University of Cambridge Local Examinations Syndicate, The Bell Educational Trust, and Cambridge University Press for their co-operation; to Downing College for providing excellent accommodation in a beautiful setting; and to Cristina Whitecross and David Wilson of Oxford University Press for their advice on the preparation of this book.

The editors
Research Centre for English and Applied Linguistics
University of Cambridge

July 1992

Introduction

1 Common ground

This collection of papers originated in a Summer Institute held in Cambridge in 1991 on the theme 'Language and Understanding' which was particularly addressed to applied linguists and to those responsible for the teaching of languages. Whereas recent developments in research in some areas are rapidly assimilated into the language learning/teaching arena because there are well-established lines of communication from researchers to influential applied linguists, developments from other areas are recognized only belatedly as relevant to language teaching. The wide range of coverage in this volume still necessarily omits important current developments in some relevant fields; and there is a deliberate bias towards research in cognitive processing, since this is an area which has made spectacular strides during the 1980s, but which has yet to make a full impact on research into language learning.

Two issues basic to any enquiry into the nature of human knowledge are how language contributes to our understanding of the world, and how our beliefs about the world inform our understanding of language. Anyone concerned with the nature of human communication—and those concerned with the teaching of language inevitably figure large in such a group—must constantly return to such issues. For each one of us, the beliefs we hold about the relationship between language and understanding will tend to be well-entrenched, so they inevitably mesh with other systems of belief. It is hardly surprising to find that many of us hold a range of beliefs which may not be perfectly coherent, because they vary depending on which aspect of language or of understanding we are currently considering.

This book brings together papers from scholars whose approaches to language and to understanding reflect a diversity of views which derive, in part at least, from the different disciplines which they represent. None the less, at many points, there is a commonality in their views about language and about understanding, a commonality which will almost certainly be shared by most readers of this book, which could by no means have been assumed thirty, or—for some of them—even ten, years ago.

All the contributors assume that a language consists, at least, of a set of forms which can be described at various levels—at the level of sounds, word-formation, sentence-formation, and discourse structure—and that some aspects of 'meaning' can be associated with each of these levels. All of them assume that it is appropriate to study the language synchronically rather than exclusively diachronically. All assume that it is proper to discuss a language not just as a collection of texts, grammars, and dictionaries, but as a vehicle of communication. Similarly, all of them take it for granted that spoken language rather than (or as well as) written language is a proper subject for scholarly study. All of them also assume that particular aspects of language or of language use are properly studied in a context of use, and that different forms will have a range of different functions.

At a fundamental level, there is a similar consensus on the nature of understanding. This is perhaps more surprising since as recently as the early 1980s the standard view of comprehension was that the listener received an auditory stimulus which was then decoded into a meaningful verbal message by a combination of 'bottom up' and 'top down' strategies, after which the listener could be said to 'have' the idea which the speaker had encoded. Indeed, this is a view still quite widely held by scholars working in a wide range of fields. The approach shared by contributors to this volume insists that there is rarely a simple 'correct' interpretation of an utterance, that listeners have to make an effort to work out what speakers mean by what they say. They believe that interpretation is a difficult and risky process with no guarantee of a satisfactory outcome, even if you have correctly identified the words and correctly worked out the syntactic structure of the sentence.

There is, then, to a remarkable degree, a consensus among these contributors about the nature of language and of understanding, despite the range of disciplines which they represent.

2   Individual differences: conflict or complementarity?

2.1   The forms of language—language variability

Most of the papers take for granted a neutral form of English which they do not even have to discuss. This neutral form is Standard English which is always most easily identified in its written form. The only paper which confronts the issues raised in trying to determine what the term 'language' might refer to, in the case of English, is Milroy's. She shows the difficulty of finding criteria for identifying 'Standard English', particularly in the spoken form. She goes on to show how understanding between native speakers can be imperilled by the diversity of forms encountered even among those who would be classified as highly educated native speakers of English. The problems which native speakers encounter in understanding each other are likely to be compounded if one of the interlocutors is a foreign learner.

The neutral form assumed by the other contributors is probably not identical for all writers since each person's construct 'language' must be, to some extent, an individual construct. For Milroy, a language is not a monolith but a complex network of variants in constant flux. What makes a language that particular language is as much a social as a linguistic question, strikingly so in the case of accents and dialects. Expressions may serve to carry their users' messages, but they also carry social values.

Two other papers focus on how the use of a particular form contributes to a particular meaning by laying down clues which the attentive listener or reader will pick up and use in the search for an interpretation. Both K. Brown and Short examine particular areas of form–meaning relationships; though Brown is concerned with examining the range of syntactic forms available for expressing a range of semantic relationships, whereas Short is concerned with explaining the effect of a particular stylistic choice in a particular context and with showing that the effect of these choices is just as pervasive in language-at-large as it is in the language of literature.

Milroy's insistence that language carries social values is certainly a view which would be shared by Aitchison, whose paper documents how the values associated with the culture of a speaker's native language are carried over into the foreign language and culture. Learners of a foreign language bring to the new language the taxonomies of their own language, so their judgements of prototypical categories of familiar lexical fields (animals, vegetables, furniture, and so on) are strikingly different from judgements made by native speakers. In a rather different form, a similar view is expressed by Bialystok, who considers the process of learning a second language to be quite unlike that of learning the first language. The reason is that in learning the first language the child learns not only that particular language, but *language* more generally conceived. Learning the first language is a cognitive problem which involves the acquisition of a cognitive system. The resulting abstract representation of the basic categories of language, the acquired conceptual system, and the ability to analyse and categorize are all already available in learning a second language, a process which, Bialystok suggests, is confined to learning the linguistic details of the new language. As Aitchison points out, the new language may be used by the learner to communicate ideas which are typically different from those available to native speakers of that language.

2.2   Language and understanding

Whereas the range of views expressed here on the nature of language can, so far, all be seen as complementary, at first sight there does appear to be a diversity in the different authors' conceptions of the relationship between language and understanding.

Milroy, for instance, again focuses centrally on an issue that is only dealt with peripherally in other papers, and that is the issue of social meaning expressed by the choice of forms of language, particularly in speech.

Speakers define their membership of particular social groups by using forms which are peculiar to them, and in choosing a form which includes them as members of the group, they exclude others from it. These subtle social meanings are quite hard even for native speakers from distant areas to pick up, and are particularly difficult for non-native speakers.

The notion of understanding emerging as a function of the social group in which it is embedded also surfaces in Brumfit's paper, though in making a rather different point. He assumes that the desired outcome of the interaction which takes place between learners and teacher in the culture created in the classroom is understanding of the language being taught and learnt. He focuses on the types of conditions most favourable to achieving the desired outcome. Here, sociocultural conditions are considered of paramount importance in directing the search for mutual understanding which is held to be the key to foreign language learning.

In Brumfit's paper, we encounter a view of the nature of understanding which seems initially to be quite different from that which is assumed by most of the other contributors (and it may actually reflect a fundamentally different view on the nature of language). Brumfit's account of understanding is that it is a basically social process. He is concerned with the role of understanding in language learning, where meaning is constructed in the classroom setting and the members of the class participate in that meaning. In a sense, understanding is seen as a social institution, like a bank owned by a social co-operative, from which contributors can borrow and to which they can contribute. Such a conceptualization often accompanies a view of language itself as a social institution, where again the bank analogy can fruitfully be drawn. This in turn often leads to an assumption that meaning is 'negotiated' between participants in an interaction, as it were 'out there' in a social space. Such an approach may be ascribed to de Saussure who wrote:

> If we could embrace the sum of word-images stored in the minds of all individuals, we could identify the social bond that constitutes language. It is a storehouse filled by the members of a given community through their active use of speaking, a grammatical system that has a potential existence in each brain, or, more specifically, in the brains of a group of individuals. For language is not complete in any speaker; it exists perfectly only within a collectivity.
> (de Saussure/Wade Baskin (trans.) 1960: 13)

De Saussure appreciated that, to include all that we know of language, it is necessary to adopt two distinct but complementary views. First, the view of language as a social institution, and second, the view of language as experienced by a single individual, which is necessarily limited by that individual's personal life-history. The first view is best represented in this collection by Brumfit and by Milroy, but the view of language as a social institution is also discussed in the papers of G. Brown and Spolsky. The complementary second view, nowadays often called the 'cognitive' view, is at least implicitly adopted by most of the other contributors with respect to language and, significantly, with respect to the processes of understanding. The papers by Aitchison, G. Brown, Bialystok, Garnham, Short, and Wilson, are all concerned, in different ways, with how individuals understand and/or learn language. Although the focus of attention is quite different, once again it can be seen that there is no conflict between the two approaches. They should ideally be seen as complementary, concentrating on different aspects of experience.

Although many of us may pay lip-service to the 'complementarity' view of the social and cognitive approaches to the study of language, few applied linguists maintain an objective bipartisan stance to the issue and are equally devoted to both views. For a variety of historical and social reasons, applied linguistics as a discipline has tended towards an emphasis on language as a social institution. The discipline will be impoverished if it fails also to take account of research into the cognitive aspects of language learning and language understanding.

2.3 Diversities of understanding

As soon as we accept that communication is a risky undertaking, requiring not simply the exchange of linguistically packaged ideas, but an effort of imagination on the part of the reader or listener, we can see why it is that the same message can be interpreted by listeners in different ways. The issue of diversity in understanding is explicitly raised in most of the papers, and dealt with at length by both Brumfit and Spolsky. Spolsky points to the variability of interpretations of the 'same' text according to who is doing the interpreting—test writers, test takers, or examiners—and according to the number of times the text is read or heard. The question of 'what a text means' is crucial to language testing, and yet, as Spolsky remarks, since so many social and cognitive aspects are involved in comprehension, over and above decoding the familiar linguistic categories, it is hard to be sure what it is that a test is measuring.

It is hard enough to be sure what are the relevant processes when testing native speakers working in their own language. It is even more difficult if they are working in a foreign language. Bialystok argues that what is crucial here is *control* of the input, to ensure that it is compatible with the learner's mental representation of the language at each stage of the learning process. This requires that teachers be able to analyse the demands that different types of task make upon the learner. G. Brown in her paper suggests that one parameter which teachers would do well to consider in this context is the different level of cognitive demands made by texts in different genres.

Once again, these diverse contributors appear to entertain compatible views on the issue of diversity of interpretation.

2.4   Language understood in context

Throughout these papers runs a common theme: that language is understood in context. Milroy and Brumfit are concerned with different aspects of the social, interactional context in which language is experienced. K. Brown discusses the way in which the choice of particular verbs sets up specific configurations of semantic roles which characterize prototypical contexts which then bring other aspects of such contexts in their train. Thus, if the verb BUY is used to describe an action of John's, it creates the context of a 'commercial exchange' which makes available other roles such as a seller, the price paid, the money used in payment, the object bought, and so on. Garnham also appeals to immediate linguistic context to give an account of the interpretation of anaphoric expressions in brief texts. And in the earlier part of his paper, where he discusses the implications of connectionism for modelling language learning, he appeals to a theory of spreading activation which might offer some hope of modelling the effect of context. Short also considers context, in particular the effect of deictic expressions in focusing upon an action from different points of view. All of these writers help themselves to as much of a notion of context as they need, without feeling obliged to explicate in detail how they conceive of the notion, or whether or not there is a general theory of context into which their approach fits (and the assumption must be that there is not).

There is, of course, the notorious problem that 'context' is a notion which seems to be impossible to constrain. If someone speaks to you of Wordsworth and then goes on to speak of 'his cottage', is it reasonable to suppose that HIS COTTAGE was somehow activated in your mind simply by mentioning Wordsworth, along with HIS SISTER, HIS FINGER-NAILS, HIS ARMCHAIR, and, literally, innumerable other features which might reasonably be associated with him? Most people would agree that it is not reasonable. But just what is activated immediately in your mind when the name 'Wordsworth' is mentioned? And how does that mention contribute to the creation of a context, and just what is 'in' that context? The only paper to address some of these problems of context directly is that of Wilson, who suggests that the listener activates no more context than is necessary to understand the utterance and that, rather than taking account of external features of context before and during the utterance, the listener only activates the necessary amount of context after having heard the utterance. The theory propounded in this paper has raised great interest because of the bold nature of the claims that it makes about cognitive processing, and it has generated animated discussion in a variety of fields (see, for instance, *Brain and Behavioural Science* 10: 697–749, which is devoted to reviews of Sperber and Wilson 1986).

Of all the areas we have discussed, that of understanding language in context is the one which may be seen as at once the most crucial to language teaching and the most controversial. In general, the other views put forward in this collection of papers, although diverse in their origins, can be seen as remarkably compatible with each other, complementary rather than in conflict.

1 Modes of understanding

Gillian Brown addresses here an issue well-known to language teachers, which is that some students find some sorts of texts extraordinarily difficult to understand. Of course, there may be many reasons for this. One reason, often overlooked, is that the processes involved in understanding different genres make different demands on the cognitive abilities of learners.

The three major genres discussed in the paper involve procedural understanding, narrative understanding, and the understanding of argument. It is frequently possible to achieve an adequate interpretation of well-contextualized instructions or directions, even if you have a limited grasp of the meaning of what was said. Where the listener has doubts about how to proceed, what is crucially important is that learners are able (and brave enough) to indicate where they do not understand, and to persist in requests for repetition or clarification. Such strategies can be learnt and practised in the classroom, ideally using a model of the range of options available to the speaker for furthering the listener's understanding—elaboration, modification, deletion, addition, paraphrase, summarizing, and so on.

Narrative understanding puts extra demands on the listener, since it is necessary to keep track of characters and objects in a mentally constructed world which does not bear a simple relationship to the immediate context. While the skills involved may, at some levels at least, be language independent, it is clear that textual markers and specific narrative conventions differ across languages and cultures.

The interpretation of extended argument demands even more of listeners (in their own or a second language) than any other genre. The learner is usually required to abandon any obvious anchorage in the present physical world, and to juggle with abstract premises which have to be related to each other in terms of what may be, for the learner, an unfamiliar logic. Advances in the field of genre analysis (for example, Swales 1990) begin to address the difficulties involved with reference to some text types which are structured along patterns which the learner can learn to predict. Similarly, Hoey's (1983) strategies for pattern identification may help in this. However, any text can contain unpredictable problems which cannot be immediately resolved but must be retained in memory awaiting later clarification. Practice in recognizing such points in a text, together with efficient note-taking and textual searching strategies, may be necessary to enable the learner to cope with such complexities.

Modes of understanding

Gillian Brown
Research Centre for English and Applied Linguistics
University of Cambridge

1 Understanding and interpretation

There are many approaches to 'understanding'. The approach that I favour is that of Bartlett's 'striving after meaning' (1932), where he insists on the effort required in the act of interpretation. I shall be more interested in the processes by which we arrive at an 'understanding', than in attempting to characterize what it is that we finally arrive at; and, indeed, my assumption is that 'understanding' will itself not be finite and fixed, but in a constant state of flux—of augmentation, of modification, of radical transformation, of restructuring of its patterns of salience, or of fading from current con-sciousness. Green and Morgan (1981: 177) point out the dangers of attempting to describe the product of a hearer's understanding. Adopting such a point of view, they warn, 'might imply a view of discourse in which communication is the simple encoding and decoding of "thoughts" or "meanings" in linguistic packages [where] a speaker packs thoughts into words or larger expressions and sends them to be unpacked (unchanged) by the addressee who then "has" them'. Such an over-simple view of com-munication is convincingly argued against by Reddy (1979), who insists that communication cannot be encapsulated by what he calls 'the conduit metaphor'. Communication is not 'a success without effort system' where communicators simply exchange well-packaged ideas, but 'an energy must be expended system' which requires each individual to try to work out what the other person must mean by a particular utterance (Reddy 1979: 308, see also Wilson, this volume).

My plan in this paper is first to discuss a mode of interpretation which seems intuitively not to impose a very considerable cognitive load on the listener or reader, and then to progress towards genres of language where the cognitive load is considerably increased.

2 Identifying and cognitive meaning

Are there examples of language use where a speaker informs a listener of something which requires nothing more than correct identification of the words used? Consider an example of Ellen Markman's (1981: 63): if I give you my telephone number, is there any sense in which you 'understand' my telephone number? This seems to be a case where you simply need to recognize the numbers, and the sequence in which they occur, to have received all that was intended to be conveyed.

At first glance, it might seem that proper names would come into a similar category, where only simple identification is required. Linguistic philosophers tend to insist that proper names have no meaning; but that is probably too strong a position, otherwise you could not meaningfully use expressions like 'the Stalin of the fourth form' or 'the Athens of the North'. Whereas most numbers seem to be uncluttered by connotational or associative meaning, proper names carry a great deal of social meaning. One might be surprised to hear of a boxer whose first name was 'Sebastian', because this is a name which is not characteristically found among the section of society from which boxers are stereotypically drawn. Similarly, there is a gamut of social information carried by place-names. If you live in Kensington, this might suggest that you have considerable social aspirations and are wealthy, whereas if you live in Potters Bar, you may have to endure an image of dull suburban existence. A great deal of British humour and anecdote depends on the ability to recognize the social implications carried by names.

This is a difficult and subtle area for second language users to come to terms with, and it is often problematic for young native speakers. It might be thought that the appreciation of such echoes is only required in arriving at a literary reading, yet I think this underestimates the stereotypes, the prejudices, and the assumptions, which names carry. None the less, you cannot reasonably say 'I understand the name Alphonse Smith', or 'I grasp the place name Wakes Colne'. If you have not identified the name correctly, we would surely not say that this is 'a failure of understanding', but rather that you 'had not heard properly'. All you can do with a name is identify its form, recognize it as a name, and identify the (sort of) individual or place appropriately called by such a name.

I conclude then that phone/car/bank-account numbers, together with proper names, are identified rather than understood.

3 Procedural understanding

It is not until we consider the use of language proper, where utterances are used to communicate specific messages and to manage the organization of knowledge, that we can really begin to talk about 'understanding' what is said or written. Even here, we can identify a genre of language use which may only require a minimum of linguistic interpretation. The philosopher Gilbert Ryle suggested that the most basic form of knowledge is not propositional knowledge about the world, 'knowing that', but procedural knowledge about how to do things, 'knowing how'. He writes that philosophers 'suppose that the primary exercise of minds consists in finding the answers to questions' in 'knowledge of true propositions or facts' (1949: 27), and suggests that 'they have for the most part ignored the question what it is for someone to know how to perform tasks' (ibid.: 28). Following Ryle, I assume that the most basic mode of language understanding, that which is least removed from simple identification, is procedural understanding.

It often happens that someone explains to you what you have to do in order to achieve something, like finding your way to the library, filling in a registration form, setting up your computer, or making short-crust pastry. It is barely necessary to understand the language in a *linguistic* mode here, in the sense of being able to repeat it back, or to construct a summary of what was said. What you need is to be able to put in train the relevant procedures. To have understood adequately is to be able to construct a mental model which matches the world sufficiently well to allow you to carry out the necessary procedures adequately. In fact, if you had a hazy idea of how to proceed even before the speaker told you how to, you might only have listened partially to what the speaker said. Even if you are listening to instructions in a foreign language which you do not fully control, you may have a sufficient basic grasp to understand what is required because the language is so well supported by the external world.

It seems reasonable to suggest that this thoroughly situated genre of language is that which is first learnt by the child, as the mother says 'into bed then' and 'up you come', suiting the action to the words. Similarly, it is procedural understanding which is exploited in many foreign language classroom activities, where familiar activities make transparent the language which accompanies them.

It may sometimes be quite unclear whether the listener has fully understood the language used, and yet the outcome, in the sense of the procedures performed in the world, can be perfectly satisfactory. I have a videotape of a little girl of eighteen months standing in the garden at the edge of the paddling pool which her three-year-old brother is splashing about in. He fills a watering-can and gives it to her. 'Go and water the flowers', he says. She looks at him, turns, looks at the garden and trots over to tip the water out on the flowers in the nearest flower bed. This instruction (and obedient response) is repeated several times, until he hands her the full watering-can with the words 'Now go and water the trees'. Again she looks at him; this time he repeats the instruction immediately. She looks at the garden and then looks at him again. He repeats it again, this time waving his hand twice, wide, away from his body, towards the trees. She turns and trots across to a tree and tips the water over the grass at the bottom of the tree. Did she understand what he said? It is impossible to know. The outcome appears to have satisfied them both.

Procedural understanding often requires only a fairly basic linguistic ability, and frequently, rather than receiving a linguistic, verbal, message, you could have been shown how to do whatever it is, simply by mimicking the actions of your instructor. If you ask someone for directions to a nearby location, he may begin to give directions verbally, and then change his mind because the route is quite complicated, and say 'Come with me and I'll take you.' Or he may draw you a map on a scrap of paper. Nothing particularly hinges on the linguistic aspect of the interaction. And only the most basic inferencing is required—like recognizing that the language refers to the current situation and that you are to do whatever it is in the order that you are instructed to do it.

Much of ordinary domestic life, of basic primary school education, and of day-to-day transactions at work, requires no more than procedural understanding. The crucial point is that the language is fully supported by the external world—so the listener can construct a mental model and match that model against the world, to test whether or not the understanding is adequate for the task in hand.

In simple cases, instructions are spaced so that they come one at a time, immediately followed by the appropriate action, which means that there is no burden on the listener's memory. The small boy in the paddling pool does not say to his sister 'Water the flowers four times and then go and water some trees'; he gives her one, new, simple instruction on each occasion, and waits until she has finished that before issuing the next command. If too much information comes in at once, the processor may become overloaded, and unable to cope with simultaneously instantiating the content of earlier instructions while processing, and memorizing for future use, later instructions. Consider the following transcript where one undergraduate (A) is instructing another (B) how to draw a route on the map of an island. Each of them has a map, which the other cannot see, of the 'same' island, where certain features are present on one map but not on the other (A has a bridge absent from B's map). Some features occur on both maps but in different locations (A and B both have woods but in different places) (see Brown 1986, 1987).

A   go round towards the wood + but you cut off between − the top of
     the river and the woods + + and then up towards the castle
B   I go up to the top of the river − right
A   you go across the bridge right − up towards the wood then go
     between the two rivers right − and then up towards the castle
B   say that again Karen
A   right you go across the bridge − and you go up towards a wood
B   wait a minute − where's your bridge + + I've not got a bridge

Here the procedural task has been complicated by introducing misleading mismatches of information. It is further complicated for B because A introduces too much information in her first and second turns, information which B, who is carefully scanning her quite complex map, simply cannot process fast enough. There is evidence that she has 'heard' and remembered, in part at least, the linguistic detail of what is said, but she sensibly refuses to move from her position on the map until she can understand what A says in terms of the physical representation in front of her.

The claim is not that procedural understanding is always simple, only that it is always simpler *all other things being equal*, than that required by the other genres that I am going on to discuss. Any genre can be made cognitively simple or more difficult by the manipulation of a small range of parameters which I shall summarize here (but cf. Brown, Anderson, Shillcock, and Yule 1984; Brown 1986; Brown 1989):

1   the number and distinguishability of the referents
    (the maps that A and B are working with have quite a large number of features, each of which looks initially quite similar to its neighbours);

2   the simplicity or complexity of spatial relationships
    ('maps' of natural idiosyncratic features are harder to locate yourself precisely on than, say, a town plan on a symmetrical grid);

3   the simplicity or complexity of temporal relations
    (irrelevant to maps but cf. section 5);

4   the simplicity or complexity of intentional/causal relationships
    (irrelevant to the map task but cf. the following sections);

5   the identity, similarity, or incompatibility of the new information with that already available to the listener/reader
    (important in the map task where crucial features are different).

4   Manipulating understanding

I have suggested that procedural understanding, 'understanding how', is perhaps not very far removed from identifying numbers and names. But it is significantly more demanding. The listener now not only has to be able to identify a referent, which is what the use of a name or a number requires, but needs also to be able to attach predicates to the mental model of the referent and interpret those with respect to the world. The eighteen-month-old child is no longer simply pointing to trees and saying 'trees', as she did three months earlier when she was establishing the relationship between the name and the referent; her brother now requires her to relate the predicate 'water' to 'the trees'.

The distinction often drawn in the psycholinguistic literature between 'recognizing' and 'grasping' (cf. Aitchison, this volume) suggests to me that you can recognize the numbers in a phone number but that there is no content, independent of these being the numbers in a phone number, that you need to grasp. There are, none the less, formal cognitive operations which you can perform upon a phone number (or a proper name).

Possible operations on the *form*:
1 perceive the utterance;
2 repeat the utterance;
3 learn it;
4 learn how to write it down;
5 recognize it upon a future occasion;
6 relate it to an individual/location and draw appropriate social inferences.

Only at your peril would you try to manipulate names or numbers in a more radical manner. However, once you enter the use of language proper, a range of additional operations becomes possible.

Additional possible operations on *form* and/or *content*:
7 elaborate the utterance (for instance, choose more specific vocabulary);
8 modify the utterance (for instance, move a phrase within the sentence);
9 delete part of the utterance;
10 add to the utterance;
11 contradict the content;
12 paraphrase the content;
13 summarize the content;
14 make temporal/causal/intentional inferences on the basis of the relationship between the content of the utterance and aspects of the co-text, context, or of background knowledge.

The competent listener does not attempt to improve upon, paraphrase, or summarize the information in a telephone number or proper name. However, in the realm of procedural interpretation, such additional operations become possible, and some may be necessary to understand the discourse (though all of them introduce some risk of misunderstanding). In understanding genres of language more demanding than procedural language, the listener must be able to undertake such operations, above all the operation of constrained inferencing.

5 Narrative understanding

Narrative understanding is involved in any genre where the content is temporally organized—technical or legal reports, historical documents, accounts of rugby matches, anecdotes, planning future events, as well as in literature, in short stories and novels. It involves the ability to understand language as depicting a temporal sequence of events in a given spatial domain, or set of domains. This requires interpreting a verbally described set of circumstances which may have no immediate representation in the real world, so that the listener is required to imagine a sequence of events, to establish in a mental discourse representation a number of distinct individuals and keep track of them through time, determining how they act or are acted upon, and envisaging the attendant circumstances. The forms of language used will determine the participant roles which are created and the viewpoint from which the listener is meant to perceive the sequence of the action (cf. K. Brown and Short, this volume).

Interpreting narratives requires the identification of each individual actor. Maintaining identity involves the ability to control anaphoric reference, to construct a mental model of the actors in this imagined world and track each individual (cf. Garnham, this volume). In addition, you have to understand (if necessary by inference) relationships of cause and effect and of intentionality on the part of human agents.

The importance of narrative understanding to a normal understanding of everyday life is beautifully illustrated by Oliver Sacks, in his book *The Man Who Mistook His Wife For a Hat* (1985), where he presents a tragic patient who appears to inhabit a world without intentionality, where events merely happen. For this man, life consists of a random sequence of unrelated and unstructured incidents. If you were to present him with E. M. Forster's narrative:

> The king died.
> Then the queen died of grief. (1927: 93)

he would not draw the inferences that normal readers draw. He would not suppose that the king and the queen inhabited the same world, living at the same period of time, nor infer a relationship between the king and queen, supposing, as we surely all suppose, that they were husband and wife, that the queen died of grief shortly after the king died, and that the cause of her grief was that the king had died. All these are inferences which are nowhere stated in the text, but which individuals capable of construing narratives will infer quite automatically (though with a risk of being wrong), without even noticing that they are thus enriching 'the bare text'. And this interpretation, note, is not supported by the physical world 'out there', but, in the case of Forster's text, is created and sustained solely by the reader establishing an imaginary world, constructing it by reference to his or her own previous experience of interpreting similar texts.

The problem for Sacks's patient is that his processes of interpretation are no longer controlled by the principle controlling normal interpretation ('the principle of local interpretation' (Brown and Yule 1983: 59) which falls out naturally from Grice's maxim of relevance (Grice 1975). This instructs us to process parsimoniously, adopting the following procedures:

1 Relate referents as closely as you can. If it is not possible to fuse them into one identity, assume a close relationship unless there is evidence against this.
2 Assume the same or closely juxtaposed time if there is no evidence against it. If I say 'he came on Tuesday', assume I am referring to the most recent past Tuesday.
3 Assume a limited location unless there is evidence against it. If you read 'Thomas went to the theatre on Wednesday. He bumped into an old friend of his' (Sanford and Garrod 1981: 6), you will assume that Thomas bumped into his old friend at the theatre (and on (the most recent) Wednesday).

Narrative understanding, like procedural understanding, can be subjected to more or less strain, depending upon the complexity of the plot and the subtlety of the language. It is easier to understand a plot told in *ordo naturalis*—in the order in which things occurred. It is no surprise that stories told to small children and by small children, like simple classic fairy tales, are of this structure. It is much harder to understand a narrative which involves flashbacks, or premonitions of the future. These require the listener to hold several embedded sub-narratives stably in a mental discourse representation, and to track characters across different time frames, without confusing the characters or misordering the events. Such a task presents a very considerable difficulty for young children, and also for older students who are relatively unsuccessful academically (cf. Oakden and Sturt 1922; Piaget 1926; Jarvella and Lubinsky 1975). They may have understood the language of each of the individual sentences correctly, but still not have achieved a stable and coherent representation in memory which they are able to access later.

The Forster narrative requires inferencing of so basic a nature that we are barely aware of enriching the text. Consider, however, how you understand this item of news, broadcast on local radio a few years ago:

The Suffolk doctor whose wife has been reported missing stayed firmly in his house today. Police have been digging in the garden.

This is reported in the way that Sacks's patient might have understood it—as a random collection of incidents. There is no obvious temporal sequence here, or explicit relationship of intentionality or of causality. Why is the Suffolk doctor not named but identified in virtue of the fact that his wife had been reported missing (by whom?)? Why did he stay 'firmly' in his house, and who might be expected to have asked him to emerge from it, and with what intention? And why should police be digging in a garden which the principle of local interpretation suggests must be the doctor's while he stays 'firmly in his house', and how do these two, apparently simultaneous, states of affairs relate to his wife having 'been reported missing'?

Understanding a narrative requires a great deal more than being able to interpret—or to paraphrase—each individual sentence, which might be an adequate test of the understanding of procedural information. Narrative understanding requires, in addition to understanding the sentences, the construction of a mental representation, where there is no structure readily available to check it against out there in the real world. Within this mentally represented world, individuals must be tracked through time, and spatial, temporal, causal, and intentional relationships must be inferred. In moving from procedural understanding to narrative understanding, there is an enormous leap in the demands made upon cognitive processing, even if parity is maintained between those aspects of discourse which contribute to extra cognitive processing—number and distinguishability of referents, relative complexity of spatial relationships, compatibility of old–new information, and so on.

In procedural understanding, you may often close off previous information which records how you arrived at the point where you now are, and no longer retain it actively in memory, thus releasing processing resources for the next step. In narrative understanding, however, you must carry relevant previous information in a readily accessible form in memory and, in order to understand fully, constantly relate what is happening now to what happened earlier.

6   Understanding argument

An even greater cognitive burden is imposed in understanding extended argument. This genre is typically not based on physical experience in the world at all. It is rarely, like procedural or narrative genres, naturally relatable to a spatial domain, and it is often not temporally or chronologically ordered. It is instead based on rational, sometimes overtly logical, sequence. Understanding an argument requires that you create a mental representation of a number of premises, that you distinguish between these and remember them accurately, and then that you track the abstract relationships established between them, until you reach the conclusion which the speaker wishes you to reach. There is little doubt that abstract arguments, explanations, justifications, theorizing, make more demands on understanding than any other genre.

Most people sometimes have problems in following extended technical exposition. All academics will have encountered students who demonstrate, in attempting to recapitulate an argument, that they have not properly understood it. We recognize the problem in graduate students, in our peers, and in ourselves. Following the steps of an argument requires an ability to concentrate on verbal input quite unsupported by experience in the physical world, to exercise selective attention on abstract constructs, and, hardest of all, to recall accurately both the constructs and the relationships into which they enter. Moreover, the amount of inferential work that a reader or listener has to do in arriving at an interpretation of argumentative language is only just beginning to be appreciated. Consider two sentences from a relatively transparent paragraph in Chomsky's *Language and Mind*:

> (1) Whitehead once described the mentality of modern science as having been forged through 'the union of passionate interest in the detailed facts with equal devotion to abstract generalisation'. (2) It is roughly accurate to describe modern linguistics as passionately interested in detailed fact, and philosophical grammar as equally devoted to abstract generalisation. (Chomsky 1968: 22, my numbering)

Assume a linguistics student reader, in the 1990s, who is given this text, out of context, and asked to read it. How would the reader approach such a text? The initial citation of Whitehead (an unfamiliar name for younger readers) provides an immediate problem, characteristic of argumentative rhetoric. Why is this individual cited? Is he (or she) a figure likely to be respected by the writer or likely to be scorned? Does he speak with authority about 'the mentality of modern science' or not? (Suppose the name had been Groucho Marx—would what followed have been read differently?) The reader will have to suspend judgement on this, waiting for more text, carrying this unresolved status in his or her mental representation, and only later infer whether or not Whitehead is being treated as an authority. Moreover, Whitehead spoke of 'modern science', which means that in order to assess the truth or contemporary relevance of this utterance (for 1968, Chomsky's time of writing) the reader needs to know whether the remark was made five, fifty, or a hundred years ago. Not knowing this, a further query must be held in memory—is the judgement true, does the judgement still apply—while the reader tries to understand Chomsky's point. I leave aside how you interpret a singular 'mentality' for science, and its being 'forged'. But consider, more mundanely, the inferencing required to determine what sort of facts the expression 'the detailed facts' might refer to here, and what sort of 'abstract generalisation' might be intended.

How does the second sentence relate to the first? What sorts of inferencing will be required to relate Chomsky's use of the expression 'modern linguistics' in the second sentence to the expression 'modern science' in the first? Does the syntactic patterning of these expressions indicate some equivalence? But then why is 'modern linguistics' only credited with one of the attributes of 'modern science'? And how does 'modern linguistics' relate to 'philosophical grammar'—are these two distinct paradigms, or is grammar part of linguistics, as the student reader has always supposed? Once again, he or she will have to hold over this problem and wait for later evidence, adding to the store of unresolved problems which must be stacked up in memory. And, for relatively unsophisticated readers, there is always the question of whether this is a part of the text which must be understood in detail, or whether this is a largely rhetorical part which is simply orientational.

I have hardly begun to approach the problems posed by the interpretation of these two sentences, let alone the general problems posed by argumentative discourse. I have tried to show, however, that whereas we can begin to give some generalizable account of the sorts of modes of interpretation which readers and listeners may employ in some genres of language, we are only beginning to grasp the massive amounts of very various inferencing which is required to understand argumentative discourse.

7   Conclusion

The implications for language teaching of research into the relative difficulties of understanding different types of genre are clear. Such research enables us to identify types of genre which will support young learners and enable them to enjoy successful experience of understanding language. It also offers a tool which permits the teacher who wants to work on a more complex text to identify where in the text conceptual difficulties are likely to lie, and to prepare activities which will ensure that students draw appropriate, constrained, inferences and arrive at plausible interpretations.

2 Understanding, language, and educational processes

Christopher Brumfit is widely recognized as an applied linguist concerned with language in education, and his paper addresses issues of direct interest to language teachers.

Brumfit's approach to understanding is the broadest of those presented here. His argument mirrors recent developments in stylistics and literary criticism and in the philosophy of language. Meaning is not seen as a stable property of texts, but as a shifting, variable phenomenon: understandings of the 'same' piece of discourse vary (a) between different readers/hearers, and (b) between several acts of reading/hearing by the same individual (cf. Spolsky, this volume).

For second language learners, the difficulties involved in making decisions about what is significant in a given stretch of discourse, and about the producer's intentions, may be greater than for native speakers for both linguistic and cultural reasons, and Brumfit calls for a conception of context which includes both the cognitive focus of Wilson (this volume), the more traditionally recognized sociocultural factors (Milroy, this volume), and also factors peculiar to individual classrooms.

The understanding generated in the language classroom is a product of the teaching/learning process. This is itself dependent on a set of processes of understanding which the culture of the language classroom—its organization and aspects of the teacher–learner relationship—may either facilitate or hamper. Brumfit calls for more empirical studies of situated discourse, both in and out of school, to supplement the existing literature in applied linguistics and the psychology of language.

Understanding, language, and educational processes

Christopher Brumfit
Centre for Language in Education
University of Southampton

1 Introduction

The purpose of this paper is to relate the concept 'understanding' to processes of language use in education. In the course of the argument, we shall see that the idea that language events take place at a particular moment in time is too limited to account for understanding and comprehension processes in typical classrooms. Indeed, a close examination of any particular setting will provide a warning against too ready an acceptance of simple models of understanding.

Every act of repetition will be an act of reinterpretation. This paper is based on a lecture presented orally some months before the final written version was prepared. That lecture was based on a written version, different from the version now being presented to the reader. And that version had its own history. Even the smallest discourse element was subject to interpretation throughout the preparatory process. Here, for example, is my original intention, itself arising from a telephone discussion, as I offered it in a letter more than a year before the lecture was given. I wrote:

(1)   'Understanding, language, and educational processes'

The relationship between studies in Discourse, Conversational Analysis, and Genre, and educational debates will be explored. Particularly, curriculum discussion on ESP, the role of literature teaching, and teaching through other subjects will be considered in relation to the methodological implications of research into understanding.

I also wrote 'Please amend as you see fit.' That was in May 1990.

In June 1990, a letter informed me that the title would appear on the programme as:

(2)   'Understanding, language and educational processes'

(note the lost comma).

In August 1990, the brochure appeared with the title as amended, and a summary as follows:

(2a)   The relationship between studies in discourse, conversational analysis, genre and educational debates and how these relate to research into understanding.

This formulation also appeared in the programme. I had agreed to the final copy (as one does, out of combination of politeness, laziness, and willing tolerance of minor variation), but there are none the less subtle shifts in meaning which the process of reinterpretation for another purpose had imposed on my original intention. A letter in May 1991, however, referred to my lecture as:

(3)   'Understanding language and educational processes'

without any commas, though the preferred form (2) reappeared in the outline programme.

If I had been pedantic, I could have corrected every comma, but I suspect that this record of minor change is typical rather than untypical and that pedantry would not have been welcome. The letters to myself were from different people and were widely spaced out in time, the changes were not usually substantial, and the general area of discussion remained clear. The extent to which individual participants on the Summer Institute might have interpreted my intentions differently from myself, and in what ways, and with what principles, is the subtext to the pedagogic theme of this paper.

I should emphasize, also, that the contributors to this correspondence were native speakers of English, not second language learners, and we tolerated this variation without necessarily realizing where meanings were being interpreted differently. If I introspect, I can report that for me commas in a list indicate discrete entities: 'Understanding, language, and educational processes' is unambiguously three elements where 'Understanding, language and educational processes' could be two. And perhaps less contentiously, from later in the text, 'X will be considered in relation to Y' is different from 'how X relates to Y'. 'Particularly . . .' is an emphasizer, which may or may not simply introduce exemplification of an earlier general category, and 'the methodological implications of research' are different from 'research'.

It will be apparent from this discussion that almost any text, however simple and apparently public, has a history. Native speakers tolerate uncertainty without even noticing it, yet changes do carry meaning, and the extent to which we allow this to matter is negotiable (I could have minded, and tried to change the reformulations; or I could have not minded and ignored them, offering my originally intended paper whether or not it was what was expected; or I could have offered a modified paper, accepting the changes implied by the alterations and assuming them to be principled —

or no doubt other options). Finally, we should note that such changes are not necessarily linguistic at all: they may be determined by the need to save space in a brochure, by aesthetically acceptable line-length requirements, or by careless typing. Even when writers publicly disagree over what they want printed, it is not always easy to interpret whether meaning is at stake. Many native speakers may object to the comma in '. . . language, and educational processes' and refuse to acknowledge a significant change in meaning.

Native speakers are constantly forced to decide what is and is not significant in linguistic variation, to interpret motives, and to decide on courses of action. More often than not, these will be courses of inaction—for we are busy people who cannot waste time renegotiating the trivial or the obvious. Our judgements may be correct assessments of intentions, but they may also be quite wrong: perhaps it was tacitly assumed that the changes to my original text would be interpreted by me as a demand for a totally different kind of presentation—I was failing to recognize an intended indirect speech act. Perhaps it was not a house style that was being adopted to enable the texts from different people to appear similar, but a carefully considered criticism of my views on the placement of commas which I was too insensitive to pick up! Because we are all free to respond in different ways, we risk misinterpreting the situation—and only subsequent reactions can enable us to judge whether we have or not.

So much emphasis on such minor changes in text may appear to be labouring the point, but it is necessary to insist that native speakers of English (and presumably of all languages) live their lives choosing whether to take any notice of such changes or whether to ignore them. They live their linguistic lives amid such potential confusion, and they generally cope. But second language learners also have to accommodate this complex linguistic process. Experience with their first languages may help; but so many of the problems we are encountering are not solely linguistic. Cultural understanding may help; but so many problems require understanding of particular individuals. Individual contact is worthwhile; but individuals are sometimes acting in response to conventions with which strangers are unfamiliar. How do we draw on research and theoretical discussion to help learners in their encounters with unstable constructs like language and culture?

Let me start by considering 'understanding' within pedagogy.

2   Understanding in education

A perennial theme in educational discussion is the distinction between education and training, and central to this issue is the concept, 'understanding'. Peters, for example, writes '. . . a person could be a trained ballet dancer

. . . without being educated. What might be lacking is something to do with knowledge and understanding.' (Peters 1973: 18).

But a great deal of educational discussion bases itself on decontextualized analysis, or psychological generalization from learning or interactional theories. In contrast with these traditions, I want to locate my discussion in this paper firmly within the area of pedagogy, or teaching methodology. I do this for two reasons. First, because teaching theory in practice realizes itself as a relationship between teachers and learners (which may be close or distant but can be neither abrogated nor abdicated). Second, because the systematic analysis of institutionalized practices is a major, and often neglected, test bed for applied linguistic theory. If classroom practices do not relate closely to the principles we advance, we should be looking closely at our principles, and be willing to consider adjusting them.

Where, then, do we find 'understanding' manifesting itself in education practices? Clearly, the sources to look to include written materials, especially textbooks and other teaching aids, widely practised classroom organizational structures intended to facilitate oral interaction, and also implicit practices reflected in syllabus and curriculum models and the models used in teacher education. Perhaps more important than any of these, however, is the practice of classroom teaching itself. Classrooms are constructed communities, with their prime function the creation of conditions for comprehension. Yet it is striking how little they have been studied with 'understanding' as an explicit concern.

General curriculum theory in the past twenty years has shown an interesting parallelism with practices in language teaching. Douglas Barnes's influential *From Communication to Curriculum*, published in 1976, stresses the role of exploratory talk and of negotiated communication between the knowledge systems brought by teachers and learners, in a very similar argument to that used by Widdowson (e.g. 1978) and others in their stress on negotiation of meaning in the language classroom. Learners are expected to create the discourse rules for the particular purposes that they share, within the constraints imposed by the teacher's structuring of classroom activity; language users both 'discover' their own rules, and receive them from the nature of the tasks they perform. Indeed, the idea that the understanding of particular disciplines is essentially a language game was explored by Hirst (1974: 83) and is implicit in much philosophy since Wittgenstein.

But our purpose here is to consider understanding in relation to language teaching rather than general pedagogy. I shall take as a starting point an analysis of the key categories that are available to teachers for the conceptualization of language teaching, because such categories reflect craft-knowledge of comprehension choices, operationalized to classroom needs. The discussion below draws on ideas on the relationship between content teaching and language teaching that were developed in Brumfit (1984: 95–6), where a diagram summarizes the pedagogic options available to language teachers (see Figure 1).

I. Analysis of product:

a. Formal analyses
    (linguists' categories):
    – phonological
    – syntactic
    – morphological
    – notional (semantico–grammatical)

b. Interactional analyses
    (social psychologists', anthropologists' and rhetoricians' categories):
    – situational
    – functional
    leading to:
    – discoursal, rhetorical, and stylistic

c. Content/topical analyses
    (technical or general categories):
    (i)   socially directed: cultural
    (ii) educationally directed: interdisciplinary
    (iii) language directed: linguistics, literature

II. Analysis of process:

a. Communicative abilities as goals:
    – conversation/discussion
    – comprehension
    – extended writing
      (extended speaking)

b. Orientation of activity:
    – accuracy
    – fluency

c. Pedagogical mode:
    – individual
    – private interactional (pairs or small groups)
    – public interactional (whole classes/large groups + teacher)

Figure 1 Basic categories for the analysis of language teaching
(from Brumfit 1984)

The categories specifying a language teaching curriculum are frequently related to the product of teaching. The first group of categories lists the types of product that are available. The selection made from this group carries implications for the manner in which teaching will be carried out. Some types of product require substantial understanding (for example, the 'content' analyses), while others may require a training, or skill-orientated model (for example, phonology). However, it is clear that the ability to combine elements into a coherent system must entail substantial, explicit understanding of both relevant world knowledge and the context of communication of each major speech event, if not of the structure of language itself.

The context of communication will include a range of 'process' elements which are also open to analysis. Language teaching can have only a limited range of real-world interactional goals. These are listed under (IIa) in Figure 1. Because the context is educational, the orientation will be either towards formal 'accuracy', or 'fluency' (where native-like effectiveness, irrespective of code-quality, will be criterial). Finally, there are only three major types of interaction possible within a classroom, each corresponding to a particular communicative macro-structure: individual (involving perhaps interaction with a written text), small-group interaction like private conversation, and large-group public interaction with formalized procedures. In each case, context understanding is crucial, and teachers have to decide how best to encourage open-ended and creative responses by learners. Now, if we move outwards from this pedagogically centred analysis, where do we find current discussion helpful? Let us start on the interface between description and practice. How do pragmatic categories link to content needs? One approach has been to develop the concept of 'genre'.

The use of 'genre' to refer to particular identifiable types of speech event is fairly recent. Swales (1990: 58) defines 'genre' as 'a class of communicative events, the members of which share some set of communicative purposes'. 'Register' is thus a way of distinguishing between styles, while 'genre' is a way of distinguishing between language events. Swales continues:

> These purposes are recognised by the expert members of the parent discourse community, and thereby constitute the rationale for the genre. This rationale shapes the schematic structure of the discourse and influences and constrains choice of content and style. Communicative purpose is both a privileged criterion and one that operates to keep the scope of a genre as here conceived narrowly focused on comparable rhetorical action. In addition to purpose, exemplars of a genre exhibit various patterns of similarity in terms of structure, style, content and intended audience.
> (ibid.: 58)

Swales is working in the context of English for Academic Purposes (EAP), and his work can be seen as an effort to pull the tradition of English for Specific Purposes (ESP) back towards textual analysis, following Widdowson's determined efforts (particularly Widdowson 1983) to move ESP from an exclusive preoccupation with style to take account of conceptual and cognitive frameworks. According to Widdowson, particular modes of thinking give rise to particular purposes which language must fulfil for its users; a simple matching of style to audience does not guarantee the fulfilment of these purposes. He suggests that there are two levels of language knowledge: systemic knowledge and schematic knowledge. These levels correspond to linguistic and communicative competence.

> Interpretative procedures are required to draw systemic knowledge into the immediate executive level of schemata and to relate these schemata to actual instances. The ability to realize particular meanings, solve particular problems, by relating them to schematic formulae stored as knowledge, constitutes . . . capacity. Capacity . . . can be understood as the ability to solve problems and, equivalently, to make meanings by interpreting a particular instance . . . as related to some formula, thereby assimilating the instance into a pre-existing pattern of knowledge.
> (Widdowson 1983: 106)

Widdowson thus wants to identify language use with processes of understanding (and it is noticeable that although Piaget is not referred to in his book, terms like 'accommodation' and 'assimilation' recur), and to tie language for specific purposes to general processes of learning. In this sense, his book is an interesting repudiation, by a major ESP theorist, of specificity for the discipline. Instead, Widdowson wishes to subsume ESP requirements under the concerns of general education. He thus proposes a sophisticated theoretical basis for the argument that what is distinctive about ESP is the homogeneity of the classes (which is an administrative matter) rather than linguistic or educational principles: the principles of ESP are the principles of good education, and vice versa.

However, in spite of the tension between Swales's concept of 'genre' and Widdowson's desire to provide a cognitive explanation of linguistic differences, we can perceive an interaction between Swales's pragmatic and Widdowson's mathetic concerns. Educational institutions do not operate in a cultural vacuum: they both reflect and contribute to their cultures. They reflect their cultures not just in their physical and organizational structures, but also through the disciplinary constructs that are made manifest in the behaviour of teachers and students. But precisely because these constructs are made manifest in individual behaviour, they are modified all the time, accidentally (as in the 'history' of the abstract for this paper discussed above), and deliberately, as when individuals decide to modify inherited expectations in the interests of a desired ideological shift.

Second language classrooms illustrate this particularly acutely, because here the code is specifically the object of study, so we should consider their role with some care.

3 Understanding in second language classrooms

We should note that, in order to make the differences between the learning conditions of first and second languages as clear as possible, this discussion will be based on a stark distinction between first and second language learning which is not always justifiable. However, for most classrooms (where second languages are being learnt in the formal education system) these generalizations seem helpful.

Differences between first and second language learning are of three main kinds. First, some derive automatically from the fact that second languages are second languages. Learners are already lingual when they approach their second language; they were not when they approached the first. Because we are already language-knowing, we can:

1 draw upon strategies for first language acquisition;
2 draw upon knowledge of likely language systems;
3 draw upon knowledge of how language operates socially, etc.

Second, some derive from the fact that second language learners are older than when they acquired their mother tongues, and thus will be more likely to:

4 think and talk about learning processes;
5 use conscious memorizing strategies;
6 (perhaps) operate substantially through reading and writing, etc.

Third, some derive inevitably from the social organization of the school. Schools are public places, whereas homes and families are private. Although the effects can be reduced, this difference is in principle unresolvable, because it derives from the fact that schooling is always chosen for children, and hence experienced by them as compulsory. Thus, interaction in school is with people who:

7 have a professional rather than a personal relationship;
8 are paid to diagnose progress, and notice errors;
9 expect active and efficient participation, discouraging opting out, etc.

These elements, and a range of others that are not necessary for establishing the principle, constitute the personal and social settings within which second language understanding occurs. However, they can all be manipulated to varying degrees by teachers and learners alike. Thus pedagogic decisions will determine to what extent explicit attention to first language strategies or forms is called upon, how much reading or memorizing is encouraged, and how punitive the attitude to errors will be. What orientations teachers take to questions such as these will constitute the 'culture' of the classroom, just as much as cultural elements in the content or subject matter of the linguistic material provided. Our earlier discussion of categories for analysis of classroom processes provides the key operational terms by which such 'culture' is created and adjusted.

Such arguments may convince us that language teachers habitually operate with non-linguistic as well as linguistic categories, but this could simply be a quirk of pedagogical history. To argue that this is significant for our understanding of 'understanding' requires us to provide an explicit link between pedagogical practice and theory. In the rest of this paper, I want to provide stronger support for the claim that understanding in educational settings demands a model that is much wider than can be provided by linguistics alone.

4   The limits of linguistic analysis

It has been claimed throughout this paper that language use is motivated behaviour. A key question for any linguistic analysis is the relationship between the categories of description provided by the linguist and the categories (if any) that are relevant to the participants in the interaction. While linguists may produce conveniently memorable category systems that have value for packaging descriptions to be read by other linguists, they cannot claim any explanatory value for these until a relationship has been established with the functioning of the human minds that participate in the interaction being described. As Taylor and Cameron (1987: 161) point out at the end of a highly critical survey of category systems for conversational analysis:

> Because of the perceived simplicity and systematicity of formalised descriptions, it is a common (but lamentable) tendency to attribute knowledge of the formulae to the actors whose behaviour was at first the object of formal description. Then, it is an equally common practice to make the epistemological leap of assuming that the formulae actually govern the production of the behaviour itself, i.e. to equate descriptive formulae with normative rules.

And, we might add, it is common to believe that teaching the descriptive rules is to teach the means of generating the behaviour itself.

They attribute the weaknesses of many descriptive studies to the presumption that speakers and hearers see their shared conversation in the same way, failing to recognize that individuals have different and competing agendas in their social interactions. These differences manifest themselves over extended periods of contact, and constitute themselves part of the shared experience of colleagues and friends. And there is a sense in which teachers are both colleagues of pupils (at least in the sense that they share much of their working lives in compulsory contact with them), and also friends (in the sense that successful relationships depend on a contact that

is more than merely professional consultation). But the numbers of participants involved, and the opportunities for competing and conflicting agendas,
are greater in the classroom than in most normal contexts. How teachers
and learners achieve mutual understanding is the subject of the final section
of this paper.

5 Understanding in the classroom

In an extended study of primary classrooms, Edwards and Mercer (1987)
attempt to show how 'common knowledge' is constructed through pedagogic interaction. 'Overt messages,' they show, '. . . are only a small part of
the total communication . . . context and continuity are essential considerations in the study of discourse' (Edwards and Mercer 1987: 160). Context,
as they define it, consists of any elements invoked by any participant, and
consequently 'participants' conceptions of each other's mental contexts may
be wrong or, more likely, only partially right . . . any physical set of circumstances could lend itself to an infinity of possible shared conceptions and
relevances' (ibid.: 161). Thus, 'context' connects with one of the key problems in interpretation: recognizing the cultural relationships between what
is referred to, as well as the linguistic relationships between elements in the
linguistic system. Speech does not consist only of linguistic items, for Swift
was right in *Gulliver's Travels*, and all speakers carry not only the language
system, but also, like the inhabitants of Lagado, everything to which the
language refers, in their lexicon. A child's 'box' encompasses that child's
idea of 'boxness' and all the relationships entailed by that concept, just as
my 'freedom' encompasses characteristics that people of different political
persuasions will exclude from theirs. Dostoyevsky's 'Catholic' is not the
Pope's, any more than the recent equation of 'democracy' with 'free mar-
kets' rather than with, say, 'equality of opportunity' is the same concept as
the 'democracy' of political discussion twenty years ago. It is not the words
that are under dispute, but all the potential associations of the concepts to
which the words refer. Insofar as concepts are socially constructed, words
and meanings will have multi-valent relationships, and the points of contact
will constantly shift over time, across speakers, and according to perceived
addressor–addressee conventions within the repertoire of a single speaker.
Thus, as ever, it seems easier to demonstrate the impossibility of communication than the possibility.

But this paradox is resolvable by recognizing the point where this paper
started. Communication does not consist of identical aims, identically formulated. Identity confuses the issue. Communication occurs as a reflection
of individuals' willingness to stay in contact with each other, and some of
the mechanisms for doing this can be charted.

As Edwards and Mercer show, teachers create a joint context for educational activity. A major means of doing this is to create a common, shared

knowledge, relying on an implicit framework which is created in the classroom.

Learners rely on 'educational ground rules' with both social and cognitive functions. These incorporate both social conventions for the presentation of knowledge and also sets of procedures for solving problems. But they tend to remain implicit, and are rarely brought out into the open. Further, some of the knowledge required of learners is routinized and ritualized, while other knowledge, not so constrained in its function, relies on principles for explanation and reflection (Edwards and Mercer 1987: 162). Picking up on traditions deriving from Vygotsky via Mehan (1979) and Bruner (1986), they emphasize a tension between the needs to induct children into 'an established, ready-made culture' and to develop 'creative and autonomous participants in a culture which is not ready-made but continually in the making' (Edwards and Mercer 1987: 164). We have already seen this conflict in our discussion both of ESP and the nature of language. But what is helpful is the insistence of Vygotsky and Bruner on the falseness of the dichotomy, because both culture and education are processes with future orientation, and processes which require a degree of distancing by learners even while the current set of values is being presented. 'Much of the process of education consists of being able to distance oneself in some way from what one knows by being able to reflect on one's own knowledge' (Bruner 1986: 127).

Where would this argument lead us in considering understanding in the second language classroom? It would primarily lead us to ask whether 'context' could be exploited more fully, whether failure to understand was attributable to the inadequacy of the referential framework provided in class. As Edwards and Mercer put it (1987: 167), 'good teaching will be reflexive, sensitive to the possibility of different kinds of understanding'. In second language classrooms, the nature of differing understanding for particular cultural and linguistic groups will become crucially important, if teachers are to develop the necessary sensitivity to individual needs.

But this argument also has implications for applied linguistic, as for psychological research. The value of experimentation, or of formally structured non-real-world encounters, will be much less than the value of studies of situated discourse, both in and out of school. The development of shared understanding rather than shared linguistic systems will become a much more important object of study, and the emphasis will have to be on knowledge as process rather than as a body of static information. This will be particularly important if we are to avoid learners simply engaging in an apparently arbitrary process. Edwards and Mercer's comment on primary classrooms will be instantly recognisable to teachers of foreign languages. They write, 'For many pupils, learning from teachers must appear to be a mysterious and arbitrarily difficult process, the solution to which may be to concentrate on trying to do and say what appears to be expected—a basically "ritual" solution' (ibid.: 169). In contrast, the effort to relate the individual to the social, seeing the relationship between creative interpretation and social convention as the central content of learning, is compatible with what we know of language learning processes in natural circumstances. But the understanding that is thus being developed arises out of the personal histories of class and teacher, and out of the provisional nature of every group-made text, as well as out of the individual contribution of each learner. The language forms that lead to idealizations by linguists will provide snapshots of speech events only, and snapshots cannot illustrate real-time processes. Because meaning is developed in real time (and because classrooms operate with meaning across time), education forces us to re-examine our concept of context.

3   Relevance and understanding

In this paper, Deirdre Wilson provides an outline of the central features of a currently high-profile theory of communication, 'relevance theory' (cf. Sperber and Wilson 1986). The theory has achieved such prominence partly because it has been asserted with the lucidity and force which characterizes the paper which you are about to read. A further reason is that whereas some scholars have embraced the potential of the theory, others from a variety of disciplines have found many of its assertions contentious. However, the most important reason for its prominence is that it makes a serious attempt to confront one of the central mysteries of communication, and that is the question 'just what is the nature of context?'.

For the past thirty years at least, applied linguists and teachers of English have talked about the importance of 'understanding language in context'. It is often unclear what is meant by 'context'. In the 1960s, the fashion was to construct taxonomies of external features of context (such as speaker, hearer, place and time of utterance, genre, etc.) often modelled on the works of Hymes (for instance, Hymes 1964). The well-known problem with such taxonomies is how, in principle, to determine which of the indeterminately large number of possibly relevant facets of any particular feature is the one which is actually relevant to the interpretation of a particular utterance. For instance, all such taxonomies include a 'speaker' feature: the facets of this feature which might be relevant on a particular occasion could include the identity of the speaker, his or her profession, age, height, nationality, degree of education, family, colour of hair/eyes, etc., clothing, political affiliation, state of health, and so on, for many pages as each facet reveals sub-facets. The classic problem in making such 'features of context' do any real work in giving an account of communication has been how to constrain the explosion of potentially relevant information.

More recently, applied linguists have turned to later theories which have attempted to show how features of the context other than those involving external features contribute to understanding language. These include 'speech act' theories deriving from the work of Austin (1962), 'mutual knowledge' theories (some of which are described in Smith (ed.) 1982), theories of knowledge representation which appeal to notions like 'frame', 'script', and 'scenario' (cf. discussion in Brown and Yule 1983) and, most significant of all for relevance theory, the 'Co-operative Principle' and its maxims, expounded in Grice (1975). Relevance theory incorporates some of the insights of all of these theories but Sperber and Wilson (1986) and, where appropriate, Wilson (this volume), argue vigorously against other aspects of each of these approaches.

The issues raised in this paper are clearly of vital importance for those concerned with trying to help students to 'understand language in context'. You may or may not agree with the conclusions which Wilson reaches, but you will certainly find your appreciation of the central questions clarified by considering her discussion of them.

Relevance and understanding

Deirdre Wilson
Department of Linguistics
University College London

1 Introduction

A certain politician—call her Margaret—is speaking to us on television. As she speaks, we are all noticing certain facts about her, interpreting these in the light of certain assumptions of our own, and coming to certain conclusions. In a sense, all of these contribute to our understanding of Margaret's speech; one might even say that they are all part of what she has communicated to us. In this paper, however, I want to think of communication, and understanding, in a rather narrower sense.

Notice first that not all the conclusions we draw were intended by Margaret. Take our conclusion that she is nervous: this is something she would have preferred us not to notice. Take our conclusion that she has no sympathy for the unemployed: this is something she would strongly dispute; if we drew it, she would feel misunderstood. Here, I will leave aside these cases of accidental information transmission and look instead at the domain of *intentional* communication and understanding.

Often, intentional communication involves a degree of manipulation or concealment. Like many politicians, Margaret, as she speaks to us, is doing her best to appear more intelligent, more sympathetic, more knowledgeable than she really is. These intentions can only succeed if they remain hidden: obviously, if we realize that Margaret wants us to think that she is nicer than she is, we are not going to be deceived. I want to leave aside these cases of covert communication and concentrate instead on a more basic, *overt* type of communication which we all engage in every time we speak.

In overt communication, there are no hidden intentions of the type described above. The speaker wants to convey a certain message, is actively helping the hearer to recognize it, and would acknowledge it if asked. During the question session after her talk, Margaret points to the back of the hall and says 'I'll take a question from the gentleman in blue.' In saying 'the gentleman in blue', she clearly intends to refer to someone, and clearly wants her intention recognized; to the extent that it is not, communication will fail. In this paper, I will take communication to mean overt, intentional communication, and understanding to mean recovering the overtly intended interpretation. I will try to show that understanding an utterance in this sense amounts to seeing its intended relevance: relevance and understanding are two sides of a single coin.

2　Understanding overt communication

Someone might claim that understanding an utterance is a simple matter of linguistic decoding. Margaret is speaking to us in English: it might be claimed that all we need to understand her is a knowledge of English. Virtually any utterance can be used to show that this hypothesis is wrong. There is a gap between knowing what a sentence of English means and understanding all that a speaker intends to communicate by uttering it on any given occasion. Communication and understanding involve more than mere linguistic encoding and decoding.

The examples that demonstrate the gap between sentence meaning and utterance interpretation fall into three main categories, corresponding to three main questions that the hearer of an utterance has to answer: (a) what did the speaker intend to say? (b) what did the speaker intend to imply, and (c) what was the speaker's intended attitude to what was said and implied? I will look at these questions in turn.

(a)　What did the speaker intend to say?

Consider (1), which was taken from an advertisement for an employment agency that used to appear in the London Underground:

(1)　If you're looking for a good job, we're offering a thousand a week.

Our knowledge of English alone will tell us that this advertisement has at least two possible interpretations: it may be offering a thousand pounds a week, or it may be offering a thousand good jobs a week. Our knowledge of English alone, however, will not tell us which interpretation was actually intended or understood. More generally, our knowledge of the language will tell us the range of linguistically *possible* interpretations of a vague, ambiguous, or ambivalent utterance, but will not tell us which interpretation was actually intended on any given occasion.

In fact, this advertisement is quite interesting from a communicative point of view. It is what psycholinguists call a 'garden path' utterance: that is, an utterance on which hearers quite systematically get the wrong interpretation first, and have to correct it. Here, the first interpretation to occur to most English readers would be that they are being offered a thousand pounds a week, which is an awful lot of money—too much, in fact, to be handed out by advertising in the London Underground. Hence, this interpretation would have to be rejected in favour of the less exciting interpretation that what was being offered was merely a thousand good jobs a week.

Indeed, it is clear that these facts were deliberately exploited by the advertisers in order to attract the audience's attention. An advertisement which merely said 'We're offering a thousand good jobs a week' would hardly have been worth a glance. An adequate theory of communication should explain not only the simple cases in which a vague, ambiguous, or ambivalent utterance is correctly understood, but also more complex cases such as (1). Why is the first interpretation to come to mind generally the 'thousand pounds' one? On what grounds is it rejected? On what grounds is the 'thousand good jobs' interpretation preferred?

In the literature on communication, following the work of Grice (1967/89), *saying* is generally contrasted with *implying*, or *implicating*. Every utterance is seen as communicating a variety of propositions, some explicitly, others implicitly. *Saying* is seen as falling on the explicit side. In order to discover what was *said* by an utterance (i.e. what proposition was explicitly expressed), the hearer must decode the sense of the sentence uttered, and then disambiguate any ambiguous expressions, assign reference to any referential expressions, restore any ellipsed material, and narrow down the interpretation of any over-vague expressions, all in the intended way. Thus, in order to know what Margaret intended to *say* in uttering the words 'I'll take a question from the gentleman in blue', we would need to decide which particular man she had in mind. The resulting proposition determines the truth conditions of her utterance: it is the one that has to be true if her utterance is to be true. As these examples show, even the recovery of this explicitly communicated proposition is not a simple matter of linguistic decoding.

(b)   What did the speaker intend to imply?

Sometimes, it is quite clear what the speaker intended to say, but less clear what she intended to imply. Consider (2), used by Mrs Thatcher in a BBC radio interview when she was still Prime Minister:

(2)   I always treat other people's money as if it were my own.

Here, there is no problem deciding what Mrs Thatcher intended to *say*, but there is a problem deciding what she intended to imply. On the assumption that she treats her own money very carefully, (2) will imply that she treats other people's money very carefully; on the other hand, on the assumption that she spends her own money any way she likes, (2) will imply that she treats other people's money any way she likes, and so on. Different assumptions lead to different implications; the hearer's task is to identify the intended ones. Clearly, in this case the intended implication was that Mrs Thatcher treats other people's money very carefully, but how do we know this? More generally, how do we recognize the intended implications of *any* utterance?

In his 'William James Lectures' (1967/89), Grice introduced the term *implicature* to refer to the intended implications of an utterance. Some utterances have a few strong, highly salient implicatures; others have a broader, less determinate range. Thus, compare (3) and (4):

(3)   a. Peter: Does Viv play cricket well?
      b. Mary: He plays for the West Indies.

(4)   a. Peter: What will you do today?
      b. Mary: I don't feel too well.

On the assumption that anyone who plays for the West Indies is a good cricketer, (3b) strongly implicates that Viv is a good cricketer, and the recovery of this implicature is essential to the understanding of (3b). (4b) has a broader and weaker range of implicatures no one of which is essential to understanding. In uttering (4b), Mary clearly encourages Peter to think that she will be less energetic, less creative than normal, but she does not commit herself to any definite course of action. Here, it might be better to talk not so much of the intended interpretation as the intended *line* of interpretation, to account for the element of indeterminacy involved. In either case—whether the implicatures are strong or weak—they cannot be discovered by linguistic decoding alone.

(c) What was the speaker's intended attitude to what was said and implied?

Sometimes, it is clear what the speaker intended to say or imply, but less clear what her attitude is to what she has said or implied. Consider a famous example from *Pride and Prejudice*. Elizabeth, the heroine, has finally agreed to marry Darcy, and her sister asks her when she first realized she was in love with him. Elizabeth replies:

(5)   I think it was when I first set eyes on his magnificent estate at Pemberley.

The question raised by Elizabeth's utterance is this: are we meant to think she believes what she said? In his review of *Pride and Prejudice*, Sir Walter Scott took the utterance literally, and condemned Elizabeth (and Jane Austen) for being mercenary. Many later readers have assumed that Elizabeth did not believe what she said: that she was indeed making fun of the idea that one might fall in love with someone for his magnificent estate. The issue, in other words, is whether Elizabeth's utterance was intended as ironical or not.

A similar issue arises at the level of implicature. Consider:

(6) a. Peter: Is John a good cook?
     b. Mary: He's English.

Given the reputation of English cooking, the most natural interpretation of Mary's utterance in (6b) is that she intended Peter to supply the assumption that the English are bad cooks, and to conclude that John is a bad cook. But while she clearly intended to commit herself to the claim that John is English, it is less clear that she seriously intended to commit herself to the truth of the assumption that the English are bad cooks, and the conclusion that therefore John is a bad cook. Perhaps she was merely being playful, encouraging her audience to entertain the stereotype without actually endorsing it? Clearly, there is room for misunderstanding here.

In deciding on the speaker's intended attitude to the propositions expressed and implied, the audience has to answer the following sorts of question. Is she endorsing these propositions or dissociating herself from them; is she asserting that they are true, wondering whether they are true, perhaps wishing or hoping that someone will make them true? To a certain extent, these attitudes can be linguistically encoded (e.g. by declarative, interrogative, or imperative syntax); but, as (5) and (6) show, in this aspect of interpretation as in any other, what is communicated generally goes well beyond what is linguistically encoded.

3 The nature and role of context

Understanding an utterance, then, involves answering three main questions: (a) what did the speaker intend to say; (b) what did the speaker intend to imply; and (c) what was the speaker's intended attitude to the propositions expressed and implied? It is obvious that *context* or background assumptions play a crucial role in answering these questions. By 'context' here, I mean not simply the preceding linguistic text, or the environment in which the utterance takes place, but the set of assumptions brought to bear in arriving at the intended interpretation. These may be drawn from the preceding text, or from observation of the speaker and what is going on in the immediate environment, but they may also be drawn from cultural or scientific knowledge, common-sense assumptions, and, more generally, any item of shared or idiosyncratic information that the hearer has access to at the time.

Selection of an appropriate set of contextual assumptions is crucial to the understanding of (1)–(6) above. With (1), the audience must have access to the assumption that jobs paying a thousand pounds a week are not handed out by advertising in the London Underground. With (2)–(4), the choice of context is crucial again: once we know what contextual assumptions we were intended to use, the intended implications follow by straightforward logical deduction. Finally, in (5)–(6), the difficulty of interpretation arises precisely because it is not clear what contextual assumptions we were intended to use: did Jane Austen in (5) mean us to assume that it is obviously ridiculous to imagine that one could fall in love with someone for his beautiful house, or did she mean us to assume that this was quite a reasonable thing to do?

Now, if contextual assumptions affect the way an utterance is understood, then in order to recognize the intended interpretation, the hearer must select and use the *intended* set of contextual assumptions. Which adds a further question to our list of questions that the hearer has to answer: (d) what was the *intended* set of contextual assumptions? And in some ways, this is the most fundamental question of all.

In most writings on communication, while it is recognized that context makes a major contribution to understanding, the problem of how the intended context is identified is not seriously addressed. The assumption is that in normal circumstances only a single set of contextual assumptions could possibly have been intended. I want to argue that this assumption is inadequate, and that the problem of context selection is a genuine and serious one.

Imagine the following scenario. I am a keen club tennis player, and you know that I have recently begun playing with a new doubles partner. When we meet, you ask me what my new doubles partner is like, and I reply:

(7)   He has much in common with John McEnroe.

At least for readers of the English tabloid press, the intended interpretation of this utterance will be immediately obvious. You are intended to use the contextual assumption that John McEnroe is extremely bad-tempered on court, and draw the conclusion that my new doubles partner is also bad-tempered on court. The question is why this is so.

Let us assume that our beliefs and assumptions about the world are organized in a sort of encyclopaedia in our minds under headings such as 'John McEnroe', 'tennis', 'doubles partner', and so on, and that in choosing a context for the interpretation of (7), the first place you will look will be under your mental heading for John McEnroe. Let us assume, too, that not all your beliefs and assumptions about John McEnroe are equally accessible, so that you do not pull out all of them at once. For most readers of the English tabloid press, as I have suggested, there is an immediate, very highly accessible assumption about John McEnroe that would come to mind in this situation: that he causes a lot of trouble on court. By using this assumption, and combining it with what was said in (7), you could derive the conclusion that my new doubles partner also causes a lot of trouble on court—which is the interpretation I have been assuming was correct.

Notice, though, that most people will have a lot more information than this stored under the heading 'John McEnroe'. You might know, for example, that John McEnroe is a very gifted tennis player, that he has a good serve-and-volley game, that he has played on the Centre Court at Wimbledon, that he is very rich, that he wears a headband when playing, that he is married to a film star, that he has a brother who plays tennis, that he enjoys rock music, and so on. By adding these assumptions to the context, you could derive a whole range of further implications: that my new doubles partner, like John McEnroe, is a very gifted tennis player, that he is very rich, that he has played on the Centre Court at Wimbledon, that he is married to a film star, and so on. What is there to stop you adding ever more contextual assumptions to the context, deriving ever more conclusions, and deciding that these were part of what I intended to imply? Notice, of course, that this is not what actual hearers would do.

This example suggests two important observations, which have to be taken account of in any adequate theory of utterance interpretation. First, it is clear that in interpreting (7) we do *not* assume that the speaker intended us to go on expanding the context indefinitely, deriving ever more implications. We do look for *some* implications, of course; but what we appear to do is choose the *minimal* set of implications that would make the utterance worth listening to, and stop there. In the case of (7), we assume that the speaker's new doubles partner is bad-tempered on court in much the same way as John McEnroe is bad-tempered on court, and stop at that. An adequate theory of communication should explain why this is so.

Second, we do not—and could not—compare all possible interpretations of an utterance before deciding on the intended one. Intuitively, we do not do this; but, as this example shows, theoretically, we could not do it either, since for any utterance there is a huge range of *possible* contexts and *possible* implications, not all of which could conceivably be considered in the very short time it takes to understand an utterance. What we need, and what hearers seem to have, is some method of recognizing the intended interpretation as soon as it presents itself, without necessarily considering any alternatives at all.

It should be clear by now that understanding an utterance involves considerably more than simply knowing the language. The class of *possible* interpretations is determined, on the one hand, by the meaning of the sentence uttered, and on the other by the set of available contextual assumptions. The hearer's task is to choose, from among this vast array of possible interpretations, the actual, intended one. In what follows, when I talk of the intended interpretation, I will mean the intended combination of explicit context, contextual assumptions and implications, and the speaker's intended attitude to these.

If the intended interpretation of an utterance is not recovered by decoding, how is it recovered? Grice, in his 'William James Lectures', suggested an answer to this question. The intended interpretation is not decoded but inferred, by a non-demonstrative inference process—a process of hypothesis formation and evaluation—in which linguistic decoding and contextual assumptions determine the class of *possible* hypotheses, and these are evaluated in the light of certain general principles of communication which speakers are expected to obey. According to Grice, speakers are expected to obey a Co-operative Principle and maxims of truthfulness, informativeness, relevance, and clarity; any hypothesis not satisfying these expectations can be automatically eliminated.

In our book *Relevance* (1986), Dan Sperber and I developed a theory of overt communication and understanding based on this fundamental idea of Grice's. In the next sections, I will explain the assumptions of relevance theory and apply them to a variety of examples. I will end by making some comparisons between relevance theory and Grice's earlier approach.[1]

4   Relevance theory

Relevance theory is based on a few very simple assumptions. First, that every utterance has a variety of possible interpretations, all compatible with the information that is linguistically encoded. Second, that not all these interpretations occur to the hearer simultaneously; some of them take more effort to think up. For instance, we saw with example (1) that the 'thousand pounds' interpretation is generally more accessible than the 'thousand jobs' interpretation, and with example (7) that, at least for most English tabloid readers, the assumption that John McEnroe is bad-tempered on court is easier to retrieve than the assumption that he has a brother who is a tennis player. As these examples also show, the order in which possible interpretations will occur to the hearer is at least to some extent predictable, though it is unlikely to be the same for all hearers at all times.

The third assumption is that hearers are equipped with a single, very general criterion for evaluating interpretations as they occur to them. In the case of (1), for instance, we know that the 'thousand pounds' interpretation will be rejected on some basis, and the 'thousand jobs' interpretation accepted. And the fourth, and final, assumption is that this criterion is powerful enough to exclude all but at most a single interpretation, so that having found an interpretation that satisfies it, the hearer need look no further: there will never be more than one.

The criterion proposed in Sperber and Wilson (1986) is based on a fundamental assumption about human cognition. The assumption is that human cognition is relevance-oriented: we pay attention to information that seems relevant to us. Now every utterance starts out as a request for the hearer's attention. As a result, it creates an expectation of relevance. It is around this expectation of relevance that the criterion for evaluating possible interpretations of an utterance is built. Different interpretations will be relevant in different ways: some will not be relevant at all; some will be fairly relevant; some will be very relevant. Which interpretation should the hearer choose? Clearly, the interpretation which best satisfies his expectation of relevance. To see how this criterion works, we need to know more about the nature of relevance and the expectation of relevance that every act of overt communication creates.

Relevance is defined in terms of *contextual effect* and *processing effort*. Contextual effects are achieved when newly presented information interacts with a context of existing assumptions in one of three ways: by strengthening an existing assumption, by contradicting and eliminating an existing assumption, or by combining with an existing assumption to yield a contextual implication: that is, a logical implication derivable neither from the new information alone, nor from the context alone, but from the new information and the context combined. We claim that newly presented information is relevant in a context when and only when it achieves contextual effects in that context, and the greater the contextual effects, the greater the relevance.

To illustrate these ideas, consider how the information in (8), given in tonight's weather forecast, might be relevant to you:

(8) It will rain in Paris tomorrow.

Suppose that you are going to Paris tomorrow, and already suspected that it was going to rain. Then (8) will achieve relevance by strengthening, or confirming, your existing assumption. Suppose instead that you are going to Paris tomorrow and were expecting it to be fine. Then, if you trust the weather forecast, (8) will achieve relevance by contradicting and eliminating your existing assumption. Finally, suppose that you are going to Paris tomorrow and have already decided to pack your raincoat if the forecast is for rain. Then (8) will achieve relevance by combining with this existing assumption to yield the contextual implication that you will pack your raincoat. All three types of contextual effect contribute to the relevance of (8), and the more contextual effects it achieves, the more relevant it will be.

Contextual effects, however, do not come free: they cost some mental effort to derive, and the greater the effort needed to derive them, the lower the relevance will be. To illustrate this idea, notice that (8) will seem more relevant to us if we really are planning to go to Paris tomorrow. In these circumstances, we will have no trouble thinking up an appropriate context, in which (8) will yield a satisfactory range of contextual effects, and hence be relevant to us. If we are not going to Paris tomorrow, we could no doubt still think up an appropriate context, but some effort of memory or imagination would be required. Intuitively, the greater the effort required, the less relevant (8) will seem to us.

The processing effort required to understand an utterance depends on two main factors. First, the effort of memory and imagination needed to construct a suitable context; second, the psychological complexity of the utterance itself. Greater complexity implies greater processing effort; gratuitous complexity detracts from relevance. Thus, compare (9a) with the longer and linguistically more complex (9b):

(9)   a. It's raining in Paris.
      b. It's raining in Paris and fish swim in the sea.

In circumstances where the hearer needs no reminding that fish swim in the sea, the extra linguistic complexity of (9b) will not be offset by any extra contextual effects, and will detract from the overall relevance of (9b) as compared with (9a).

The linguistic structure of an utterance is not the only source of psychological complexity. In fact, a linguistically simpler utterance may none the less be psychologically more complex. For instance, it is well known from psycholinguistic experiments that frequently encountered words are easier to process than rarely encountered ones. Thus, compare (10a) and (10b):

(10) a. I have no brothers or sisters.
      b. I have no siblings.

Although (10a) is linguistically more complex than (10b), most English speakers in most circumstances would regard it as stylistically preferable. The reason is that although (10b) is linguistically less complex, it contains the very rare word 'sibling', which generally requires more processing effort than the longer, but more familiar, 'brothers or sisters'.

Relevance, then, depends on contextual effects and processing effort. The greater the contextual effects, the greater the relevance; but the greater the processing effort needed to obtain these effects, the *lower* the relevance. The connection between relevance and understanding should now be clear. To see the intended relevance of an utterance, the hearer must identify the proposition and propositional attitude expressed, and combine these with the intended set of contextual assumptions to obtain the intended contextual effects; the intended set of contextual effects will include the intended contextual implications of the utterance, or what we have been calling its implicatures. To see the intended relevance of an utterance, then, amounts to recovering the intended combination of content, context, attitude, and implications. Relevance and understanding are two sides of a single coin.

The most basic assumption of relevance theory is that every aspect of communication and cognition is governed by the search for relevance. What is unique to overt communication is that, approaching an utterance addressed to us, we are entitled to have not just hopes but steady expectations of relevance. In the next section, I will argue that the expectation of relevance created by every utterance is precise enough, and powerful enough, to exclude all but at most a single interpretation, so that if we find an interpretation that satisfies our expectation of relevance, we can be sure that it will be the only one.

A word of caution here. Precisely because utterance interpretation is not a simple matter of decoding, but a fallible process of hypothesis formation and evaluation, there is no *guarantee* that the interpretation that satisfies the hearer's expectation of relevance will be the correct, i.e. the intended, one. Because of mismatches in memory and perceptual systems, the hearer may overlook a hypothesis that the speaker thought would be highly salient, or notice a hypothesis that the speaker had overlooked. Misunderstandings occur. The aim of a theory of communication is to identify the principles underlying the hearer's (fallible) choices. Relevance theory claims that the interpretation that satisfies the expectation of relevance is the only one that the hearer has any rational basis for choosing. To claim that a choice is rationally justified, however, is not the same as claiming that it is invariably correct.

5   The criterion of consistency with the principle of relevance

The principle of relevance is the principle that every utterance (or other act of overt communication) creates an expectation of relevance. What exactly does this expectation amount to, in terms of effort and effect? Here, there is an obvious hypothesis: that what the hearer is looking for is the most relevant interpretation: that is, the one that yields the greatest possible contextual effects in return for the smallest amount of processing effort. It is worth seeing why this hypothesis is wrong. In order to find the *most* relevant interpretation of an utterance, the hearer would have to consider and compare all *possible* interpretations; but, as we saw when discussing the McEnroe example above, it is clear for both intuitive and theoretical reasons that hearers do not compare all possible interpretations of an utterance before deciding on the intended one.

In Sperber and Wilson (1986), Dan Sperber and I define a notion of *optimal* relevance which is meant to spell out what the hearer is looking for in terms of effort and effect. An utterance, on a given interpretation, is optimally relevant if and only if:

(a)   it achieves enough contextual effects to be worth the hearer's attention;
(b)   it puts the hearer to no gratuitous processing effort in achieving those effects.

A word of explanation about each of these clauses. On the effect side, what the hearer is entitled to look for is enough effects to make the utterance worth his while to process. In general, what this means is that he is entitled to expect more effects than he would have got from any other information that he could have been processing at the time. How much that is depends on what is going on elsewhere in his cognitive environment. Thus, suppose that someone walks into an important lecture and says (11):

(11)   Ladies and gentlemen, I have to tell you that the building's on fire.

'The building' is a referential expression, and different assignments of reference lead to different levels of contextual effect. In the circumstances, the
first hypothesis to come to the audience's mind should be that 'the building'
means the building where the lecture is taking place. Clearly, the utterance,
on this interpretation, would achieve enough effects to be worth the audience's attention: their minds would be immediately filled with thoughts of
how to get out. Given that at a formal lecture the audience is supposed to
be entirely absorbed in what the lecturer is saying, it is hard to see what
other interpretation would achieve enough effects to justify the interrup-
tion; and in these circumstances, the interpretation just suggested is basically the only possible one.
might be thought that in other circumstances the intended interpretation
would be harder to pin down. Surely there might be several radically different combinations of content and context, each of which would yield enough
contextual effects to make the utterance worth the audience's attention?
This is where clause (b) of the definition of optimal relevance comes in.
Recall that we are talking about overt communication, where the speaker
is anxious to avoid misunderstanding, and is actively helping the hearer to
recognize the intended interpretation. Clearly, it is in such a speaker's interest to make sure that there is no interpretation which is both easier for the
hearer to construct than the intended one, and has enough effects to be
worth his attention, since such an interpretation is likely to lead him astray.
Clause (b) of the definition of optimal relevance, which excludes gratuitous
calls on the hearer's processing effort, covers this type of case: that is, it
excludes the possibility that the hearer will be expected to recover, process,
and accept the wrong interpretation before lighting on the intended one.
From clause (b), it follows that a speaker aiming at optimal relevance
should try to formulate her utterance in such a way that the first acceptable
interpretation to occur to the hearer is the one she intended to convey.
From the hearer's point of view, this clause has an immediate practical
consequence. Having found an interpretation which satisfies his expectation
of relevance in a way the speaker might manifestly have foreseen, he need
look no further. The first such interpretation is the only such interpretation,
and is the one the hearer should choose.

   I should note in passing that in order to be acceptable and comprehensible, an utterance does not actually have to *be* optimally relevant. Suppose
that, as you are about to leave the house, I warn you that it is raining; as
it happens, this is something you already know. In the circumstances, the
proposition I have expressed will have no contextual effects and hence be
irrelevant to you. None the less, my utterance will be both comprehensible
and acceptable as long as you can see how I might reasonably have expected
it to be relevant. The actual criterion proposed in Sperber and Wilson

(1986), then, is a criterion of consistency with the principle of relevance which takes account of this type of case:

> An utterance, on a given interpretation, is consistent with the principle of relevance if and only if the speaker might rationally have expected it to be optimally relevant to the hearer on that interpretation.

Vague as this criterion may sound, it makes one important prediction not matched by other theories. This follows from clause (b) of the definition of optimal relevance and its consequence that the first interpretation tested and found consistent with the principle of relevance is the only interpretation consistent with the principle of relevance. Let us assume that, in interpreting an utterance, the hearer starts with a small initial context left over, say, from his processing of the previous utterance: he computes the contextual effects of the utterance in that initial context; if these are not enough to make the utterance worth his attention, he expands the context, obtaining further effects, and repeats the process until he has enough effects to make the utterance optimally relevant in a way the speaker could manifestly have foreseen. At that point, he has an interpretation consistent with the principle of relevance, and it follows that he should stop; or, at least, he is entitled to continue on his own account, but is not entitled to assume that the speaker intended to communicate anything more. In other words, all the hearer is entitled to impute as part of the intended interpretation is the *minimal* (i.e. smallest, most accessible) context and contextual effects that would be enough to make the utterance worth his attention. Thus, the interpretation process has an in-built stopping place.

6   Some consequences of relevance theory

In this section, I will look at some practical applications of relevance theory to the analysis of a variety of examples. These will be grouped under two headings, to illustrate the two main strategies of analysis that relevance theory provides. Under the first heading fall analyses hinging on the assumption that the first interpretation tested and found consistent with the principle of relevance is the only interpretation consistent with the principle of relevance; under the second heading fall analyses hinging on the assumption that any extra processing effort demanded will be offset by extra effects. Both strategies ultimately derive from clause (b) of the definition of optimal relevance, which excludes gratuitous demands on the hearer's processing effort.

(a)   The first acceptable interpretation is the only acceptable interpretation

This set of analyses all rest on the same point: that if an utterance has a highly salient (i.e. immediately accessible) interpretation which the speaker *could* have intended, then, by clause (b) of the definition of optimal relevance, this is the one she *should* have intended: she cannot rationally have intended to communicate anything else.

My first example is adapted from Katz (1972: 449–50). Suppose someone walks up and down outside the White House in America with a placard saying:

(12)   George Bush is a crook.

He is then prosecuted for libelling the then President of the United States. His defence lawyer argues that he was not intending to refer to the President, but was talking about a shopkeeper who had cheated him in his home town. As Katz (ibid.) says:

> It seems clear that such a defense would probably fail ... The court would reason that the speaker must have known or can be assumed to have known that a national audience would inevitably take the occurrence of ['George Bush'] to refer to the President, and thus he ought to have employed a qualifying expression (e.g. 'who runs the grocery store in my neighborhood') to make the statement that he says he intended to make.

In other words, if, in the circumstances, your utterance has a manifestly satisfactory and immediately accessible interpretation, that is the only interpretation you can rationally intend to communicate.

How does this follow from the definition of optimal relevance? Clause (b) of the definition says that the speaker should put the hearer to no gratuitous processing effort in achieving the intended effects. But it is clear that, in the circumstances described above, the speaker of (12) *would* have put his audience to some gratuitous effort if he intended to refer to anyone other than George Bush. He would have put them to the unjustifiable effort of first recovering, processing, and accepting the wrong interpretation (i.e. the interpretation in which he was referring to the President of the United States), then wondering whether this was, in fact, the intended one, looking around for an alternative interpretation, and then, presumably, engaging in some further form of inference to decide between the two. Moreover, he could have spared his audience all this effort by reformulating his utterance in the way suggested by Katz, thus eliminating the unintended interpretation. It follows that the first interpretation consistent with the principle of relevance is the only interpretation consistent with the principle of relevance: all other interpretations are disallowed.

My second example involves disambiguation. Suppose we are writing the plot of a television thriller, and I am giving you instructions about how the scenes should go. At one point, I say:

(13)   In scene 10, when the police come in, the criminal makes a bolt for the door.

This utterance is ambiguous, with the two linguistically possible interpretations (14a) and (14b):

(14)   a. When the police come in, the criminal runs for the door.
      b. When the police come in, the criminal gets out his tool-kit and constructs a door-bolt.

In normal circumstances, the only legitimate interpretation would be on the lines of (14a). How can this be explained?

Relevance theory suggests the following explanation. In the circumstances, the first interpretation to occur to the hearer should be (14a); moreover, this interpretation will be consistent with the principle of relevance: i.e. it will yield adequate effects for no unjustifiable effort in a way the speaker could manifestly have foreseen. Why should it be the first interpretation to occur to the hearer? Because it is based on a very stereotypical scenario. We have all frequently seen thrillers in which such a scene occurs; we should thus have easy access to a ready-made context in which to process the utterance on this interpretation: the police come in, the criminal runs to the door to escape the police, the police give chase, and so on. As a result, we should be able to achieve adequate effects for very little effort. By contrast, although we might all be able to think up a scenario in which the police arrive and the criminal, who happens to have a tool-kit handy, sits down and hammers out a door-bolt, it would take some effort of imagination to do so. Hence, an overall interpretation along the lines of (14a) will be easier to construct, and, once constructed, will prove satisfactory.

It follows from clause (b) of the definition of optimal relevance that a speaker, knowing this, is not free to intend an interpretation along the lines of (14b), and a hearer, knowing this, is not free to choose an interpretation along the lines of (14b). That is, on hearing my utterance in (13), you are not free to go out and shoot a scene based on (14b). In disambiguation, as in reference assignment, the first interpretation tested and found consistent with the principle of relevance is the only interpretation consistent with the principle of relevance: all other interpretations are disallowed.

Exactly parallel arguments apply to the selection of intended context and implicatures. Thus, consider the following exchange:

(15)   a. Peter: Would you like some coffee?
      b. Mary: Coffee would keep me awake.

In interpreting Mary's utterance, Peter would normally be expected to supply the contextual assumption in (16) and derive the contextual implication in (17):

(16)   Mary doesn't want to be kept awake.

(17)   Mary doesn't want any coffee.

Notice that this is not the only possible interpretation. In certain circumstances—for instance, if Peter and Mary are just about to attend a boring lecture—an interpretation along the lines of (18) and (19) might be both intended and understood:

(18)   Mary wants to stay awake.

(19)   Mary wants some coffee.

How does the hearer know which interpretation was intended? The answer again follows from clause (b) of the definition of optimal relevance. If, in the circumstances, the contextual assumption in (16) is highly salient, and leads on to a satisfactory interpretation, then *this* is the only interpretation that the speaker is free to intend and the hearer to choose. Similarly, if, in the circumstances, the contextual assumption in (18) is highly salient, then this is the only interpretation that the speaker is free to intend and the hearer to choose. The first interpretation tested and found consistent with the principle of relevance is the only interpretation consistent with the principle of relevance: all other interpretations are disallowed. Returning to the McEnroe example, we can now explain why the hearer, having found a satisfactory interpretation based on the highly salient assumption that John McEnroe is bad-tempered on court, is not free to expand the context indefinitely, deriving ever more implicatures. By clause (b) of the definition of optimal relevance, as soon as this highly salient and satisfactory interpretation is discovered, all other interpretations are disallowed. The criterion of consistency with the principle of relevance thus explains the observation made earlier in connection with this example: that the *minimal* satisfactory interpretation is the one the hearer should choose.

(b)   Extra effort implies extra effect

Let us look a little more closely at example (15) above, in which Mary says 'Coffee would keep me awake', intending Peter to supply the assumption that she does not want to stay awake and derive the conclusion that she does not want any coffee. Would Mary's utterance, on this interpretation, be consistent with the principle of relevance? If this were all she wanted to communicate, the answer would be 'No'.

To see why this is so, we need to ask ourselves two questions, corresponding to the two clauses of the definition of optimal relevance: (a) could Mary have expected her utterance, on this interpretation, to achieve adequate effects? and (b) was there some other utterance (equally easy for Mary to produce) which would have achieved the intended effects more economically? It seems clear that the answer to question (a) is 'Yes'. After all, by asking the question in (17a), Peter has indicated that a 'yes' or a 'no' answer would be adequately relevant to him. It seems equally clear, though, that if all Mary wanted to communicate was that she did not want any coffee, she could have communicated it more economically by saying, simply, 'No'. Her utterance, on this interpretation, fails clause (b) of the definition of optimal relevance: it puts the hearer to some gratuitous effort.

It follows that if Mary was aiming at optimal relevance, she must have intended the indirect answer in (17b) to achieve some additional contextual effects, not achievable by the direct answer 'No'. Once alerted, we can see that this is so. By saying that coffee would keep her awake, Mary not only refuses the coffee, but gives an explanation for her refusal—an explanation which would not have been communicated by the simple answer 'No'.

This example illustrates a very pervasive feature of utterance interpretation. Any element of indirectness in an utterance demands additional processing effort, and thus, by clause (b) of the definition of optimal relevance, encourages a search for additional effects—effects that a more direct formulation would not have achieved. Returning to the McEnroe example, we can see that a similar sort of indirectness argument applies. I have suggested that the hearer of (7) is intended to supply the assumption in (20) and derive the conclusion in (21):

(7)   He has much in common with John McEnroe.

(20)   John McEnroe behaves badly on court.

(21)   The new doubles partner behaves badly on court.

But if the only information the speaker wanted to communicate was that her new doubles partner behaved badly on court, why not say so directly? Why put her hearer to the additional effort of processing (7), looking into his encyclopaedic entry for John McEnroe, retrieving assumption (20) and then performing a step of logical inference to arrive at (21)? It follows from clause (b) of the definition of optimal relevance that by putting her hearer to this additional effort, she must have intended to achieve some additional effect not achievable by saying simply (21). Here, the most likely line of interpretation is that she has in mind a particular degree and type of bad-temperedness: in other words, that she is encouraging her hearer to draw the conclusion:

(22)   The new doubles partner is bad-tempered on court in a similar way to John McEnroe.

And that, of course, is something that would not have been achieved by saying simply (21).

Metaphor provides a further type of indirectness argument. Consider (23) and (24):

(23)   John is a lion.

(24)   Bill is a donkey.

Many analysts of metaphor argue that these utterances communicate (25) and (26), respectively:

(25) John is brave.

(26) Bill is stupid.

Certainly, given stereotypical assumptions about lions and donkeys, these conclusions could be derived as contextual implications from (23) and (24). Within the framework of relevance theory, however, there is an indirectness argument to show that these analyses are inadequate as they stand. If all the speaker of (23) wanted to communicate was that John was brave, why not say so directly? Why put the hearer to the additional effort of processing (23), accessing the contextual assumption that lions are brave, and deriving (25) as a contextual implication? A speaker aiming at optimal relevance must have intended to achieve some additional effects not achievable simply by saying (25): she might have intended to communicate, for example, not only that John is brave, but that he is brave in the way a lion is: the courage is physical rather than mental, depends on physical rather than moral strength, and so on; that is, she might have intended to communicate something more like (27):

(27) John is brave in the way a lion is brave.

And (23) might well have been a more economical way of achieving *these* effects than saying (27) directly. Parallel arguments apply to (24) and (26).

Indirectness involves making the hearer derive as a contextual implication something that could have been said directly. Not all arguments based on effort involve indirectness. Compare (28) and (29), for example:

(28) That was a stupid thing to do.

(29) That was a stupid, stupid thing to do.

It has often been noted that repetition can have an intensifying effect. Thus (29) might be understood as communicating something like (30):

(30) That was a very stupid thing to do.

Relevance theory suggests a natural explanation. By repeating 'stupid', the speaker puts the hearer to some additional effort. By clause (b) of the definition of optimal relevance, she must therefore have intended to achieve some additional effects, not achievable by use of the simpler (28). The most natural assumption—and hence the one favoured by considerations of optimal relevance—is that she thought the action described was stupider than would have been indicated by the use of (28). On this interpretation, (29) would indeed have been equivalent to (30).[2]

7 Relevance theory and Gricean pragmatics

Grice's 'William James Lectures', delivered in 1967, offered the first systematic alternative to a code theory of communication and understanding.

Focusing on the implicit aspects of communication, Grice argued that the implicatures of an utterance are not decoded but inferred, by a non-demonstrative inference process in which contextual assumptions and general principles of communication play an important role. His account of implicatures as beliefs that have to be attributed to the speaker in order to preserve the assumption that she has obeyed a Co-operative Principle and maxims of truthfulness, informativeness, relevance, and clarity, had instant appeal, provoked a flood of research, and is the starting point for most pragmatic theories today.

Grice's insights left many questions unanswered. There were questions, in particular, about the nature and source of the Co-operative Principle and maxims. Is co-operation essential to communication? Do speakers really aim at truthfulness, informativeness, relevance, and clarity? What is relevance? Grice left this undefined. Where do the Co-operative Principle and maxims come from? Are they universal? If so, are they innate? Are they culture-specific? If so, why do they vary, and how are they acquired? In Sperber and Wilson (1986), Dan Sperber and I set out to answer these questions. The resulting theory, sketched above, looks rather different from Grice's.

There is a difference, first, over the role of the Co-operative Principle and maxims. For Grice, the fundamental principle of communication is the Co-operative Principle, according to which the speaker should try to make her contribution 'such as is required, at the stage at which it occurs, by the accepted purpose or direction of the talk exchange'. Grice assumed that every utterance, every conversation, has an accepted purpose or direction whose identification plays a crucial role in comprehension. This raises two questions: how is the accepted purpose of the utterance identified? and, once identified, how does it help with comprehension? Neither question has received a satisfactory answer.

Consider example (1) above ('If you're looking for a good job, we're offering a thousand a week'). The purpose of this advertisement is to attract people to the employment agency in question. As far as I can see, this purpose could be equally well achieved on either of the interpretations mentioned: how, then, does knowing the purpose of the advertisement help to choose between them? Consider the McEnroe example. The purpose of this utterance is to inform the hearer about the speaker's new doubles partner. It could equally well achieve this purpose on either the minimal, correct interpretation, or any of the more expansive interpretations which we have seen are incorrect. How, then, does knowing the purpose of the utterance help with the identification of the intended context and implicatures? These questions have not been satisfactorily answered within the Gricean framework.

There is a more serious problem with the Co-operative Principle. To the extent that the purpose of an utterance does play a role in comprehension, this merely adds a further question to the list of questions that the hearer has to answer: how is the accepted purpose of an utterance identified? Grice gives no answer to this. Like many theorists of communication, he seems to have assumed that the purpose of an utterance, like the set of intended contextual assumptions, is somehow given in advance of the comprehension process, or identifiable independently of it. In fact, it could not be identified by use of the Co-operative Principle itself, on pain of circularity: to identify the purpose of an utterance by use of the Co-operative Principle, one would already have to know it. Grice's theory of communication thus rests on the assumption that the purpose of an utterance is identifiable by some process that falls outside the scope of comprehension proper, and that is never satisfactorily explained.

Relevance theory suggests the following explanation. There is no Co-operative Principle, and hence no circularity in assuming that the purpose of an utterance can be identified, where necessary, as part of the comprehension process. To the extent that the purpose of an utterance does contribute to comprehension, it is identifiable as a contextual assumption like any other, via the criterion of consistency with the principle of relevance. In this framework, there is room for a notion of purpose, but the real burden of explanation lies elsewhere.

Among the maxims, Grice sees truthfulness as the most important; relevance theory argues that there is no maxim of truthfulness, and indeed no maxims at all.[3] Relevance theory is not a rule-based or maxim-based system. In this framework, relevance is fundamental to communication not because speakers obey a maxim of relevance, but because relevance is fundamental to cognition. As a result, the questions that arise in Grice's framework about the number of the maxims, their universality or culture dependence, their acquisition, and the relative weight attached to each of them, do not arise.

Another difference between the two frameworks is over the role of maxim violation. Grice listed a number of ways in which a speaker could violate the maxims: she could *opt out*, explicitly or implicitly, thus suspending a maxim; she could *covertly violate* a maxim, with intent to deceive; or she could *overtly violate* a maxim, thus creating an implicature. Although the mechanisms involved were unclear, the assumption that overt violation can create an implicature plays a crucial role in Grice's framework, and in particular in his account of metaphor and irony. This assumption has rarely been questioned (though see Hugly and Sayward (1979), for an excellent discussion). Relevance theory rejects it.

The principle of relevance is not a maxim: it is not a rule that speakers can obey or disobey: it is an exceptionless generalization about what happens when someone is addressed. In such a framework, it makes no sense to claim that the principle of relevance can be overtly violated to create an implicature. How, then, do metaphor, irony, and the other phenomena that Grice analysed in terms of maxim violation arise?

Sperber and Wilson argue that metaphor is simply a variety of loose talk. In a framework with no maxim of truthfulness, where speakers are not constrained to say only what is strictly speaking true, speaking loosely is often the best way of achieving optimal relevance. Hence, metaphor should arise naturally in such a framework. As we saw in section 6 above, the interpretation of metaphor involves an element of indirectness. This calls for extra processing effort, which, according to clause (b) of the definition of optimal relevance, must be offset by extra effects. In this framework, indirectness, with its resulting increase in processing effort demanded and contextual effects achieved, does much of the work that maxim-violation was supposed to do for Grice.[4]

A further difference between the Gricean approach and relevance theory is that whereas Grice was mainly concerned with the implicit side of communication, relevance theory has been equally concerned with the explicit side. Relevance theorists have looked in particular at the role of contextual factors in disambiguation, reference assignment, and other processes that contribute, in Grice's terms, to what was *said* rather than what was implicated: that is, to the truth conditional content of utterances. Much work has been done on distinguishing explicit from implicit communication, and truth conditional from non-truth conditional meaning; this seems to me to have been a particularly fruitful line of research.[5]

Having drawn attention to some of the differences between Gricean pragmatics and relevance theory, I would like to end by underlining what they have in common. Relevance theory rests squarely on Gricean foundations: Sperber and Wilson accept Grice's view that the goal of pragmatic theory is to explain how the hearer recognizes the overtly intended interpretation of an utterance; they acknowledge the importance of non-demonstrative inference in comprehension, and agree with Grice that general principles of communication play a major role in the inference process, though not, perhaps, in quite the way Grice thought.

Notes

1 An excellent textbook on relevance theory is Blakemore (1992). For further discussion, see the multiple review of Sperber and Wilson (1986) in *Behavioural and Brain Sciences* 10/4 (1987), and the reply in Sperber and Wilson (1987). For applications of relevance theory, see Blakemore (1987); Blass (1990); and Gutt (1991).

2 For further discussion of the effects of repetition, see Sperber and Wilson (1986) Chapter 4: 219–22.

3 For discussion of the maxim of truthfulness, see Sperber and Wilson (1986); Wilson and Sperber (1988).

4 For discussion of metaphor and irony within the relevance theoretic framework, see Sperber and Wilson (1985/6, 1990); Wilson and Sperber (1988, 1992).

5 See, for example, Blakemore (1987, 1992); Carston (1988); Wilson and Sperber (forthcoming). Several papers on relevance theory are collected in Davis (1991); see also Volume 87, Parts 1 and 2 of *Lingua*, which are devoted to recent work on relevance theory.

4   Syntactic clues to understanding

In this paper, Keith Brown is concerned to give an account of how it is that we can know, having heard or read a sentence taken out of context, much more than is directly asserted in the sentence. He draws attention to a range of related syntactic phenomena which have specific semantic implications. They give rise to what he calls 'implicatures', a term which he uses very generally to embrace not only non-cancellable entailments and presuppositions but also conventional implicatures and what have hitherto been treated as rather loose implications which he shows can be seen as systematically derivable from a generalizable analytic framework.

These implicatures not only fill the communicative stage with unmentioned agents, patients, and instruments, they also contribute crucially to the structuring of 'point of view' discussed in Short's paper (this volume). They may also indicate, sometimes only subtly, such aspects of meaning as whether or not an action was intentional and whether or not it was completed successfully.

Brown's strategy is to take one verb HIT and submit it to a fine-grained analysis, drawing out in detail the types of 'implicature' which derive from its use in a given type of construction. As the paper progresses, Brown teases apart the implicatures which are derived from the generalized sentence type, the generalized verb type, and those which are derived from the lexis of the verb itself. He contrasts the implicatures of HIT with those derived from other, semantically related, verbs, and proposes generalized lexical rules which show how these implicatures are derived. In an Appendix, he demonstrates briefly how the same treatment might be applied to other verbs. It seems clear that such an analysis can be fruitfully applied far more generally throughout the vocabulary.

It is an approach which sees the verb as establishing a cognitive framework which would be quite compatible with the notions of *scenario* or *script* mentioned by Aitchison and Garnham (this volume). One could think of a 'hitting' scenario which involves an agent, a patient, something used to hit with, some degree of violence, a location in which it occurs, someone who starts off not having been hit and who finishes up having been hit, and so on.

Similarly, imagine the scenario for 'buying' which would involve a person having money ('the price'), an object ('the thing (desired and) bought') in the possession of someone else ('the seller'), and a temporal transaction during which the person who had the money but not the object comes to have the desired object but not the money.

Short (this volume) remarks that it is rarely the case that it is appropriate to teach grammar directly to students, unless they are advanced students. He would agree, however, that what is important is that teachers of a language should have a thorough grasp of how syntax operates to provide clues to semantic understanding. If they have such a grasp, they can explain on a particular occasion to a student how it is that a particular sentence can mean more than it explicitly states, or why it is that the verb that the student has chosen to use, which may be perfectly grammatical, none the less carries with it inappropriate semantic implicatures which leads to the student appearing to say something not in the least intended.

A number of papers in this collection (those by G. Brown, Brumfit, and Spolsky, for instance) have insisted on the riskiness of communication as texts are re-read and re-interpreted, and of the dangers of misunderstanding. This paper (like that by Milroy) is concerned with the basic building blocks of meaning, what you need to get straight before you even get to the point of developing a misunderstanding. If you do not appreciate the difference in point of view which a young delinquent tries to establish by saying 'My ball hit the window' rather than 'I hit the window with my ball', you will be ill-equipped not only to read literary works and newspaper articles, but also to do business in English and to hold easy social interactions. Because the study of syntax involves careful attention to grammatical detail, there are those who hope that they can avoid syntax and leap straight to meaning. This chapter shows the dangers of adopting such a view.

Syntactic clues to understanding

Keith Brown
Research Centre for English and Applied Linguistics
University of Cambridge, and

Department of Language and Linguistics
University of Essex

A speaker can present an event from a variety of different perspectives. An old joke declares that a politician's attitude towards the giving and receiving of favours is reflected in the paradigm:

I receive an occasional small gift
You accept too many expensive presents
He takes bribes

Different perspectives on the same event can be communicated lexically, by the speaker's choice of words as in the example, or grammatically, by exploiting various grammatical patterns. This chapter explores some of the ways in which a reader or writer can exploit grammatical patterns as clues to communicative effects which the reader or listener needs to be able to interpret in order to recover the intended meaning. Some of these effects are very subtle.

Lexical meaning is the sense attributed to items in the dictionary. Grammatical meaning is associated with those elements of meaning that derive from grammatical categories like tense and aspect, sentence forms like active and passive and syntactic functions like subject of and object of. Lexical and grammatical meaning are closely related, and particularly so in the area of transitivity: the description of the number, nature, and order of the arguments of a verb. The traditional distinction classifies verbs as transitive, intransitive, and the like, but this description is not fine-grained enough.

In this chapter, we will examine some of the inter-relationships between the sense of a verb and the various syntactic patterns in which it can be found. We will explore these issues as they affect a single verb, HIT[1]. In the Appendix, the reader is invited to explore the extent to which our findings can be generalized to other verbs.

1   A 'hitting' event

Imagine a situation where an individual, who we will refer to as Kim, hits a table with a stick:

(1)   Kim   hit   the table   with a stick
       agent   *patient/goal*   *instrument*

A prototypical hitting event involves three *participants*: an *agent* (Kim) who delivers a blow with an *instrument* (a stick) on a *patient* or *goal* (the table), which receives the blow. HIT has the sense 'strike with a blow'[2]. STRIKE has the sense 'subject something to an impact', which we could analyse as 'cause something to receive an impact'. In (1) *Kim* (the agent) is the causer, *the table* (the patient or goal) is the something which receives the impact, and a stick is the instrument that delivers the blow.

The description of events is usually focused on verbs, which can be assigned to a variety of *aspectual types* on the basis of the kind of the event they describe and the number and nature of the participants involved. The aspectual type of HIT is an *activity* verb and if we assume that the event described in (1) involves the intentional action of an agent directed at a goal we can further characterize it as a verb of *directed activity*.[3]

The description of the participants involved is the *argument structure* of the verb and is typically focused on the noun phrase (NP) and the prepositional phrase (PP) associated with the verb. In (1) we have characterized the function of the various arguments as agent, patient/goal, and instrument.[4] The agent is the active participant, the causer of the impact who used the instrument to deliver the blow. The third participant in (1) is characterized as patient/goal to capture its dual function, as the patient that suffers the action of the verb and the goal that receives the impact. The two roles can be dissociated, as they are in:

(2)   Kim   hit   Shane   on the head   with a book
       agent   *patient*   *goal*   *instrument*

and in other examples to which we will turn in due course.

HIT is traditionally characterized as a transitive verb. This means that it occurs with an obligatory object NP, *the table* in (1), and may also occur with various optional PPs, like the instrumental *with a stick*. This traditional *constituent selection* refers only to the verb and its sister constituents within the VP—the object NP and associated PPs. For reasons which will shortly become clear, it will be helpful to expand the traditional constituent selection frame to the representation in (3) which also includes the subject expression. Paired round brackets indicate an optional constituent, paired square brackets show constituent structure: thus (PP[*with* NP$_3$]) means that the PP is optional, but if it is chosen it must have the constituents [*with* NP].

(3) a. NP₁   V   NP₂   (PP[*with* NP₃])
     b. Kim   hit   the table   (with a stick)

Statements of constituent selection are important since they specify the category of the constituents that must or may occur with a verb, but they need to be supplemented by a statement about *argument selection*: how the arguments are distributed to the various constituents. In (3), argument selection is handled by subscripting the NPs: we can then say that agent has been selected as NP₁, patient/goal as NP₂, and instrument as NP₃ in a *with* PP. The subscriptions relate to argument selection and not to grammatical functions like subject and object. These functions are implicit in the ordering shown in (3a): the subject is the NP immediately preceding the verb and the object the NP immediately following the verb.

In an active sentence like (1), the agent and patient/goal arguments are obligatory, as (4a) shows, but the instrument is optional: we will return to sentences like (4b) when we discuss (12).

(4) a. *Kim   hit   (with a stick)
     b. Kim   hit   the table

The description is summarized in (5):

(5) HIT:
         sense: cause to receive an impact
                                             'strike with a blow'

         aspectual type: directed activity
         argument structure: agent; patient/goal; instrument
         constituent selection: NP₁ V NP₂ (PP[*with* NP₃])
         argument selection for active: agent: NP₁ (subject)
                                             patient/goal NP₂ (object)
                                             instrument: PP[*with* NP₃]

A sentence like (1) has a variety of *implicatures*[5], among them those in (6):

(6) a. Kim did something
     b. Kim did something to the table
     c. Kim had a stick
     d. Kim used a stick to hit the table
     e. Kim caused a stick to hit the table
     f. The table received the blow
     g. The stick hit the table with some force
     h. The table was affected by Kim's action
     i. Kim acted intentionally

With respect to (1), (6a–e) have the force of entailments since we cannot simultaneously assert (1) and deny any of (6a–e):

(7)   a. *Kim hit the table with a stick but didn't do anything
              (1 but not 6a)
      b. *Kim hit the table with a stick, but didn't use a stick
              (1 but not 6c)
      c. *Kim hit the table with a stick, but missed
              (1 but not 6d).

By contrast, although the default interpretation of (1) is that it describes an intentional act, (6i) can be cancelled, overtly by an adverb, as in (8), or covertly in an appropriate context.

(8)   Kim accidentally hit the table with a stick

There are other ways of indicating a non-volitional 'hitting', as we shall see when we discuss (27) below.

   We are supposing that in (1) HIT has the sense 'strike with a blow': (6g) accounts for the oddness of (9):

(9)   Kim hit the table with a feather

A blow implies force and a feather is an inappropriate instrument. Using a feather as instrument we would be more likely to STROKE or CARESS. (6e,g) assert that in (1) it is the instrument, *the stick*, rather than the agent, *Kim*, that actually comes into direct contact with the table. The implicature of (6h) arises from the selection of the patient/goal argument as the direct object[6].

   These implicatures can also account for paraphrases of (1) like:

(10)   a. Kim used a stick to hit the table
       b. Kim hit the table and he did so with a stick
       c. Kim had a stick and used it to hit the table

and so on.

   The implicatures derive from a number of sources, some general in the language and others specific to the particular verb. Some of the general implicatures derive from the aspectual class of the verb and its argument structure. With a verb of directed activity, (6a,i) are implicatures of the agent argument; (6g) is an implicature of the patient/goal argument and (6c,d,e) are implicatures of agent and instrument arguments. The implicature of force in (6f) derives from the specific lexical item HIT. The implicature in (6h) arises from the way arguments are selected as grammatical subject and object. Some implicatures derive from more than one of these sources: (6b), for example, is a combination of argument structure and argument selection.

   In (6), the implicatures are expressed in the specific terms that apply to the example sentence (1). It will be more helpful to think of them in the more general terms shown in (11):

(11) a. agent does something
     b. agent does something to grammatical object
     c. agent has instrument
     d. agent uses instrument
     e. agent causes instrument to contact patient/goal
     f. instrument contacts patient/goal with some force
     g. goal receives the action of verb
     h. grammatical object affected by activity of agent
     i. agent acts intentionally (deliberately etc.)

implicature derived from:

a. agent in directed activity
b. agent and grammatical object in directed activity
c,d. agent and instrument in directed activity
e. HIT, agent, instrument and goal in directed activity
f. HIT
g. goal in directed activity
h. argument selection for grammatical object
i. agent in directed activity

2 Understood arguments

We began by declaring that a verb of directed activity like HIT intrinsically involves three participants: in (1) all three are selected. We have also observed, example (4b), repeated below as (12a), that we can omit the instrument and the sentence is still well formed. If, however, 'hitting' intrinsically involves three arguments, it should be the case that (12a) maintains all the implicatures of HIT shown in (11) except that an instrument is understood: that is, (12a) should imply (12b–d):

(12) a. Kim hit the table
     b. Kim used something to hit the table (cf. 6d, 11d)
     c. Kim caused something to hit the table (cf. 6e, 11e)
     d. Something hit the table with some force (cf. 6f, 11f)

An understood instrument is sometimes recoverable from the context, explicitly (13a), or implicitly, (13b):

(13) a. Kim had a stick and used it to hit the table
     b. Kim picked up a stick and hit the table

Frequently, the precise nature of the instrument is immaterial, but an instrument of some sort is implicated, as the bracketed addition in (14) is intended to suggest:

(14) Parents should not hit their children (with anything)

Sometimes when no instrument is mentioned the hearer will assume a body part is involved, a hand perhaps in (14) or (15):

(15)   To emphasize his point, Kim hit the table

Note that (15) is not usually understood reflexively, i.e. as 'Kim hit the table with himself', where the agent is also the instrument: we will look at reflexive uses of HIT in discussing (25).

In some cases, the language provides particular lexical items where a specific instrument is absorbed, as it were, into the lexical structure of the verb itself. (16a) involves body parts, and (16b) other more or less specific instruments:

(16) a. KICK   'hit with the foot'
         PUNCH   'strike hard with the fist'
         SLAP   'strike with the palm of the hand'
     b. HAMMER   'hit or beat with a hammer'
         FLOG   'beat severely especially with a rod or whip'

The examples in (12)–(15) involve understood instrument. Passive sentences can involve understood agents. Corresponding to (1) is the full passive, (17a), and the short passive, (17b):

(17)   a. The table was hit (with a stick) by Kim
       b. The table was hit (with a stick)

The syntactic difference between (1) and (17) lies in argument selection. In the active sentence (1) the agent must be selected as subject; in the corresponding passive, (17), the patient/goal argument is selected as subject. In the passive sentence, the agent is optional and, if it is chosen, will be realized in a PP[*by*].

We have said that as a verb of directed activity HIT intrinsically involves an agent, a patient/goal, and an instrument. In discussing (12), we supposed that when an instrument is not overtly specified it is implied. For the same reasons, we assume that the implicatures in (11), which hold for the active sentence (1), also hold for the corresponding passive. In the short passive, an understood agent can be recovered from the context, textual or situational, or, if the agent's precise identity is irrelevant to the communicative purpose of the speaker one is understood. (18a) implies (18b):

(18)   a. The table was hit
       b. Somebody did something to the table (cf. 11b)
           Somebody used something to hit the table (cf. 11d,e)
           Somebody acted intentionally (cf. 11i) and so on.

The active and passive sentences differ in their focus. The question in (19a) focuses on the agent: (19b) responds appropriately, but (19c) does not:

(19)   a. What did Kim do?
        b. He hit the table with a stick
        c. The table was hit with a stick by him

In (20), the question focuses on the patient/goal, and the agent can either be omitted altogether by using the short passive, (20b), or be indefinite, (20c):

(20)   a. What happened to the table?
        b. It was hit (with a stick)
        c. Someone hit it (with a stick)

3   Focusing on the instrument

The event in (1) can be described from a subtly different perspective. In (21), the *stick*, the instrument, is selected as grammatical object and *the table* occurs in a PP[7].

(21)   Kim hit the stick on/against the table

This pattern of argument selection has a number of consequences for the way we must characterize the arguments and for whether or not they can be omitted from the sentence. *The table* loses its dual role as patient/goal and becomes a goal only. It remains, however, a primary participant and cannot be omitted:

(22)   Kim hit the stick

is not construed with an understood patient/goal (i.e. as 'Kim hit something with a stick'). Like (12), it is construed with an understood instrument (i.e. as 'Kim hit the stick with something'). We can omit the instrument

(23)   Kim hit against the table

but if we do so, then the sentence can only be interpreted as reflexive 'Kim hit herself against the table', an interpretation to which we return in (25).

In an act of hitting, the instrument contacts the patient/goal (cf. 11e,f,g). When all three arguments are realized in the order shown in (21), then the implicatures of (11) remain, but the perspective from which the event is viewed subtly shifts. (1) focuses on the effect on the patient/goal, whereas (21) focuses on the effect on the instrument. The difference between (1) and (21) lies in which argument is selected as grammatical object: in (1) it is the patient/goal, and in (21) it is the instrument. The implicature in (11h) is phrased to reflect this: it stipulates that the argument chosen as grammatical object is the argument most affected by the action of the verb.

The focusing effect of argument selection can be seen more clearly with some other verbs of directed activity. SMASH has the sense 'cause something to be broken violently into pieces', 'hitting' with additional components of meaning, one of which is the absorption of the implicature in (11h) into the lexical structure of the verb.

(24)   a. He smashed the table with the stick
       b. He smashed the stick against the table

In both cases, it is the grammatical object that is most affected by the action of the verb. In (24a), it is the table, the patient/goal, that is broken violently into pieces with the stick used as an instrument. In (24b), it is the stick that is broken violently into pieces and the table is the goal of the action.

With the pattern of argument selection shown in (21), i.e. with the instrument as grammatical object, all three arguments are usually selected. We have already remarked that it is possible to omit the instrument argument and that when this happens the sentence is understood reflexively: (25a) is understood as (25b):

(25)   a. Kim hit against the table
       b. Kim hit herself against the table

These observations are summarized in (26). As we have already observed, the subscripting on the NPs relates to the distribution of the participants to the various NPs and not to grammatical functions like subject, object (cf. remarks on 3). (26) is identical to (5) and (11), except for the characterization of the goal argument (cf. remarks following 21) and the statement on constituent selection and argument selection (which affect the ordering of the arguments):

(26) HIT:

sense:	cause to receive an impact 'strike with a blow'
aspectual type:	directed activity
argument structure:	agent; goal; instrument
constituent selection:	NP_1 V NP_3 PP[*on/against* NP_2]
argument selection for active:	agent: NP_1 (subject)
	instrument: NP_3 (object)
	goal: PP[*on/against* NP_2]
implicatures:	a–i as in (11)

4   Suppressing the agent

Let us now turn to yet another perspective on a 'hitting' event:

(27)   The stick hit the table

(27) could have a number of interpretations, all of which, to a greater or lesser extent, disclaim the voluntary action of an agent.

The most agentless interpretation would arise in a circumstance when, for example, the stick simply fell from a tree and happened to hit the table.

Accidental agency seems to be involved in (28):

(28)   Kim threw a stick down the garden for the dog to chase and *it hit the table*

In (29), we could imagine a situation where a child walking through the house carrying a stick inadvertently strikes a valuable vase which falls and breaks. The child, disclaiming responsibility, might protest:

(29)   I didn't hit the vase, *my stick did*

Neither (27) nor (28) could reasonably be held to have the agentive implications of (11a–e) or (11i). In the case of (29), whatever an adult observer may think, the child chooses to represent the situation as not implying (11a–e) and particularly not (11i). Indeed, (29) seems to invite an interpretation where the instrument has, as it were, a quasi agentive function (cf. *what my stick* DID), even though an inanimate object cannot be credited with the implicatures of deliberate activity that are carried by the typically animate and human agent. (31) tries to reflect this.

Note that with this argument selection, i.e. when the instrument is selected as subject in an active sentence, an agent cannot also be selected: there is no (30a) or anything like it

(30)   a.   *The stick hit the table by Kim
       b.   Kim's stick hit the table

Perhaps the possessive modifier, *Kim's* in (30b) or *my* in (29), are a reflex of the agent.

Suppressing the agent clearly has a variety of consequences. Our particular interest is in the consequences for argument structure and selection. The argument structure changes by the loss of the agent participant, which affects the verb's aspectual type: HIT remains an activity verb but ceases to be a verb of directed activity. Some of the implicatures of (11) are retained but others, most obviously those derived from the agent, are discarded or changed. One effect of this is that HIT loses its causative sense — 'cause to receive an impact' becomes 'receive an impact' — a fact reflected in the dictionary; 'strike with a blow' becomes 'come against with force'. This is summarized in (31):

(31)   HIT:

sense:	receive an impact
	'come against with force'
aspectual type:	activity
argument structure:	patient/goal; instrument
constituent selection:	NP_3 V NP_2
argument selection for active:	instrument: NP_3 (subject)
	patient/goal: NP_2 (object)

implicatures (cf. 11):

a.   instrument does something
b.   instrument does something to grammatical object
c, d.   cancelled
e.   instrument contacts patient/goal
f.   instrument contacts patient/goal with some force
g.   goal receives the action of the verb
h.   grammatical object affected by activity of instrument
i.   cancelled

5   An interim summary and some lexical rules

Let us summarize the position so far. We started with the assumption that a 'hitting' event is an activity that inherently involves an agent, a patient/goal, and an instrument. This is perhaps the prototypical perspective for HIT, and it is directly reflected in the aspectual type and argument structure of the verb as presented in (5). It is not, however, the only possible way in which a hitting event can be conceptualized and in particular contexts the same event could be described by any of the other sentences we have looked at. The speaker of any particular sentence chooses to conceptualize the event with a slightly different emphasis and to describe it from a slightly different perspective. These different perspectives involve different argument selections: whether the event is to be presented as a voluntary, involuntary, or accidental act, whether the speaker wishes to mention the agent or not, which of the participants is seen as being primarily affected by the action of the verb, and so on. These choices affect the aspectual type of the verb, its argument structure, and its constituent selection possibilities. And all of them affect the implicatures that a sentence can convey and hence the sense of the verb itself.

The traditional way of describing relationships of this kind is by ascribing different dictionary senses to the different uses of the verb, and the lexicon does indeed seem to be the appropriate place to describe such relationships. We will explore the possibility of handling them through a set of lexical rules. The position we have adopted supposes that the basic lexical entry for HIT, as in (5) and (11), describes a prototypical 'hitting'. The relevant changes can be described by assuming this structure as a base and proposing various lexical rules that operate on this basic structure adjusting aspectual type, sense, implicatures, and so forth. The implications of using lexical rules is that these changes are not *ad hoc* manipulations of the sense of HIT but are generalizable across a set of verbs. We will return to this issue at the end of the chapter.

In this spirit, the entry in (26) can be derived by a rule like that in (32), which can be referred to as the *instrument focus* derivation:

(32) instrument focus

sense:	no change
aspectual type:	no change
argument structure:	no change
constituent selection:	NP$_1$ V NP$_2$ (PP[*with* NP$_3$]) => NP$_1$ V NP$_3$ PP[*on/against* NP$_2$]
argument selection for active:	agent: NP$_1$ (subject) instrument: NP$_3$ (object) goal: PP[*on/ against* NP$_2$]
implicatures:	no change

This supposes, as the discussion has suggested, that instrument focus retains the sense and implicatures of the base structure. This seems to be right for HIT, but not necessarily for all verbs, as we have seen, with SMASH, cf. (24). We will return to this question. In a similar vein, the entry in (31) can be derived by a rule like that in (33):

(33) agent suppression

sense:	loss of causative
cause to receive an impact =>	receive an impact
'strike with a blow' =>	'come against with force'
aspectual type:	directed activity => activity
argument structure:	lose agent patient/goal to patient otherwise no change
constituent selection:	NP$_1$ V NP$_2$ PP[*with* NP$_3$] => NP$_3$ V NP$_2$
argument selection for active:	instrument NP$_3$ (subject) patient/goal NP$_2$ (object)
implicatures:	no change f,g,h delete c,d,e,i agent => instrument in a,b

A passive lexical rule operating on the derived structures will accommodate passives where they are possible.

6 Modifying the manner of the action

The examples we have looked at thus far have involved the aspectual type of a verb, the number and nature of its arguments, the way the arguments are distributed to subjects, objects and PPs, and how all this affects the verb's implicatures and hence its sense. We should now consider another kind of modification to the verb, the addition of particles of various kinds. In (34):

(34)   Kim hit at the table (with a stick)

the addition of *at* modifies the basic sense of HIT from 'strike with a blow' to 'aim a blow at'. In verbal combinations of this kind, *at* seems to have a basic directional sense, it adds to a verb the implicature that the 'action is carried out in the direction of or towards the goal'. With verbs of hitting, attacking etc., there is the additional implication, that 'somebody tries to do something, but does not succeed or complete it'. The implication of (34) is that the blow does not make contact: a consequence of failing actually to make contact is that the goal NP is not affected by the action of the verb: compare (35a) with (7c). This default interpretation, like other default interpretations, can be cancelled, as (35b) shows:

(35)   a. Kim hit at the table but missed
         b. The pensioner hit at her assailant and caught him a nasty blow over the ear

Note, too, that there is no longer a corresponding passive sentence:

(36)   *The table was hit at by Kim

HIT in (1) involved action on a goal and we described it as a verb of directed activity: HIT AT remains a verb of activity, but undirected in that it involves action towards a goal. In (34), agent and goal are obligatory and must occur in the order shown; the instrument is optional, but, as with sentences like (1), it is understood if it is not overt.

We can derive this sense too by lexical rule:

(37) attempt activity

sense:	add: attempt to . . .
cause to receive an impact =>	attempt to cause to . . .
'strike with a blow' =>	'aim a blow at'
aspectual type:	directed => undirected activity
argument structure:	patient/goal => goal
	otherwise no change
constituent selection:	NP_1 V NP_2 (PP[*with* NP_3]) =>
	NP_1 V PP[*at* NP_2] (PP[*with* NP_3])
argument selection for active:	agent: NP_1 (subject)
	patient/goal: PP[*at* NP_2] (object)
	instrument: PP[*with* NP_3]

no passive
implicatures: no change a,c,d,i

b => agent does something in direction of grammatical object
e => agent attempts to cause instrument to contact patient/goal
f => agent attempts to contact patient/goal with some force
g cancel
h => agent attempts to affect grammatical object

HIT AT can be further modified by the addition of OUT, which implies violent and uncontrolled action: to HIT OUT (AT) is to 'attack violently'.

(38)   Kim hit out (at the table) (with a stick)

The participants remain the same, except that now only the agent is obligatory. HIT OUT AT also involves undirected activity, with the additional implication that the activity is violent and perhaps uncontrolled. If the patient is not overt then the verb describes general rather than specific activity. As before, the instrument is optional, but understood when it is not selected. As with (34), there is no grammatical object and no corresponding passive. Some entailments and implicatures remain, others are further modified. The lexical rule in (39) assumes HIT AT, the output of the violent activity lexical rule, (37), rather than HIT as base:

(39)   violent activity

sense:	add: violently . . .
attempt to cause to . . . =>	violently attempt to cause to . . .
'aim a blow at' =>	'attack violently'
aspectual type:	no change (from HIT AT)
argument structure:	no change (from HIT AT)
constituent selection:	NP$_1$ V PP(*at* NP$_2$) (PP[*with* NP$_3$]) => NP$_1$ V out (PP[*at* NP$_2$]) (PP[*with* NP$_3$])
argument selection for active:	agent: NP$_1$ (subject) patient/goal: PP[*at*NP$_2$] (object) instrument: PP[*with* NP$_3$]
no passive	
implicatures of HIT AT:	a => agent does something in a violent manner no change b–i

The formulation chosen in (37) and (39) implies that, in the sense intended, (39) should only apply to the output of (37): i.e. that if a verb can be modified to V+*at* then it may be able to be further modified to V+*out*+*at*, but that if it cannot be modified to V+*at*, then there should be no form V+*out*+*at*. The data presented in the appendix seem to support this.

7   The result of the action

The first set of modifications we examined (instrument focus and agent suppression) focused on the way in which participants are perceived to be affected by the action of the verb. The second set (attempt activity and violent activity) focused on ways in which the nature of the action can be modified.

In this section, we will look at further modifications which draw attention to the results of the action. A sentence like (40) might be used to describe an event in a cricket or baseball match:

(40)   Kim hit the ball out of the ground

The additional argument realized by the PP *out of the ground* changes a simple aspectual type, a directed activity, into a complex aspectual type, a directed activity together with a transition.

Transitions can be illustrated with a simple transitional verb like GO, illustrated in (41):

(41)   Kim is going from Cambridge to Colchester

The argument structure of a transitional verb typically involves an agent (*Kim*), a source (*from Cambridge*), and a goal (*to Colchester*), and typically involves implicatures of a kind illustrated in (42): before the transition the state described in (42a) held and afterwards, providing the transition is successfully accomplished, the state in (42b), which includes the negation of (42a), will hold:

(42)   a.   Kim was in Cambridge
       b.   Kim will be in Colchester and not in Cambridge

We can state these implicatures more generally as:

(43)   implicatures of transitional event:
       j.   before event: state—patient is 'at source'
       k.   agent causes patient to 'go' from 'source'
       l.   agent causes patient to 'go' to 'goal'
       m.   after event: state—patient is 'at goal'
                        state—patient is not 'at source'

(40) involves both a directed action, the agent strikes with a blow (cf. 5), and a transitional event, the agent causes the ball to go from in the ground to out of the ground (cf. 43k, l). HIT in this sense tends to focus on the transition itself, i.e. on the implicatures in (43k, l). The reader is invited to try out the implicatures of (9) and (43). The dictionary glosses this sense as 'drive forward by striking': a transition (drive forward) plus an activity (by striking). A lexical rule of the following kind seems appropriate:

(44)   activity plus transition
       HIT:
           sense: cause to receive an impact and go from source to goal
                    (directed activity)   (transition)
                                                     'drive forward by striking'
                                                     (transition)   (activity)
           aspectual type: directed activity and transition
           argument structure: patient/goal => patient
                                                      add source
                                                      otherwise no change
           constituent selection: NP$_1$ V NP$_2$ (PP[*with*
                                                      NP$_3$]) =>
       NP$_1$ V NP$_2$ (PP[source NP$_4$]) (PP[goal NP$_5$]) (PP[*with* NP$_3$])
           argument selection for active: agent: NP$_1$ (subject)
                                                     patient: NP$_2$ (object)
                                                     instrument: PP[*with* NP$_3$]
                                                     source: PP[source NP$_4$]
                                                     goal: PP[goal NP$_5$]
           implicatures: directed activity: a–i as in
                                                     (11)
                                                     transition: j–m as in (43)

As a final example consider (45):

(45)   Kim hit Shane unconscious

This again involves the complex aspectual type of directed activity plus
transitional, but whereas HIT with a directional PP, as in (40), focuses on
the transition, on the implicature in (43k, l); HIT with an AP complement,
as in (45), focuses on the consequent state, the result of the transition, the
implicature in (43m). (46a) implies (46b):

(46)   a. Kim has hit Shane unconscious
       b. Shane is unconscious

In a statement of argument structure, we will describe the AP as an attribute. The following lexical rule is proposed:

(47)   activity plus consequent state
       HIT:
           sense: cause to receive an impact and enter resultant state
                    (directed activity)   (result of transition)
                                                     'reduce to a state by striking'
           aspectual type: directed activity and resultant state
           argument structure: patient/goal => patient
                                                      add attribute

constituent selection:	NP_1 V NP_2 (PP[*with* NP_3]) =>
	NP_1 V NP_2 AP (PP[*with* NP_3])
argument selection for active:	agent: NP_1 (subject)
	patient: NP_2 (object)
	attribute: AP
	instrument: PP[*with* NP_3]
implicatures:	directed activity: a–i as in (11)
transition:	

j.   before event: state—patient does not have attribute
k.   agent causes patient to 'go' from not having attribute
l.   agent causes patient to 'go' to having attribute
m.   after event: state—patient has attribute

We have observed that some verbs absorb some implicatures into their lexical structure (HAMMER absorbs the instrument argument; SMASH the implicatures of objecthood). It will be no surprise that there are verbs that absorb the resultant state:

(48)   PULP 'cause something to become pulp'
       MASH 'beat or crush something into a mash'

8   Summary

We started by describing various interrelated syntactic–semantic properties of HIT, summarized in (5): its aspectual type, argument structure, constituent selection, and the way its arguments are assigned to the subject, object, etc. We also looked at some of the implicatures of HIT, summarized in (11), and saw that some derive from the aspectual type, some from the argument structure and some from subject and object selection processes.

We then considered the syntactic and semantic effects of altering one or other of these descriptive parameters: changing the aspectual type, adding or removing arguments, adding particles, altering the way arguments are assigned to subject, object, etc. Some of these processes modify the way participants are perceived as being involved in the event. Is it the deliberate act of an agent, or is it involuntary or even non-agentive (cf. agent suppression)? Which of the participants is primarily affected by the action (cf. instrument focus and passive)? Other processes modify the nature of the act itself (cf. attempt activity and violent activity). Yet others concentrate on the consequences of the action, rather than on the action itself (cf. plus transition and plus consequent state).

We have seen that manipulating various aspects of the grammar of HIT produces a range of ways in which a 'hitting' event can be presented. The discussion and exemplification has been deliberately restricted to the verb

HIT. The question obviously arises as to whether the processes are restricted to HIT or whether they can be generalized to other verbs. The chapter proposes that the various processes can be formulated as lexical rules and this suggests that they can indeed be generalized. The Appendix begins to explore this issue.

The role of syntactic structure in the communication of meanings has been insufficiently explored in language teaching. It may not be appropriate for younger students to study the type of information called implicatures in this chapter, but there seems little doubt that advanced students need to understand the kinds of mechanisms that can be employed in texts to convey more than is explicitly asserted. The approach explored here could help them approach these issues in a systematic manner in the interpretation of texts.

Notes

1 HIT and related verbs are discussed in Fillmore (1970) and Dixon (1991).
2 Word senses recorded in single quotes, i.e. as 'strike with a blow' and the like, are taken from the *Oxford Advanced Learner's Dictionary*.
3 Vendler (1967) is one of the first and still one of the most approachable introductions to the literature on aspectual types. See also Baker (1989) and Comrie (1976). Halliday (1985) and especially Dixon (1991) have descriptions of English in which the notion is central.
4 There is an extensive literature on participant roles, also known as case, thematic roles, etc. Fillmore (1968) is an early article; Brown and Miller (1980, 1991) contains a tutorial introduction; Dowty (1991) is a recent contribution.
5 In this chapter, we will not distinguish between the various kinds of entailments and implicatures that have been recognized in the literature. We will use 'implicature' to cover all those non-truth-conditional inferences that are attached by convention to particular sentence types (see Smith and Wilson (1979) for an introductory account) to aspectual types and elements of argument structure (cf. Dowty 1991) or to particular lexical items (cf. Grice 1975).
6 See Kilby (1984) and Dixon (1991) for some discussion on argument selection and the direct object and the effect of the passive.
7 Jespersen (1927: 236ff.) refers to an 'instrumental object' in such cases.

Appendix

In Table 1 the labels on the columns correspond to the sentence patterns illustrated. In the rows there are pairs of letters: in the first of each pair 'y' indicates that there is and 'n' that there is not a dictionary entry for the appropriate sense in the *Oxford Advanced Learner's Dictionary*; in the second of each pair 'y' and 'n' are my judgements as to whether the relevant sense can be generated by rule. The rows explore the grammatical distribution of some selected subclasses of verbs of directed activity. Following Table 1 are notes on each row.

A   Kim hit the table with a stick
B   Kim hit the stick on the table
C   The stick hit the table
D   Kim hit at the table
E   Kim hit out at the table

		A	B	C	D	E
1	HIT	y y	y y	y y	y y	y y
2	SLAP	y y	n some	n n	n some	n some
3	SMASH	y y	? y	n y	n n	n n
4	CUT	y y	n n	y y	n y	n n
5	SMEAR	y y	y y	n y	n n	n n
6	STROKE	y y	n y	n y	n n	n n
7	FONDLE	y y	n n	n n	n n	n n

Table 1

1   Other verbs like HIT are BANG, STRIKE, KNOCK, POUND, BEAT. All have the implicature of (11f) that the agent acted with some force.
2   SLAP, 'strike with the palm of the hand', involves a typical instrument, often a body part. Other verbs like this include WALLOP, PUNCH, SWAT, LICK, etc. The specific instrument is typically absorbed into the sense of the verb, (cf. 16 above), and is therefore not usually mentioned explicitly: some of these verbs, however, allow both the A and B patterns:

> He slapped his hand on his forehead
> He slapped his forehead with his hand

> A few allow patterns D and/or E:

> He punched out at me wildly

3   As we noted in discussing (24), with SMASH the implicature in (11h) is absorbed into the sense of the verb. Other similar verbs include BREAK, SHATTER, SPLIT, and DEMOLISH.
4   With verbs like CUT, 'make an incision with a sharp-edged tool', the instrument is usually 'sharp-edged'. Other verbs are PRICK, PUNCTURE, SLIT, and PIERCE, etc. They do not appear in pattern B.

5 SMEAR verbs usually involve 'covering something with something'. They have an extensive literature. There is usually an additional implicature of 'completion' affecting the grammatical object:

> Kim smeared the wall with paint (= covered it)
> Kim smeared paint over the wall (does not = covered it)

6 STROKE, 'pass the hand gently over', appears necessarily to involve contact, and gentle contact at that: i.e. implicature (11f) cannot hold. The instrument is usually a body part and, as with SLAP, usually absorbed into the verb. Other verbs are BRUSH, TOUCH, and SCRAPE. The sense inhibits STROKE AT and STROKE OUT.

7 FONDLE 'touch or stroke gently or lovingly' is like STROKE, except that it does not occur in columns B or C. Similar verbs include CARESS and FEEL.

5 Understanding words

Jean Aitchison, like Garnham (this volume) takes a psychological approach to considering comprehension processes. Here she examines some of the phenomena which have influenced the way psychologists think about the processes of word recognition and the mental representation of meaning.

In studying how words are recognized in speech, experiments reveal that listeners use 'top-down' expectations to combine with the auditory stimulus (which is often inadequate) in identifying particular phonemes or words. (Garnham also explores the theoretical consequences of such phenomena and discusses their compatibility with recently developed models of word recognition such as 'connectionism'.)

The importance of top-down expectations for the language-learner cannot be overstated. Once the understanding process falters, the word recognition process no longer receives crucial contextual information, which means that the likelihood of recognizing subsequent words is reduced and so the likelihood of recovery from the failure gets into a downwards spiral leading to the breakdown of comprehension. It is for this reason that researchers in the field of L1 reading ability have laid so much stress on basic word recognition skills (e.g. Perfetti 1985) and on the importance of maximal contextual support to facilitate understanding. (Garnham's paper shows that context also supports syntactic and textual processing.)

In her discussion of word meaning, Aitchison concentrates on the 'prototype' approach deriving from the work of Rosch (1975). It is now widely accepted that prototype effects are real (that is, that people find it easy to decide whether examples are 'good' members of a category, thus a carrot is judged better than a tomato as a member of the class 'vegetable') but it is still not clear how such results contribute to our understanding of the mental representation of words. None the less, this approach allows us to see, in a way that the traditional definitional approach did not, that prototypical judgements vary between individuals and may vary widely between speakers of different languages. If, as Aitchison suggests, the causes of such differences lie in complex webs of cultural beliefs about what it is to be a 'good' vegetable, bird, or mother, this approach contributes directly to a current debate in language teaching; where is the boundary between the meaning of a word and knowledge of the cultural matrix in which it is used? Is it possible to conceive of a 'language for specific purposes' which ignores the cultural values from which the language derives? (Compare Bialystok's discussion (this volume) of the way conceptual distinctions in L1 development may be unconsciously inferred from the way a particular word is used. Mere exposure to expressions like 'John's blood boiled' or 'He blew up' may be enough to induce a conceptual organization which supports a set of interlocking cultural expectations, 'the body is a container / anger is a hot liquid / overheated liquids naturally burst out of their containers' which, taken together, may lead to the expectation that it is natural to express anger violently (cf. Lakoff and Johnson 1980).)

Understanding words

Jean Aitchison
Faculty of English
University of Oxford

1 Introduction

Understanding words is hard work. People often assume that a hearer behaves somewhat like a tape recorder, passively registering another person's speech. But this is a fallacy. The hearer is involved in an active, and highly complex process.

This process can be divided into two main stages: recognizing and grasping. That is, recognizing the word which has been spoken, and grasping its meaning. This paper will deal in outline with word recognition, and will then discuss some of the problems involved in grasping the meaning.

2 Recognizing words

2.1 Impossibility of hearing everything

Word recognition is a remarkable feat, for two main reasons. First, speed of speech: people talk too fast for the human ear to hear the details. Second, acoustic variance: there is no fixed sound wave pattern for each sound. A sound such as [k] differs depending on its neighbours, the person who said it, and the care with which it was pronounced. This has been known for a long time, at least since a famous series of experiments in the 1950s (for a useful summary, see Garman 1990).

Word recognition therefore involves imposing expectations on to a sketchy outline. A hearer is in a similar situation to someone trying to complete a partially solved crossword puzzle: a few pieces of a word are likely to be in place, but the rest has to be guessed with the help of diverse clues.

2.2 Imposing expectations

In recognizing words, hearers' guesses are aided by their knowledge of the language, and by exploitation of the surrounding context. Let us consider how people use these to impose their expectations (for a summary, see Aitchison 1987).

Experiments with single words have shown that hearers seek in their minds for the nearest plausible word, even though they could not possibly have heard this. Take the 'blanket' experiment: subjects were asked to wear headphones, and the sequence *lanket* was played into one ear a fraction of a second before *banket* was relayed into the other. They therefore were exposed to a sequence *lbanket*. But when quizzed, they reported hearing *blanket*. And this result was repeated with other sequences, such as *psin*, when subjects claimed to have heard *spin* (R. S. Day 1968; 1970 cited in Clark and Clark 1977). A more modern variant of this is the 'kiss' experiment, more usually called the 'Ganong effect' after the experimenter. A synthesized (artificial) sound was produced, halfway between [k] and [g], then various sound sequences were added on after it. When this [k]/[g] was followed by *iss*, subjects reported hearing *kiss* (never *giss*). But when it was followed by *ift*, they identified the word as *gift* (not *kift*) (Ganong 1980).

The 'ate' experiment showed the importance of context. An indistinct sound followed by the sequence *ate* was presented to listeners in a variety of settings. In 'paint the fence and the ?ate', listeners thought they heard *gate*; 'check the calendar and the ?ate' elicited *date*; and 'here's the fishing gear and the ?ate' produced *bait* (Garnes and Bond 1980). In the 'legislature' experiment subjects were asked to write down what they had heard when exposed to 'the state governors met with their respective legislatures convening in the capital city'. But in fact, a portion of the word *legislature* was obliterated by a cough. Yet subjects not only reported the whole word, they also claimed not to have noticed a cough, when asked where one had occurred (Warren 1970).

Further experiments have shown that, if all context is removed, and an unlikely but well-formed sequence of words is presented, hearers are unable to report accurately on this. On hearing: 'in mud eels are, in clay none are', native speakers of English produced bizarre renderings such as 'in muddies sar in clay nanar', 'in my deals are in clainanar' (Cole and Jakimik 1980).

These, then, are a sample of the experiments which show that hearers use a variety of clues to actively reconstruct the words they recognize, only part of which they could genuinely have heard.

2.3   Multiple activation, then narrowing down

But how do hearers match the outline they have heard against the possible words in their mental lexicon? There are, in theory, two radically different possibilities, a *serial* search or a *parallel* search. As in doing a crossword, one could think up a plausible word, and check it against the clues. If it fitted, one would decide on it as the 'answer'. If it did not, one would reject it, and seek another candidate, and so on. This so-called serial model of recognition is plausible, on the assumption that hearers check out commonly used words first, and only later move on to less likely ones. But in recent years, serial models have mostly given way to parallel search models. In these, hearers subconsciously contemplate a large number of words, and then suppress those they do not want.

The 'bug' experiment of Swinney shows how psycholinguists have established this type of information (Swinney 1979). He read out sentences to subjects, such as *for years the government building had been plagued with problems. The man was not surprised when he found several spiders, roaches and other bugs in the corner of the room.* As soon as the word *bugs* was spoken, three letters were flashed up onto a screen, and the subject had to decide whether they formed a word or not. Swinney found that subjects responded faster to ANT, a type of bug, than they did to an unrelated word such as SEW. Furthermore, they responded as fast to SPY as they did to ANT, suggesting that both kinds of bug had been subconsciously activated. Further experiments by Swinney and others showed that this was not a freak result based on the prevalence of all types of bugs in government buildings, but a genuine phenomenon (e.g. Seidenberg *et al.* 1982). And the effect worked across different word classes. In one experiment, the sequence *rose* appeared to activate both the noun ('type of flower') and the verb ('stand up'). Subjects were played a sentence containing the word *rose*, either *they bought a rose* or *they all rose.* Immediately afterwards, they were asked to judge whether a sequence of letters was a word. They answered equally fast to both FLOWER and STOOD, whatever the previous meaning of *rose* (Tanenhaus *et al.* 1979).

These and similar experiments have shown that recognizing words is not just a question of finding the word required, it is also a matter of suppressing those which are not needed. A variety of candidate words are automatically activated, perhaps more than many people realize, though exactly how the selection process works is unclear (some possibilities are summarized in Aitchison 1987; Marslen-Wilson 1989).

In short, recognizing words involves using a variety of clues to set up a host of possible candidates, which are then narrowed down to the most plausible one. Word recognition indicates that linguistic processes in the mind involve far more complex procedures than was once thought. And this complexity increases as the problem of grasping the meaning is considered, which is the topic of the next section.

3 Grasping the meaning

3.1 The fuzziness of word meaning

A definition, according to Samuel Butler in his *Notebooks* (1912), is 'the enclosing a wilderness of ideas within a wall of words'. And from Aristotle onwards, scholars have believed that it was possible to do this, to find a definition which in modern terminology listed the 'necessary and sufficient conditions' for a word: that is, to draw up a list which specifies any conditions which are necessary for its meaning, and which taken together are sufficient to distinguish the word from all other words (e.g. A *square* is a closed flat figure, with four sides, with all sides equal, and all interior angles equal). This is sometimes known as the check-list viewpoint, since one can (in theory) check off the essential properties one by one. According to this view, grasping the meaning involves being aware of the check-list. One might have further information about something, such as (say) that squares are important in the design of strong buildings. But this general knowledge would not be part of the core meaning of *square*, it would be an optional extra. In practice, however, this simple notion works for relatively few words.

For the vast majority of vocabulary, check-lists are difficult or impossible to assemble for a variety of reasons (summary in Aitchison 1987). First, it is often impossible to tell where 'core' meaning ends, and general knowledge begins. Is it an essential property of a cow that it has horns? Or is this general knowledge, useful for recognizing cows, but not part of the central definition? Second, there are some words which do not seem to have a core at all. Take the word *tiger*. Many people are quite flexible about what constitutes a tiger, so much so that they are prepared to accept 'three legged, lame, toothless, albino tigers, that are tigers all the same'. But, as these researchers ask, 'what keeps them tigers?' (Armstrong, Gleitman, and Gleitman 1983). Third, many words have fuzzy edges. In a famous experiment, the sociolinguist William Labov asked students to label a range of containers: some were tall and thin, others were low and flat, others were in the middle range. He demonstrated that there were no hard-and-fast lines between vases, cups, and bowls, they merged into one another (Labov 1973). People were sure about only a few clear-cut examples. Otherwise, they differed from each other, and were inconsistent from day to day. They also varied depending on what the container was used for: the same object might be labelled a 'bowl' if it was filled with soup, and a 'vase' if it contained roses. Fourthly, many words involve the 'family resemblance' problem, a point emphasized by the philosopher Wittgenstein in his famous discussion of the word *game* (Wittgenstein 1958). Games are like members of a family: every game has some feature in common with some other game, but there is no one definition which links them all (e.g. tennis and canasta are both competitive games played by two to four players, but in one, the participants run around after a ball, in the other, they sit at a table and manipulate packs of cards. Another card game, patience, does not involve competition, and is played by one person alone).

Faced with these four problems: the overlap of core meaning with general knowledge, apparently coreless concepts, fuzziness, and the family resemblance phenomenon, the check-list viewpoint seems untenable as a way in which humans understand the meaning of words.

Up till the mid-1970s, researchers mostly tried to ignore these problems, many assuming that if they simply tried a little harder, sooner or later it would be possible to find a satisfactory definition for every word. But, in 1975, a radical new approach sprang from psychology: prototype theory.

3.2 Prototype theory

In 1975, Eleanor Rosch at the University of Berkeley conducted an experiment in which she asked students to rank items within a category (Rosch 1975). She gave subjects a list of birds, for example, which had to be ranked on a scale of 1–7: 1 for a really 'birdy' bird, down to 7 for a truly bad example of a bird. She found that most of them were able to do this, and that there was significant agreement from person to person. For each category, it was therefore possible to point to a 'best exemplar' which Rosch labelled the 'prototype', and to draw up a relative ranking for the other category members. Americans regarded a robin as a prototypical bird, canaries were slightly less good, parrots were ranked lower, and emus and penguins were ranked lowest of all. All of these were birds, but some were 'better' birds than others. Similarly, tables and chairs were regarded as prototypical furniture, items such as cupboards were somewhat less good, and benches, ottomans, and davenports were further down still.

The results of this famous experiment were confirmed by other, later experiments (e.g. Rosch and Lloyd 1978; Armstrong, Gleitman, and Gleitman 1983). They suggest that when humans group objects into categories, they set up a prototype—the most typical example. And they subconsciously rank all other items in the category in relation to the prototype. Consequently, when they grasp the meaning of a word, they automatically activate their subconscious ranking system. According to this view, concepts and words are inextricably linked, and cannot be disentangled.

3.3 Advantages of prototype theory

Prototype theory seems, at a stroke, to eliminate many of the difficulties caused by a check-list approach. It deals with fuzziness by suggesting that problem cases are simply not very good examples of the category under discussion. It shows how tigers can lack stripiness and still be tigers, they are just not very good examples of tigers. It works not only with nouns, but also with other parts of speech. Take the verb *go*: this has inspired an immense amount of discussion about whether it should be treated as one lexical item or two, since sometimes it implies movement ('on Mondays, Paul goes from London to Oxford'), and at other times it does not ('the road goes from London to Oxford'). Prototype theory suggests that the road going to Oxford is still a case of *go*, but just not a prototypical one. And adopting this viewpoint means that there is no need to make decisions about borderline cases, such as rivers 'The Ganges goes from the Himalayas to the Indian Ocean', where it is unclear whether this is movement 'go', or static 'go': it is clearly not a prototypical instance of *go*.

Prototype theory explains how people cope with extended usages and metaphor: 'The children tobogganed downstairs on a tea tray' is an example of *toboggan*, but not a prototypical one, which would involve ice or snow. 'The whisky tobogganed down Bill's throat' is an even less good example, so bad, in fact, that it must be regarded as a 'metaphor', a use in which important typicality conditions are broken: there is no sledge, and no ice or snow, simply fast downward movement.

At first sight, therefore, prototype theory seemed to be a model which explained almost everything, a new paradigm which swept the old one away. At last, it seemed, we understood how human beings grasp the meaning of words. On closer examination, however, prototype theory raises not only a number of interesting questions, but also a whole set of problems, some of them serious. These are the topics which will discussed in the remainder of the paper. The next section will look at some questions about the development of prototypes whose answers might be important for language learning. The final section will outline some unsolved problems.

4   Development of prototypes

4.1   Questions about language learners

Prototype theory raises a number of questions about how prototypes are acquired. Three questions in particular are likely to be interesting:

1   Borderline items. How quickly do language learners discover whether borderline items are just bad examples, or are outside the category? How soon do they realise, for example, that a penguin is a bad example of a bird, but a bat is not a bird at all, even though it can fly?

2   Learning stages. Do language learners go through predictable stages as they learn to rank items?

3   Type of learner. Do adult language learners behave in the same way as native-speaking children?

These are the topics which were explored in quizzes presented to 11- to 14-year-old English speaking children (200 children, 50 in each age range), to 45 non-British adults who were fluent speakers of English, and to a control group of 12 English students (Aitchison 1992).

4.2   Borderline items

Four borderline items were considered. Subjects were asked the following questions:

1 'Is a lettuce a vegetable?'
2 'Is a goose a bird?'
3 'Is a walnut a fruit?'
4 'Is a washing machine a piece of furniture?'

They were instructed to answer either *yes, no,* or *don't know.*

Not surprisingly, the children grew progressively more confident about borderline items as they grew older, and they gradually moved closer to the adult categorization. Lettuces obtained the highest measure of agreement: 89 per cent of 11-year-olds said that a lettuce was a vegetable, but this figure moved up to 98 per cent at age 14. Next came geese: 85 per cent of 11-year-olds said a goose was a bird; but this rose to 92 per cent of 14-year-olds.

The children were somewhat less sure about walnuts as fruit. At age 11, 57 per cent said 'no', but 30 per cent said 'yes'. By age 14, 81 per cent said 'no', and 15 per cent said 'yes'. This is still somewhat short of the typical response for British adults, since all the control group said 'no'. The washing machine responses showed less agreement. All ages were undecided whether this was a piece of furniture, though those saying 'no' predominated within each age group. For example, 41 per cent of 14-year-olds said 'yes', and 53 per cent said 'no'. Interestingly, this is an item on which British adults are divided—most of the control group said 'no', though some said 'yes', perhaps because of the recent fashion of putting fake wooden fronts on anything in the kitchen.

The children's results, then, indicate that borderline items are categorized relatively late, in line with other studies which indicate that central items are assigned to a category before non-central ones. Furthermore, an adult type categorization appeared to correlate with a reasonable-sized vocabulary, since 20,000 was the approximate average number of words potentially actively usable by the 14-year-olds (based on testing dictionary samples). There may be no direct relationship between categorization ability and vocabulary size: both may simply be useful indicators of linguistic facility.

Adult non-British speakers differed somewhat from the children. Although they were all fluent speakers, many of them teachers of English, they were subconsciously influenced by their native language, especially over geese and walnuts. Over 20 per cent denied that a goose was a bird, claiming that instead it was a fowl (these speakers coming from Italy, Spain, and China). Almost 40 per cent claimed that a walnut was a fruit, explaining that it was a dried fruit (these speakers being predominantly Italian and Spanish).

Over borderline items, then, native British children gradually approximate to the adult norm, but foreign adults, even fluent speakers, are affected by their own native language, even though they may be unaware of it: in this study most had not realized that in their own language category membership differed in some degree from that of English.

4.3   Ranking

In this part of the quiz, the subjects were presented with six items in each of four categories, and were asked to choose the 'best' in the following way:

> Suppose you had to explain to a foreigner what a VEGETABLE was. Out of the following words, which do you think would be the best example of a vegetable? POTATO, CARROT, CAULIFLOWER, CABBAGE, TOMATO, PEAS.

> Please underline your choice. If you can't decide, please underline all the ones which you think would be very good examples.

The other categories were:

> Fruit: CHERRY, BANANA, MANGO, APPLE, DATE, ORANGE
> Furniture: BED, CHAIR, CUPBOARD, TELEVISION, TABLE, REFRIGERATOR
> Bird: PEACOCK, BLACKBIRD, ROBIN, PENGUIN, PARROT, DUCK

In this section of the quiz, children achieved an adult type grading at different ages for different categories, based on an analysis of the percentage of items underlined. Furniture and fruit were those in which the children were closest to the adult norm. All ages agreed that a *chair* was the 'best' example of furniture (it scored over 30 per cent), followed by *table*, though the 11-year-olds regarded *bed* as equal to *table*, perhaps because *bed* ranks more highly in the lives of younger children. Not surprisingly, *cupboard* came next, followed by *telephone* and *refrigerator*, which scored very low. The fruits also were ranked similarly by the children and the British adults. First, *apple* closely followed by *orange* and *banana*, then *mango*, then *cherry*, finally *date*.

There was some difference between children and British adults in the vegetable and bird categories. Over vegetables, the youngest children had a relatively small range of scores, indicating that for them, vegetables were all much of a muchness. But there were some surprises in the 12- to 14-year-olds. All of them ranked a *potato* as being the 'best' example, perhaps because of children's predilection for chips. This indicates that personal preferences can affect the ranking system—though the wording of the question may also have affected the response, with the word 'best' being interpreted as 'like best'. *Carrot*, *cabbage*, and *cauliflower* came next (with slight variations in order from year to year), then *peas* and *tomato*. British adults all ranked *potato* after *carrot*, *cabbage*, and *cauliflower*.

All ages regarded *robin* and *blackbird* as good examples of *bird*, and *peacock* and *penguin* as bad examples, in line with adult rankings. But the other two birds, *parrot* and *duck*, were somewhat oddly ranked by the children. *Parrot* was ranked as high as *robin* and higher than *blackbird* by the 12-year-olds, and it was also ranked not much below *robin* by 13-year-olds. Meanwhile, *duck* was ranked fairly highly by the 14-year-olds. These oddnesses need to be accounted for.

One possibility is that city school children do not know very much about birds, and therefore rank highly those they do know. However, this explanation may be over-simple. When quizzed about the *parrot* preference, some said simply: 'I like them', suggesting that personal preferences affected the responses. But others indicated that the *parrot* response had been triggered by a picture of a parrot in a school book. This raises an interesting pedagogical dilemma. Perhaps, in order to be eye-catching, books and teachers pick colourful, but non-prototypical examples to exemplify categories, which in the long run may delay the development of an adult type ranking.

The adult learners of English had some overlaps with the children's responses. In particular, they ranked highly items that were important to them in their culture, without being aware that these were strange to British ears. For example, the adult learners, most of whom came from Europe, ranked *cupboard* highly as a piece of furniture, alongside *table* and *chair*. This may be due to the very beautiful antique cupboards which are far more prevalent in continental Europe than in England. It is also possibly due to the fact that English has an extra word *wardrobe*, which is usually translated as the equivalent of *cupboard* in most European languages. But the non-native adults were mostly unaware that their responses differed from those of native English speakers, even though they spoke English fluently.

The vegetable response also differed from that of the native speakers, with cabbage coming out top, mainly in this case because of the unanimous placing of cabbage as the best example of a vegetable by the German speakers.

These results, then, indicate that speakers of a language are able to rank items within a category, though language learners, both children and fluent non-natives, are affected by various factors which means their ranking differs from native adults.

However, these differing rankings raise the following serious questions. On what factors is the selection of a prototype 'normally' based? And if it can be altered by people's preferences, what exactly are 'prototypes'? Such questions raise serious difficulties for prototype theory, and the answers are still hotly debated. These problems form the topic of the next section.

5 Prototype problems

5.1 Some basic difficulties

Within a culture, there is sufficient agreement on choice of prototypes for the phenomenon to be taken seriously. Yet the more closely prototypes are examined, the more elusive they seem to be. Above all, it is hard to see the basis on which they are selected: frequency, appearance, function, are all important, but none is critical (Aitchison 1987). In the furniture category, items in most American homes such as *television* and *icebox* were ranked lower than 'better' examples of furniture such as *bench* and *ottoman* which are by no means universally owned. Appearance cannot be crucial, since *carrot* and *pea* were the top American vegetables, but look different, and vegetables similar in appearance to carrot such as *parsnip* were lower ranked. Function cannot be supreme because *chair* came (with *table*) at the top of the American furniture list, but *bench*, which is also used to sit on, came much lower down.

Furthermore, even if a prototype can be unambiguously identified, such as the American choice of *robin*, and the British selection of *blackbird* as a prototypical bird, it is unclear how to arrange its features in order of importance. Clearly, feathers and ability to fly are important, but what about possession of a beak, nest-building, small size, or stick-like legs? The ordering of features presumably has some effect on the ranking of the other birds, yet there is no easy way to assess it.

A further serious challenge to prototype theory is the 'odd number' problem. Subjects were able to rank odd numbers in the same way as birds or vegetables. Three was considered better than 23, which was in turn better than 127 (Armstrong, Gleitman, and Gleitman 1983). This is peculiar, at first sight, since all odd numbers should be equally 'good'. This finding has for some people cast doubts on the whole of prototype theory. Yet the most probable solution is that it is easier to identify 3 as an odd number than 23 or 127. The consequence of this is that either prototypes reflect identification strategies, as some people claim, or that prototypes involve a combination of identification strategies and knowledge, as seems most likely: there is no need actually to see feathers before identifying a blackbird at the end of the garden, one just knows they are there.

Yet another problem is that of multiple meanings: if one asks subjects to rank vegetables, then the word *vegetable* has several overlapping meanings: at its broadest, it refers to any plant life, as in the phrase 'animal, vegetable, mineral'. And it has two narrower senses: on restaurant menus, 'meat and two veg' usually includes potatoes as one of the veg, but a menu which offers 'meat, a veg, and either rice or potatoes' is apparently excluding potatoes. In fact, a prototypical vegetable is likely to be one in which all meanings are covered; but, in an experiment, a subject might use one of the other interpretations.

Context provides another difficulty. It is possible to elicit the notion of a prototypical *boot*, usually regarded as a fairly heavy leather shoe which laces up. But if a context is provided, such as gardening, skiing, or sailing, then the nature of this boot changes considerably (Barsalou 1983).

A further possibility, according to some, is that prototypes work best with 'basic-level' terms, that is, words in the middle of a hierarchy which goes upward to more general terms, and downward to more specific ones. So one might be able to talk about a prototypical *chair*, a basic-level term, but find it much more difficult to produce a reliable ranking for the collective term *furniture* (Wierzbicka 1985, 1990).

Finally, the term *prototype* itself has been claimed to show the 'family resemblance syndrome': there are different types of prototype, and no one definition covers them all (Geeraerts 1989).

All these difficulties show that prototype theory, while solving some problems, raises considerable difficulties of its own, in particular, what exactly prototypes represent. This will be discussed further below.

5.2 Causes of prototype effects

The numerous difficulties with the nature of prototypes have led to a reluctance to speak of straightforward 'prototypes', and a tendency to replace the term 'prototype' with the notion of 'prototype effects'. In short, prototype effects, rather than prototypes, are real, but what is causing them?

Children learning about prototypes have shown the importance of clusters of properties. That is, children do not learn the features of a typical bird one by one. Instead, they learn to recognize a combination of properties—feathers, wings, beak, flying ability, small size—as representing a bird. But these clusters could be interpreted in different ways (Markman 1989).

One viewpoint is that this cluster of properties is the result of a non-analytic, holistic approach. The learner has focused on the overall picture, rather than on any one individual feature. This is consistent with the input-driven connectionist attitude towards prototypes. The notion of bird, for example, is regarded as the end-product of cumulative exposures to creatures which have feathers, wings, beak, and an ability to fly.

Another viewpoint takes the opposite approach: that prototypes are the end result of a highly analytic process. They represent an attempt to reconcile the variability within a category with the classical view. In order to avoid the cognitive dissonance associated with a messy bird category, people have selected as a 'proper' bird one which could fit the check-list approach.

A third viewpoint suggests that prototypes represent a person's naïve beliefs about the world. People handle the world by building mental models which incorporate their assumptions about its nature and workings. Prototypes are just such models, and like all naïve beliefs, they are varied and partially inconsistent. This viewpoint also seems to be supported by mental models which go beyond the 'real' world, and beyond single words, as outlined below.

5.3   Beyond single words: frames and idealized cognitive models

A *week* provides a lucid example of a prototype which extends beyond the 'real' world (Lakoff 1987). In England, most people have a mental image of a prototypical *week*, which consists of five working days labelled Monday, Tuesday, Wednesday, Thursday, Friday, followed by two days off, Saturday and Sunday. They maintain this model, even if it might not correspond to their own week. Yet this is an intangible cultural artefact. Other cultures split up time differently. An Inca 'week' involved nine working days followed by market day, on which the king changed wives.

Other mental models also known as 'idealized cognitive models' (ICMs), Lakoff 1987) involve the notion of a 'script' or 'scenario', a prototypical sequence of events. *Having a bath* in England involves filling a bathtub with water, climbing in and washing with soap, then climbing out and drying off with a towel. In India, *having a bath* involves throwing the contents of a bucket of water over oneself. Such scripts are difficult to formalize as semantic analyses, but have sufficient recurring features and enough consistency to justify labelling with the notion of 'prototype'.

Such mental models are not just passive pictures. They can have an active effect on life. In particular, they can get handed down from generation to generation, and reinforce cultural norms. For example, the notion of *mother* lies at the centre of a cluster of different mental models: the birth model, in which the mother gives birth to the child, the nurturing model, in which the mother is the one who looks after the child, and the marital model, in which the mother is married to the father (Lakoff 1987). This has led to a model of a 'proper mother' being one who after giving birth stays at home and nurtures and is married to the father in a nuclear family. This therefore reinforces a stereotype which is now largely unjustified in modern British society. Similarly, many British citizens have a belief that we live in a layer cake society, with rich upper class at the top, comfortably-off middle class in the middle, and poor working class at the bottom. In fact, numerous socio-economic publications have shown that the middle class versus working class divide is largely one of differing lifestyles, rather than position in an economic hierarchy. Yet the cultural stereotype of Britain as a layer cake society persists in the minds of many.

Finally, covert ICMs may even predict people's behaviour. According to Lakoff (1987), metaphors can reveal subconscious ICMs. An emotion such as anger is often envisaged as the heat of liquid in a container, as shown by phrases such as 'John's blood boiled', 'Pamela seethed with rage'. Since containers under pressure are liable to burst, then so does anger erupt: 'Dan blew up', 'Marigold exploded with fury'. This may lead people to assume that it is normal to erupt, if placed under pressure, not only when angry, but in other emotional situations also, such as lust, leading even perhaps to rape.

Fear provides another example. Physiologically, there is a tendency to either freeze or flee. Yet English metaphors emphasize freezing, not fleeing: 'he froze with fear', 'he was rooted to the ground with terror'. Perhaps such metaphors incorporate mental models which subconsciously persuade the average person to stand still, rather than run away when faced with a threat.

Such examples show the potential power of mental models. Understanding words, therefore, is not just a case of sorting out the meaning of individual lexical items: a true grasp of the meaning involves understanding the mental models of a culture.

6 Conclusion

This paper has pointed out that understanding words is hard work, comprised of two facets, recognizing and grasping. Word recognition involves reconstructing a candidate set of possible words from a variety of clues, then narrowing these down to the most plausible one. Grasping the meaning involves knowing the prototype, and the ranking of items in relation to it. But understanding the prototype is in fact a more complex process than was once thought, since prototype effects may have different causes. Above all, they possibly represent the naïve mental models of the native speakers of the language, which need to be understood in order for hearers fully to comprehend the meaning.

6 Psychological processes and understanding

In this paper, Alan Garnham highlights a number of issues which are currently of prime concern in constructing an approach to language understanding in terms of cognitive processing.

One of these issues relates to the ways of modelling psychological processes developed in 'connectionism', which takes a radically different approach to language processing from that adopted by previous psychological models. Conventional models assume that linguistic rules, together with the symbols (sentences, phrases, morphemes, etc.) which are manipulated by the rules, are the proper objects of psycholinguistic investigation, since they must in some way be directly represented in the brain. This 'rules and symbols' approach is usually studied by constructing a theoretical model which will give a good account of observed human behaviour, and then testing crucial points in the model by controlled experiments.

The connectionist approach, in contrast, assumes that linguistic symbols and rules are not represented directly in the brain, but are categories invented to describe the complex structure of the 'fall-out' from processes which are themselves much simpler and more basic. These fundamental processes are conceived of in terms of neural networks, where the suggestion is that these resemble, or at least symbolize, what is known about the physical behaviour of the brain. These neural networks have to be modelled on computers since there are far too many simple operations happening at once for a human being to be able to calculate them. Their properties have been the subject of intense research not only in psychology but also in artificial intelligence and, more generally, in computational engineering. Many features of such networks are only just beginning to emerge and they are the subject of considerable controversy. In the application of this approach to language processing, the most striking successes so far have been achieved in word-level processing, though these too are the subject of debate.

From the point of view of modelling human learning and human understanding, the connectionist approach has many attractive features, as Garnham explains. Particularly striking is the ability to cope with partial information and distorted input (see also Aitchison's discussion of 'multiple activation' and Bialystok's account of the 'competition model' of human understanding). Unlike conventional approaches, the connectionist model offers a way of explaining variability in language performance, especially during the course of learning. It is this aspect of the model which must be of particular interest to applied linguists, since it offers a potentially illuminating framework for accounting for variability of performance in understanding a foreign language.

Garnham's discussion of syntactic processing highlights another central debate in psycholinguistics: is there a level of purely syntactic processing which precedes a semantic/pragmatic analysis? This is a question of obvious importance in language teaching. If, in the course of normal language processing, syntactic processing is inextricably linked with semantic processes then it may be more profitable to teach these aspects of language in as integrated a way as possible (see also K. Brown, this volume, whose proposals give support to this approach). The 'modular' as opposed to 'interactive' issue is, ten years after the publication of Fodor's provocative proposals (Fodor 1983), still producing animated discussion. Garnham briefly outlines some of his recent work on syntactic processing and on the resolution of anaphors in discourse, producing in both cases support for the view that different levels of processing interact with each other and influence each other during the course of understanding (see also Aitchison's discussion of context effects in auditory word recognition). Such findings would support the explicit appeal to context at all levels of language teaching, not only because different levels of skills appear to need to be integrated during language comprehension, but also because the learner can use information from one level to compensate for lack of competence at another level.

Psychological processes and understanding

Alan Garnham
Laboratory of Experimental Psychology
University of Sussex

1 Introduction

Psychology and, in particular, psycholinguistics—the psychological study of the mental mechanisms and processes that underlie our ability to use language—is a relatively young science. The teaching of foreign languages is a much older practice, and one whose practitioners have met with a certain amount of success, despite having no technical knowledge of psycholinguistics. Nevertheless, an understanding of psycholinguistics—of what our mental apparatus accomplishes with ease and what only with difficulty—is potentially of great value in teaching. And knowledge about the learning of language, in particular, is likely to be important. Of course, the mere possession of psycholinguistic knowledge is not enough. Its applications have to be thought through and, almost always, to be verified by empirical research. Nevertheless, those who do not have the knowledge cannot even think about its applications. This chapter, therefore, provides an outline—and in the space provided it can only be an outline—of work on language understanding within the psycholinguistic framework. One set of ideas that it focuses on is connectionism, a new approach to modelling cognitive processes that has become increasingly important in the last decade. One crucial aspect of connectionist research is that it emphasizes the importance of learning, and for this reason it has already attracted interest in the applied linguistics community (e.g. Spolsky 1988).

For reasons that are largely historical and methodological, psycholinguistics is usually divided into the study of language acquisition, language production (speaking and writing), and language understanding (listening and reading). The focus of this chapter is language understanding, but, as has already been said, some attention will be paid to questions about language learning. Psycholinguists divide the processes of language understanding into three main groups: word-level processes, syntactic processes, and message-level processes.

Corresponding to these three sets of processes are three research questions:

—How do listeners and readers decide which of the words that they already know is encoded in the current perceptual input?
—How and at what point in processing do they group words into phrases, clauses, and sentences?
—How do they extract the information that the speaker or writer is trying to convey to them?

In trying to answer these questions, psycholinguists construct models, which they aim to make as plausible as possible, given the range of empirical evidence about the psychological processes they are modelling. Although the predictions of these models may have to be tested on a narrow range of seemingly arcane examples, the models are, of course, intended to explain how people process all linguistic items of the relevant kind (words, sentences, or texts).

It must be stressed that the mental processes that psycholinguists study are, for the most part *unconscious* ones, which happen 'automatically', without conscious control. We are not aware of the complex activity that takes place in our minds (and brains) when we take part in a conversation, or read a book, newspaper, or magazine. All we are aware of is the end product of this activity, our understanding (or lack of it) of what we have been told or what we have read. One thing that psycholinguists have established is that, although we understand utterances very quickly, there is, indeed, a huge amount of (unconscious) mental activity taking place, just as there is when a person looks at an everyday scene and 'immediately' sees all the objects in it as the objects that they are.

This chapter will focus in turn on each of the three main sets of psycholinguistic processes identified above, with primary emphasis on language understanding rather than on production or acquisition. The section on word-level processing will be prefaced with a general discussion of connectionist models, which will be followed by descriptions of particular connectionist models that have had an important impact in this field.

Connectionist models have been much less successful in the domains of syntactic and message-level processing. As an illustration of work on these two topics I will provide an account of some of my own recent research. This account will be couched in traditional (symbolic, non-connectionist) terms, though it will be apparent that much of the theorizing in these domains is rather informal. In my discussion of syntactic processing, I will present some research on the resolution of syntactic ambiguities, and in particular on the question of whether contextual information can influence the initial decision about the structure of a locally ambiguous stretch of a sentence. In the domain of message-level processing I will discuss the interpretation of anaphoric expressions as an example of research on discourse comprehension within a framework known as 'mental models' (Johnson-Laird 1983; Garnham 1987).

2 Modelling mental processes

Linguists try to describe both particular languages and, in their study of so-called 'universal grammar', language in general (see K. Brown, this volume). In doing so, they formulate descriptions, sometimes instantiated as rules, at many levels—for example, phonetic, phonological, morphological, syntactic, semantic, pragmatic.

The traditional psycholinguistic approach to explaining our ability to use language is, roughly speaking, to postulate that these rules are encoded into our mental apparatus and that there are processes that can use these rules to analyse an input (in the case of language understanding) or to generate an output (in the case of language production). In the last decade, this traditional *symbolic* approach has been challenged by a different one, which is sometimes referred to as *subsymbolic*, and which is known by a variety of names: *connectionism, parallel distributed processing (PDP)*, and *neural network modelling*. In one interpretation of this approach, linguistic rules are epiphenomena. A connectionist model behaves as if it is following rules, but those rules are not directly encoded into it. Not unnaturally, connectionist models in psycholinguistics look very different from traditional symbolic models.

2.1 What are connectionist models like?

Connectionist models have their origins in the computer modelling of behaviour and are almost always implemented as computer programs. They are built up out of simple processing units, whose behaviour is somewhat similar to that of a nerve cell, or group of nerve cells, in the brain. The units are divided into three groups: input units, hidden units (which make connectionist models more powerful than they otherwise would be), and output units (see Figure 1).

Activation passes from one unit to another along the *connections* from which the models get their name. Each connection has a weight, which determines how easily it carries activation between the units it links. Like nerve cells, the units add up the amount of activation reaching them, and the activation that they pass on is based on the total input.

Connectionist models can carry out a wide variety of tasks, not just language processing. The trick is to come up with a scheme for coding the input as a set of activation levels of the input units, and another scheme for interpreting activation in the output units as the result of processing the input. The network then has to be 'set up' (either manually, or using a learning procedure such as the one described below) so that with the same configuration of the network, a wide variety of inputs can be transformed into the appropriate outputs.

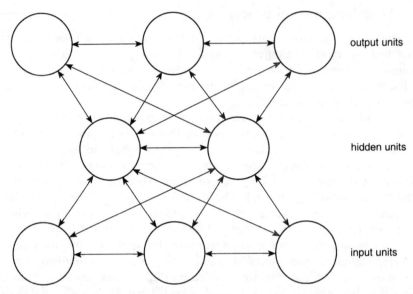

output units

hidden units

input units

Figure 1   A simple connectionist network showing input, hidden, and output units

In carrying out a particular task—say, the identification of a word on the basis of its physical properties—the network behaves as follows. First, the input is encoded as a pattern of activation in the input units. In the case of word identification, this pattern might represent the perceptual appearance of a printed word (in terms of visual features) or the sound of a spoken word (in terms of its phonetic features). That activation then spreads along the connections between the units, from the input units to the hidden units and then to the output units. The amount of activation passing from one unit to another depends on the strength of the connection between them (its weight). Weights can be positive, corresponding to an excitatory connection, or negative, corresponding to an inhibitory connection. At any moment, the activation of each unit depends on the total amount of activation arriving along its connections. Activation is passed in a series of processing cycles. The output units quickly settle to a steady pattern of activation, which represents the response of the system to the current input. In the example under consideration, it should represent the identity of the word actually presented.

As has already been said, one of the primary reasons for interest in connectionist models is that they not only carry out tasks, they also learn how to perform them. Learning is, generally speaking, a lengthy procedure for a connectionist machine—much more time-consuming than carrying out a particular task. However, it must be remembered that the comparison being made is between, say, the identification of a particular word on a particular occasion, and learning to be able to identify all the words of (some substantial subset of) a language on any occasion.

The most popular learning method for connectionist models has the daunting name of *backwards error propagation using the generalized delta rule (back propagation* for short). Back propagation is a supervised learning method that requires a 'teacher'. In back propagation, the weights on the connections are initially set to random values. An input (a *written* word, say), chosen from a *training set*, is presented to the machine and it is allowed to produce a response (the *pronunciation* of the word, say). At first, the responses are almost always hopelessly wrong. The 'teacher' tells the machine the correct response, and the machine calculates the difference (known as the error) between its response, as encoded in its output units, and the correct response. This error is then propagated backwards through the network and used to adjust first the weights of the connections between the output units and the hidden units and then those on the connections between the hidden units and the input units. The weights are adjusted so that if the same input were re-presented, the machine's response would be closer to the correct one. Another item from the training set is then presented to the network, the error calculated, and the weights on the connections are again adjusted. The adjustments made are small. It is no good changing the machine so it can deal with the last input properly, if that stops it from dealing properly with other inputs. Items from the training set are processed over and over again, usually in cycles. Eventually, the weights settle to steady values, which should allow the machine to process all items in the training set successfully, and *may* allow it to process other items of the same kind (e.g. words) that were not in the training set. However, even when it is successful, learning by back propagation is a slow process. When a connectionist machine has learned to carry out a task by back propagation, the knowledge that it embodies is *distributed* across the whole network. It is not possible to localize the representation of, say, the pronunciation of a particular word.

Advocates of connectionist models claim many advantages for them. The first of these, already mentioned above, is biological plausibility. The processing units from which connectionist models are constructed bear some resemblance in their mode of operation to nerve cells (or groups of nerve cells) in the brain. Also, massively parallel models can carry out complex computations on a time scale that is compatible with what is known about neural firing rates. Nerve cells are *very* much slower in operation than the electronic components of a digital computer, but standard digital computers effectively carry out just one operation at a time.

A second advantage of connectionist models is their ability to learn. A connectionist model will actually learn to perform a task (at least approximately), whereas traditional symbolic models of language processing are usually so vaguely specified that it is not even possible to implement them as computer models, let alone to determine how they might provide an account of language learning.

A third advantage of these models is a property known as *graceful degradation*. If a connectionist model suffers from changes in activity level not associated with changes in input ('internal noise'), as the brain undoubtedly does, or if some of it is damaged, as the brain can be, its performance deteriorates, but not necessarily very badly. This property is related to the fact that the representation of knowledge is distributed in a connectionist machine. Damage to individual units degrades any particular piece of information only slightly. Most traditional (symbolic) models simply stop working if they are 'damaged'.

A fourth advantage has already been hinted at. Although linguistic rules are not encoded into connectionist models, particularly those that learn, those models learn to behave in a predictable way, as if they were following rules. This aspect of connectionist models is often expressed by saying that rule-governed behaviour is an *emergent property* of them.

A fifth advantage is that, at least in principle, connectionist models can make simultaneous use of information from a wide variety of sources. As long as the different kinds of information can feed into the same network, they can influence the network's behaviour. Those who believe that language understanding is a process in which many types of information—lexical, syntactic, semantic, and pragmatic, for example—work together, find this property of connectionist models attractive.

There are a number of technical problems with connectionist models (see e.g. Norris 1991). One of these problems is the problem of local minima, which is illustrated graphically in Figure 2.

The optimal solution is represented by the lowest point in a 'terrain' of possible states of the model (each state corresponds to a set of values for the weights on the connections). Using this analogy, the way that back propagation works is by always trying to go downhill. However, there are points (the local minima) which are not the optimal solution, but where all small changes involve going uphill (e.g. the point where the 'ball' is resting in Figure 2).

A more serious problem is that connectionist models, as currently formulated, are unable to represent the *systematicity* of mental representations. For example, if a person can understand the sentence 'John loves Mary' they will be able to understand the sentence 'Mary loves John'. A connectionist model in which this link is broken is just as easy to set up as one in which it holds. Related to this problem is the suspicion that connectionist models are unable to learn highly structured tasks. In language, structure

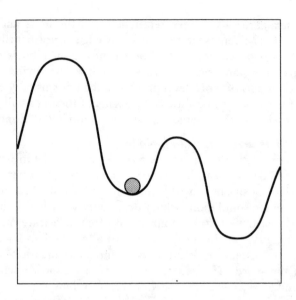

Figure 2   Graphical representation of the notion of a local minimum—a non-optimal solution to a problem for which all 'neighbouring' solutions are worse.

and systematicity tend to go hand in hand, so connectionist machines may be unable to carry out many of the complex processes that comprise language understanding.

2.2   Word-level processing

In the domain of language processing, connectionist models have been at their most successful in modelling our ability to identify words. Influential connectionist models of word-level processing include:

1   the interactive activation model of the identification of written words (McClelland and Rumelhart 1981);
2   the TRACE model; of the identification of spoken words (McClelland and Elman 1986);
3   The Rumelhart and McClelland (1986) model of past tense learning;
4   NETtalk (Sejnowski and Rosenberg 1986);
5   The Seidenberg and McClelland (1989) model of written word recognition and naming.

All these models were formulated primarily with English in mind. The first two are so-called 'hard-wired' models that do not learn. The others learn by the standard back propagation technique. Hard-wired models are easier to understand than models that learn, because the modeller can assign relatively straightforward interpretations to all the units and connections of the model. The representation of knowledge is *not* distributed in such models, though processing *is* distributed, just as in models that learn by back propagation, and the two types of model share many properties. In hard-wired models of word-level processes, the units usually correspond to detectors for words or linguistic components of them, as will become clear in the discussion of the interactive activation and TRACE models, below.

2.2.1 The interactive activation model

The interactive activation model is a hard-wired model in which the units correspond to detectors at the level of visual features of letters (input units), letters at given positions in words (hidden units), and words (output units). In the computer simulation, which deals only with words of four letters written in a particular stylized upper-case font, a feature might be a full-height vertical line at the left-hand side of a letter (as in D, E, F, H, etc.). A separate set of feature detectors is required for each letter position (1–4) within the word. The general organization is shown schematically in Figure 3 and a *very* few of the individual connections are shown in Figure 4.

The model contains both excitatory and inhibitory connections. Within any one of the three levels connections are usually inhibitory. The interpretation of this fact is that, for example, evidence that the first letter of a word is, say, R is evidence that it is *not* any of the other 25 letters. This is not to say that letters do not share features, but it is nevertheless true that there can only be one letter at a given position in a word. The situation at the word level is the same as at the letter level. A given piece of text can only be one word. At the feature level things are more complex, and in their computer simulation McClelland and Rumelhart omit feature-to-feature connections.

Connections between levels have two interesting properties: they run in either direction and they can be either excitatory or inhibitory. Evidence for an 'S' in the first letter position is positive evidence in favour of the word being, among other possibilities, *stop* or *slow*, but negative evidence that the word is, for example, *talk*. Furthermore, once evidence begins to build up that the word is *stop*, that in turn is evidence that the first letter, which may not yet have been definitely identified, is an 'S'. This feeding back of information from the 'higher' levels of the system to the 'lower' levels explains a well-established finding in the psychological literature: letters are easier to identify in words than on their own.

2.2.2 The TRACE model

The TRACE model of spoken word identification is closely related to the interactive activation model of written word recognition. It is a hard-wired model with detectors at the (phonetic) feature, phoneme, and word levels. Its input is a sequence of time slices of speech, which are one two-hundredth of a second long in one version (TRACE 1) and one fortieth of a second

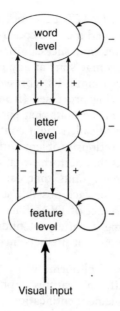

Figure 3   General organization of the interactive activation model of printed word identification (after McClelland and Rumelhart 1981).

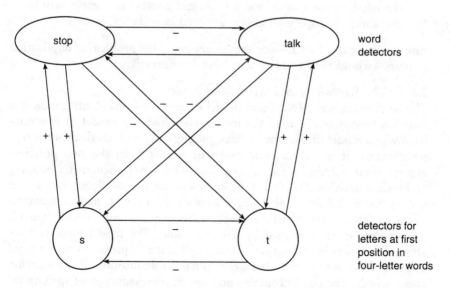

Figure 4   Individual connections in the interactive activation model of printed word identification.

long in another (TRACE 2). TRACE 2 has mock speech for its input, which cannot be directly perceived and must be coded into its input units. It looks for phonemes spanning three time slices. Initially, it hypothesizes that any of the (211) words it knows may start at any phoneme position.

Once a time slice has been input, its representation remains in the *trace* of the part of the input being processed (from which the model gets its name), and the activation of the units that encode it continues to change, thus allowing for effects of so-called 'right context' on the identification of previous words. The most serious problem with TRACE is that it requires massive duplication of units that perform what appears to be the same task. For example, there are many units that can recognize each word that TRACE knows about, one for each possible starting position in the trace.

The reason for the importance of TRACE has been its remarkable success in predicting and modelling a variety of findings about the way people identify spoken words. Findings it predicts include:

1   categorical perception of phonemes;
2   trade-offs between different features in phoneme identification;
3   lexical effects on phoneme identification;
4   preference for phonologically regular patterns;
5   co-articulation effects (in TRACE 1, with its input of real speech);
6   preference for short words (e.g. 'cat' v. 'caterpillar');
7   the strong, though not decisive, influence of word beginnings;
8   use of lexical information to identify word boundaries;
9   the need, in some cases, for use of right context to identify words;
10 the ability to cope with elision at word boundaries.

Any successor to TRACE—one that might avoid the problem of duplication of units—would need to behave at least as impressively.

2.2.3   *The Seidenberg and McClelland model*
The Seidenberg and McClelland model of written word identification is a more ambitious model than the interactive activation model. It is a non-hard-wired model that learns by back propagation and has distributed representations. It models a wide range of results from the two principal experimental paradigms for investigating word-level phenomena: naming and lexical decision. So far, it only knows about monosyllabic words, and it does not model effects that depend on word meaning, such as semantic and associative priming, where a word is recognized more quickly when it is preceded or accompanied by a related one. The model predicts facts about differences in reading skill (including the major problems experienced in acquired dyslexia) and about the course of acquisition of information about words. The model contains no explicit representation of spelling-to-sound rules and, furthermore, it has no 'lexical entries'. All the information is stored in connections between 400 orthographic (input) units, 460

phonological (output) units, and the hidden units (100 in one simulation, 200 in another). In this respect, the model contrasts with almost all other models of word-level processes, in which the notion of lexical entries has been taken as crucial.

2.2.4 *The Rumelhart and McClelland past tense learning model*

The Rumelhart and McClelland past tense learning model has attracted widespread interest, because it not only appears to learn English past tense morphology without encoding morphological rules, but it also goes through the same stages of learning that children go through. The model has, however, been sharply criticized, most notably by Pinker and Prince (1988). Some of the criticisms are specific to the model itself, which by recent standards is somewhat unsophisticated. Other criticisms are more general, and would apply to any model that tried to learn the mixture of regular and irregular past tenses found in English. The most important of these criticisms is that connectionist models group items by similarity, but the English regular verbs have nothing in common except that they are regular.

2.3 Syntactic processing

Although there have been attempts to model syntactic processing within a connectionist framework, they have enjoyed neither the success nor the influence of connectionist models of word-level processing. Questions about syntactic processing tend to be formulated and addressed within the traditional symbolic framework. Over the past decade or so, the most important research in this field has addressed the question of how *local* syntactic ambiguities are resolved. I will illustrate this type of research by describing some studies that I have carried out in collaboration with Gerry Altmann, Yvette Dennis, and Judith Henstra (Altmann, Garnham, and Dennis 1992; Altmann, Garnham, and Henstra 1994).

A locally ambiguous sentence is one with a part that might be parsed in two different ways. The ambiguity is local, since it is resolved before the end of the sentence, by purely structural information—the final part of the sentence is only compatible with one of the two possible structures for the first part. For example, in a sentence that begins:

The fireman told the woman that he had saved . . .

the words *that he had saved* might begin a complement clause that tells the reader what the fireman told the woman (. . . *that he had saved many people in similar fires*), or a relative clause that identifies one of two or more women (. . . *that he had saved to install a smoke detector*). *That he had saved* is locally ambiguous, but the ambiguity is resolved in different ways by the two endings given to the sentence.

If sentences such as these are presented out of context, those in which the ambiguous part turns out to be a complement clause are easier to understand than those that turn out to contain a relative clause (see e.g. Altmann, Garnham, and Dennis 1992). Two main types of symbolic model have been proposed to explain how local syntactic ambiguities are resolved. One type of model suggests the human sentence parser follows a set of principles that cause it to construct, in the first instance, simple structures (e.g. ones with smaller parse trees) rather than complex ones. In the example given above, the complement clause has a simpler structure than the relative, and so is favoured. The second type of model suggests that people build the structure that carries the most appropriate meaning in the context—structural ambiguities are almost inevitably associated with differences in meaning. On this view, when there is no context, the relative clause is 'unexpected' in the example above, because there is no reason to think that the woman needs to be distinguished from other women by information in a relative clause. According to this second kind of model, the difficulty of the relative clause version should disappear entirely if the sentence is put in a context in which there are two women, between whom it is necessary to distinguish, for example:

> An off-duty fireman was talking to two women. He was telling them how serious the situation had been when their house had caught fire. The fireman had risked his life for one of the women while the other had waited outside.

It is crucial that the difference should completely disappear in context. If context only reduces the difference, the explanation could be that the complement structure is always tried first. When that structure is incompatible with the end of the sentence, an explicit context might make it easier to reanalyse the sentence as one containing a relative clause, since it explicitly provides the information that there are two women, and it provides information that allows them to be distinguished. The alternative account is that the language processor immediately tries to interpret the *that* clause as a relative, because, in a context in which there are two women, the simple noun phrase *the woman* is referentially indeterminate.

In the first set of experiments (Altmann, Garnham, and Dennis 1992) we used an eye movement monitoring technique to record the amount of time people spent looking at the ambiguous region of such sentences, in their first sweep through them, and the likelihood that they would look back. We found that, in the majority of cases (around 70 to 80 per cent) the relative clause in context was no more difficult that the complement clause (in its appropriate context). In the remaining 20 to 30 per cent of cases people both spent longer reading the ambiguous part of the sentence, indicating a difficulty in understanding it properly, and looked back to the previous part of the sentence, indicating an attempt to reanalyse. We concluded that, in the normal case, when contextual information is properly processed, it has an immediate effect on which of two competing analyses is chosen for a locally ambiguous stretch of a sentence. Thus, the results favoured the second kind of model described above.

In a more recent series of experiments (Altmann, Garnham, and Henstra 1994) we have investigated structures in which the same ambiguity (between a complement clause and a relative clause) is resolved more quickly, indeed within one word. The importance of this move is that in a relatively long stretch such as *that he'd risked his life for* there is the opportunity for initial analysis and subsequent reanalysis to take place (although our first series of experiments provided no definite evidence in favour of this idea). Thus, the evidence for the kind of parsing model we favour was not as strong as it might have been. The relative clauses in the experiments described above were object relatives. By switching to subject relatives (e.g. *the woman that had risked . . .*) we were able to examine a case in which the ambiguity is resolved on the word following *that*, since a complement clause must have a subject. Again, we found that the difficulty of the relative clause over the complement out of context was entirely eliminated with a context appropriate to the (subject) relative, providing further support for the idea that the ambiguity is resolved by using information about the appropriate form of reference in the context.

2.4   Message-level processing

As in work on syntactic processing, psycholinguistic research on message-level processing is conceptualized almost entirely within the symbolic framework. However, the range of questions that can be asked is much broader. Although I will again illustrate research in this area with work from my own lab (this time carried out with Jane Oakhill and Kate Cain), the piece of research I will describe addresses just one among many sets of questions about the comprehension of text and discourse.

The information in the different parts of a text or conversation is highly interconnected, and one set of devices that indicates these interconnections is anaphoric expressions, such as definite pronouns and verbal ellipses. Within the mental models framework, it has long been recognized that the traditional idea that an anaphoric expression takes its meaning from an antecedent element in the text (see e.g. Halliday and Hasan 1976) cannot be translated into a processing theory (see also Brown and Yule 1983, for some further problems with this idea). In the mental models framework, an influential theory of anaphor interpretation (Sag and Hankamer 1984) has suggested a link between two broad classes of anaphoric expressions and the two main aspects of the mental representation of texts that have been postulated by psycholinguists. The types of anaphor are called *model-interpretive anaphors* and *ellipses*. Sag and Hankamer propose that the former are interpreted directly from a representation of the content of a text, whereas the latter are interpreted using a representation of surface features of the text, and are only assigned a meaning indirectly. Although this theory seems plausible, we have evidence against both parts of it. To anticipate, this evidence shows that both types of representation are involved in the interpretation of both types of anaphora.

Hankamer and Sag (1976) had previously established that ellipses 'require' antecedents that are parallel in form to the elided material. However, although this finding reflects the considered judgements of linguists, ellipses in natural texts do not always obey this constraint. Garnham and Oakhill (1989) have demonstrated this fact from a corpus of ellipses from published texts. But if the parallelism requirement breaks down, ellipses cannot be interpreted solely from representations of surface form. This conclusion was supported in experimental work (Garnham and Oakhill 1987) in which we compared texts in which the linguistically *correct* interpretation and the most plausible interpretations coincided, with those in which they did not. For example, in:

> It had been a busy morning at the hospital. The elderly patient had been examined by the doctor during the ward round. The child had too.

it is plausible that a child had been examined by the doctor during the ward round as well as an elderly patient. However, if the final sentence is replaced by

> The nurse had too.

then it is more plausible that a nurse examined an elderly patient during a ward round than that a doctor examined a nurse during a ward round. We found that people took longer to read the last sentence in the second case, and more often misinterpreted it (as determined by their answers to a subsequent question). The plausible reading, which was suggested only by the representation of content, was influencing their interpretation of an ellipsis.

Thus, one half of Sag and Hankamer's (1984) claim—that ellipses are interpreted via a superficial representation—appears to be incorrect. A (more plausible) reading of the passages, that would never be considered if interpretation were via surface form, affects the understanding of these texts. The converse part of this counter-claim to Sag and Hankamer, that a superficial representation is implicated in the interpretation of model-interpretive anaphors, is more difficult to establish in English. Nevertheless, Garnham and Oakhill (1988) did produce some indirect evidence for this hypothesis in a study of anaphoric reference into so-called *anaphoric islands*. Subjects found such references less acceptable and took longer to understand them even when they were acceptable, than they took to understand parallel anaphoric references with normal noun phrase antecedents for definite pronouns. For example, they found the second of the two following sentences easier than the first.

(1) Tom dreams a lot, but he never remembers them.
(2) Tom has a lot of dreams, but he never remembers them.

More importantly in the current context, this effect was accentuated when the sentences were changed to the past tense:

(1) Tom dreamed a lot, but he never remembered them.
(2) Tom had a lot of dreams, but he never remembered them.

The most obvious change here is the breaking of the superficial match between the verb *dreams* and the plural noun *dreams*. Thus, a property of a superficial representation affects the interpretation of a model-interpretive anaphor.

Clearer evidence against Sag and Hankamer's claim comes from languages with non-semantic gender, in which a pronoun can be interpreted as co-referential with a previous noun phrase when the only information that selects one referent over another is the syntactic gender of the noun and the pronoun. For example, in the French sentence:

J'ai acheté une chaise et un tapis. Elle était belle.

elle must refer to the chair not the carpet. Furthermore, in a series of experiments conducted in conjunction with Jane Oakhill, Manuel Carreiras, and Marie-France Ehrlich, we have established, both in French and in Spanish, that the interpretation of pronouns referring to objects is faster when there is a syntactic cue to the antecedent of the pronoun (it only matches one of the potential antecedent noun phrases in gender) compared with the case where there is no cue (it matches both). For example, we compared in French the comprehension of sentences such as:

(1) La cape a protegé la veste parce qu'elle est imperméable.
(2) La cape a protegé le manteau parce qu'elle est imperméable.

(1) Jacqueline a vendu ses bijoux à Béatrice parce qu'elle voulait partir en vacances.
(2) Jacqueline a vendu ses bijoux à Thomas parce qu'elle voulait partir en vacances.

In each pair, the second was understood faster than the first, and the difference between the pairs was approximately the same in the two cases.

3 Conclusions

Psycholinguists have made great advances in understanding language processing over the last thirty years. Connectionist models have been particularly successful in the domain of word-level processing. However, even in this domain they have been the subject of intense debate. Pinker and Prince (1988) have shown how one particular model fails to deal with the rule-governed nature of the English past tense system, and Fodor and Pylyshyn (1988) have shown that connectionist models are bound to have trouble in accounting for complex rule-governed behaviour. There is, however, a way in which some of the advantages of connectionist models can be combined with those of traditional symbolic ones. Neural networks can be used, not as a framework in which to model cognition, but as a particular kind of computational device on which traditional models can be *implemented*. And, since the brain is a neural network *par excellence*, if Fodor and Pylyshyn are right that symbolic models are needed, those models must run on human brains. Formal results in the theory of computation show that neural network implementations of symbolic models are always possible.

As far as second language learning is concerned, the gap between psycholinguistic accounts of language understanding—at least those of the kind described in this chapter, which are produced primarily by psychologists—and their application in pedagogical programmes remains a large one. At the word level, the crucial question in second language learning is whether the learner knows the word at all, not what the detailed mechanism of identification might be. At the syntactic level, there are interesting questions about the universality of the parsing principles discussed in section 2.3, questions which are just beginning to be considered seriously. At the discourse level, a wealth of evidence points to the importance of background knowledge, both general and specific to the topic of the current conversation or text, in language understanding. Language teachers know that students can often use background knowledge to get round deficiencies in knowledge of the language that is being learned. An interesting set of questions which have yet to have much impact on 'mental models' researchers concern cross-cultural differences in text and discourse structure and how they might affect the understanding of material in a second language.

Acknowledgements

My work on syntactic processing is supported by grant SPG 8920151 'Parsing in Context' from the ESRC/MRC/SERC Joint Initiative on Human Computer Interaction and Cognitive Science. My work on the interpretation of anaphoric expressions is supported by grant C00232439 'Mental Models and the Interpretation of Anaphora' from the ESRC and by NATO Collaborative Research Grant CRG 890527 'A Cross-Linguistic Study of Anaphor Interpretation'. I would like to thank the editors, and in particular Gillian Brown and John Williams, for their comments on an earlier version of this paper.

7 Towards an explanation of second language acquisition

Ellen Bialystok's paper begins by outlining three approaches to the study of language acquisition—neurolinguistic, linguistic, and psycholinguistic—and then goes on to consider the role that understanding plays in language acquisition. For each approach to the study of language, she describes the most important contribution which she believes each could make to a general theory of second language acquisition. Different approaches have different ways of theorizing, examine different types of data, and so are best suited to different types of problem, and only through a recognition of this fact can the myriad approaches to second language acquisition be unified in a single theory.

A recurrent theme throughout the chapter is the extent to which L1 and L2 acquisition are the same or different. Bialystok's conclusion is that they are essentially different, although the nature of this difference depends on whether one is considering phonology, syntax, or semantics. For example, in the case of syntax, although she assumes that the L2 learner has access to the principles of universal grammar, advances made in the *analysis* of this knowledge during the course of L1 acquisition serve to facilitate L2 acquisition. This view should be contrasted with that of writers such as Bley-Vroman (1989) who argue that universal grammar is no longer available after a certain critical period (see also Johnson and Newport 1991), and that L2 learners are only aided by knowledge of their native language. Instead, Bialystok's position is close to that expressed in Flynn's parameter-setting model of L2 acquisition (1989) in which universal grammar is still available to the L2 learner (although its interaction with the input data might be affected by the L1 parameter settings). In addition, Bialystok stresses that the representation of universal grammar might itself undergo change over time. She argues that a major cause of this change would be the interactions between universal grammar and the conceptual system, an interaction that takes place during the course of L1 acquisition.

Although Bialystok's chapter is primarily theoretical, she considers some practical implications in the final section on 'Common-sense views of second language acquisition'. Two of these, simplified input and the role of listening, will be familiar as Krashen's (1985) notions of 'comprehensible input' and the 'silent period'. Bialystok provides theoretical justification for these ideas in terms of the need to make input commensurate with the learner's current level of analysis of the target language, and its role in triggering parametric changes in the learner's grammatical knowledge. Hence, given that the input is comprehensible, certain types of learning can take place through listening tasks alone. However, as should be clear from the other papers in this volume, the factors affecting the comprehensibility of the input will reach far beyond the degree to which it matches the learner's current level of grammatical competence, and must take into account the particular genre (G. Brown), and the degree of contextual support (Aitchison, Garnham).

One further implication of Bialystok's view of acquisition may be drawn for language testers. If there is as little scope as she claims for cognitive influence in the development of the second language's phonological system, then is it fair to give as much weight as we usually do to 'pronunciation' in oral testing? Perhaps oral proficiency scales should take care to ensure that students are penalized only if their pronunciation or use of stress actually causes the examiner to fail to understand what was said; otherwise, the proficiency of the Conrads of the world may always be underestimated.

Towards an explanation of second language acquisition[1]

Ellen Bialystok
Department of Psychology
York University, Ontario

Today we have naming of parts
(HENRY REED)

Introduction

The past two decades have seen an escalation in both the quantity and quality of research in second language acquisition. None the less, the question of *how* learners learn a second language has rarely been addressed directly.

Much of the research into second language acquisition has reformulated the question in an attempt to make solutions more accessible. Instead of asking *how* learners learn a second language, most research has explored *what* learners learn during second language acquisition. This revised question is easier to answer and more amenable to empirical study.

Focusing attention on the product question is a natural step in the development of explanation. As with first language acquisition studies (e.g. R. Brown 1973), a great deal of second language acquisition research has followed the paradigm: 'How do speakers of X learn the Y of Z?', where X is the native language, Y is a specific grammatical structure, and Z is a target language. What gets documented, then, are the forms of speech produced by speakers of X as they progressively master the Y of Z.

As long as we resist accepting this body of data as the answer to the process question, these product-oriented studies are an important contribution to the enterprise because they provide a detailed description of what it is that is in need of explanation. However, at some point description must be re-evaluated, not for what it directly reveals, but for what it indirectly insinuates. As both Chandler (1991) and Overton (1991) argue, scientific explanation is ultimately advanced through the abduction of patterns that capture the universal features of performance and understanding. Second language acquisition has reached this point.

Detecting the common patterns in second language acquisition has not been easy. The frustration of researchers attempting this is exacerbated by a popular sense that the questions about the process of second language acquisition should be easy to answer. There is a body of 'common-sense' knowledge regarding how learners go about learning a second language that pre-empts the process question and leaves little of interest for researchers to quibble about. For example, those who have informal conversational interactions with non-native speakers will insist that the key to teaching someone a language is to present them with *simplified input*. This intuition leads to various modifications and mutilations in the speech addressed to non-native speakers. Teachers tell you that by pointing to things and *naming* them, the students will soon be speaking. Students tell you that they *listen* to the language for a while and at some point they just start speaking.

An evaluation of these intuitive claims turns out to be a complicated matter. One problem is that the standard form of the question 'How do learners learn a second language?' leaves unspecified many factors that may influence the answer. The complexity of the question belies any simple response.

The research that has addressed the problem of how learners learn a second language has been conducted from different disciplinary traditions. These differences potentially make the resulting pieces of wisdom gained through each of the investigations incommensurate with each other. Each discipline brings its own theoretical traditions and empirical methods to an investigation, and these presuppositions are influential in determining what questions are posed for study. Only when variations in the disciplinary methods and criteria for proficiency within each discipline are made explicit, does it become possible to set out the conditions for a more unified explanation of second language acquisition. It becomes, essentially, a problem of division of labour. Unlike simple delegation, however, the overarching principle must be that the separate portions of the whole must be rationally related to each other and must be motivated by a consistent principle.

The main claim of this paper is that each of the major approaches used in second language acquisition research has contributed essential but different knowledge to understanding that process. The reason is that each discipline confronts the problem with different purposes, different assumptions, and different instruments. Each is therefore poised to explain different phenomena. A coherent description of second language learning will need to integrate the insights obtained through all of the relevant disciplinary approaches.

The purpose of this discussion is to document some of the pieces that will inevitably be part of a more complete explanation of second language acquisition. Each approach influences the kind of theory or model of second language acquisition that one holds. In that sense, all the approaches are fundamental to a description of the process. My intention, however, is not to endorse a method of unrestrained relativism in which all competing descriptions would be considered equally valid. Rather, my purpose is to set the basis for establishing an integration of competing rigorous perspectives. Ultimately, the explanation for how learners learn a second language will need to be an interdisciplinary enterprise.

The analogy to first language acquisition

One place to begin the examination of a difficult question is in the exploration of solutions to a similar problem. The most obvious candidate for inspection in this regard is the process of first language acquisition by young children. The possible relation between first and second language acquisition has long captured the imagination of second language researchers. In spite of this, there is no consensus regarding either the utility of first language research for second language acquisition, or the general applicability of the first language paradigm to the issues of second language research. Indeed, the experience of young naive children tentatively grasping the earliest crumbs of their first language in the context of their nurturing home environment seems on the surface to bear little resemblance to the laboured efforts of adults struggling with the complexities of syntax in a language class. None the less, the parallels should not be overlooked. After all, the learning machine is the same, if a little more worn for the adult, and the content that is to be learned for both groups of apprentices is essentially identical. In both cases, this content is so complex as to defy explanation by the usual mechanisms for learning at our disposal. Hence, if there is some magic in learning a language, it just may apply equally to children's first language acquisition and adults' learning of a second language.

Most models of second language acquisition are, in fact, based on some (usually implicit) assumption regarding the similarity or difference between first and second language acquisition. This assumption is critical to the nature of explanation that is developed for second language acquisition. If the two are the same, then we need look no further than models of first language acquisition for a complete explanation of second language acquisition. If the two are different, then we must begin anew to construct a description for second language acquisition.

Some early theories of second language acquisition differed in precisely this regard. The contrastive analysis hypothesis advanced by Lado (1957), for example, claimed that second language acquisition involved replacing the habits acquired during first language acquisition; acquiring a second language was thus not at all like acquiring the first. Later, the creative construction hypothesis advocated by Dulay and Burt (1974) claimed that second language learners begin again in the same way as young children learning their first language. Whatever happened during first language acquisition happens again when someone learns a second language. Second language acquisition is first language acquisition revisited.

It is clear now that the truth is considerably more complex than either of these dichotomous views allowed. Second language acquisition is both the same as and different from first language acquisition. The paradigms for first language acquisition cannot be imported directly into accounts of second language acquisition, but neither can they be ignored.

My plan is to consider three approaches to language learning research: the neurolinguistic, linguistic, and psycholinguistic traditions. I will consider the contribution each has made to explanations of first language acquisition and then extend that line of reasoning to second language acquisition. Differences in the effect that each approach might have on the two language learning situations will be noted. These differences will then be summarized in an attempt to develop a general description for the relation between the processes of first and second language learning.

Neurolinguistic approach

The study of language acquisition, both first and second, has always included an interest in finding the relation between the neurological structures that provide the material location for language learning and the behavioural indices of that learning. Early successes by the nineteenth-century neurologists Wernicke and Broca were instrumental in motivating subsequent efforts to locate specific language functions in specific brain positions. Ensuing study has continued the effort to map linguistic functions throughout the brain. Most of this research has proceeded by studying the patterns of language impairment that are found in patients with particular types of brain damage.

One application of this research concerns the localization of language functions in the brain. According to Albert and Obler (1978), for example, bilingual brains are more bilateral and less fixed with respect to cerebral dominance than are those of monolinguals. Such claims have strong implications for theories of acquisition.

A second issue taken up by the neurolinguistic approach is the search for evidence that the development of the brain constrains the acquisition of language. This possibility was most clearly formulated by Lenneberg (1967), who argued that changes occurring in the brain at around puberty make it more difficult to learn a language after that time.

If there are maturational constraints on language acquisition, then they would likely apply to the learning of both first and second languages. The correspondence, however, need not be direct; while biological influences may continue to shape language acquisition throughout life, there is no reason to assume that the influence remains constant or that the shape of the emerging language remains identical. At the same time, constraints are merely probabilistic—they do not guarantee a particular developmental form or timetable. The problem of evaluating biological constraints, therefore, is to identify the areas of language proficiency that appear to be most rigorously governed by these constraints and the time period during which this biological influence is most prominent.

Critical period for language learning

The operationalization of potential biological influence on language acquisition is in the question of an optimal age for learning. This question needs to be examined in two steps. The first is to establish whether or not any age group is privileged in its ability to learn language; the second is to account for differences that might have been found.

Evidence supporting the notion of a critical period in first language learning has been ambiguous. The most widely documented case in recent times of a child deprived of normal language experiences and exposed to language only post-pubescently is Genie (Curtiss 1977). Yet intensive study of Genie's progress has failed to resolve the issue of whether or not the ability to learn language atrophies. Genie learned some language, but it was far from perfect.

The aspect of first language acquisition that shows the most promising relation to biological factors is the acquisition of phonological systems. Eimas *et al.* (1971) showed that infants as young as one month of age were capable of distinguishing between phonemes on the basis of minute differences in sound quality, such as the voice onset time that differentiates 'p' from 'b'. It may be that phonetic distinctions are under the control of innate perceptual processes. At the very least, the results suggest a strongly-determined 'preparedness' for human infants to process language they hear and to make the necessary distinctions in the auditory signal.

Claims such as this have direct implications for second language learning. The greater the role of neurological factors in second language learning, the more second language learning will be the same as first language acquisition, and the more constrained second language learning will be to a biological timetable.

The popular view for second language learning is that younger children have an advantage over older children or adults in mastering the target language. Logically, this view depends on the bulk of first language acquisition being dominated by biological factors which cease to control language learning later in life. The view is generally justified by a variety of neurological and quasi-neurological arguments, such as the completion of hemispheric lateralization, myelination of cortical cells, and decreasing plasticity of the brain regarding localization, all of which occur at or around puberty. Even here, however, the evidence is controversial, as some researchers report the completion of lateralization as early as two years of age, yet no-one suggests that the language learning ability begins to atrophy at that time.

Age and second language acquisition

Empirical studies have produced mixed evidence. Cummins (1981) and others (see Collier 1989 for a review) failed to find any advantage for younger learners; Cummins attributed the majority of the variance in achieved language proficiency to length of residence in the new country. On the other hand, Newport (1990) and Johnson and Newport (1989) reported that age of initial exposure to the second language is the single most important factor in determining eventual proficiency.

Differences between the studies may help to resolve the disparity in the results. The first is age: in general, Newport's subjects were adults while Cummins's subjects were schoolchildren. It would be expected that small differences in length of residence would be able to account for differences in the language abilities of children, whereas much larger differences would be needed to explain the differing proficiencies of adult learners. The difference in length of residence for children who have been in the new country for one year or four years is three years, and is likely to be significant. A three-year difference in length of residence for adults who have been in the new country for eleven years or fourteen years is not likely to be significant. A larger difference, say fifteen years, however, might affect proficiency. None the less, these differences in length of residency were not examined in the study by Johnson and Newport. Any spurious correlation between age of arrival and length of residency would show up as an effect of age of arrival, as their data were plotted only on this dimension. Both sets of studies do converge, however, in finding an important effect of age of arrival before about five years old.[2]

A second difference is in the aspect of language proficiency examined. Newport, as well as Johnson and Newport, showed that the age-related effects in the acquisition of syntax are confined to only the more complex structural aspects of morphology, while simpler features such as basic word order showed no such relationship. It is possible, then, that sources of influence for language learning vary with different aspects of language proficiency.

Finally, the subjects in the two sets of studies had different types of exposure to the second language. Cummins' children learned the language in academic settings and a variety of language and academic measures were obtained. Collier (1989) points out that any study of age effects for second language learning must consider first language and cognitive proficiency as intervening variables. This information is lacking for the Newport and Johnson subjects, and it is consequently difficult to evaluate the results.

A comprehensive integration and interpretation of the literature regarding the problem of age in second language learning is provided by Scovel (1988). He defines the critical period as a convergence of genetic and environmental factors over time. Changes in learning that occur at specific points in time, therefore, will only partly be explained by neurological factors. Sociocultural and cognitive explanations will need to be considered as well. In this way, he avoids the perils of the usual dichotomous conceptualization.

By considering research evidence in terms of a more complex array of factors, Scovel finds no evidence to support the idea that there is a critical period for the acquisition of syntax or lexicon. Adult second language learners routinely achieve high levels of proficiency in these aspects of a foreign language. He labels this competence the 'Joseph Conrad effect', after the Polish-born writer whose command of English syntax and lexicon was indistinguishable from that of a native speaker. Clearly, adults can master certain aspects of a foreign language even well into adulthood.

Scovel's survey, however, points to an aspect of language proficiency that falls outside this general model. Conrad's English, proficient as it was, was heavily marked by a foreign accent. Here Scovel attributes an influential role to a biologically-determined critical period. After puberty, he argues, an adult second language learner will never master the phonological system of the target language to the level of a native speaker.

Scovel sees puberty as a cross-over point at which phonology becomes more difficult and perhaps impossible to acquire while lexical and syntactic competence become easier. Even though there may be biological contributions to the learning of syntax, via something like universal grammar, and to lexicon, via innately specified meaning primitives, these aspects of language can also be learned on their own. Hence, increasing cognitive sophistication can compensate for and possibly even supplant the dwindling neurological support enjoyed by young children in first language acquisition. Leather and James (1991), however, describe exceptions to this generalization both before and after puberty. They argue that a complete explanation will require a description of auditory processing strategies as well as of the individual and social conditions that influence second language learning.

The neurolinguistic approach demonstrates that there are important biological constraints on the ability of humans to learn a second language. In spite of contradictory research findings, there is a persistent effect of age in some portion of second language acquisition. Evidence for this biological influence is revealed most clearly in the domain of phonology. Access to a completely native pronunciation in both first and second language learning is restricted by the age at which learners are first exposed to the language. Other evidence continues to suggest a biological role in the native-like acquisition of certain aspects of syntax. The influence here appears to focus on the more complex linguistic structures, but the data are inconclusive in several respects.

For those aspects of language that are controlled by biological constraints, the processes of first and second language acquisition are identical. Hence, it is in phonology that these two learning experiences are most similar. There is less evidence that biological factors control the acquisition of syntax or semantics. For these domains, first and second language learning may need different kinds of explanations.

Linguistic approach

Linguistic theories are not typically or necessarily theories of acquisition, but each linguistic theory has implications for the kind of cognitive or psycholinguistic acquisition theory that is compatible with it. Two broad categories of acquisition theory make different assumptions about language structure. Connectionist theories, on the one hand, take an empiricist approach to acquisition: language structure is determined by the linguistic environment that exists outside the learner. Learnability theories, on the other hand, take a nativist approach: language structure is traced to a biologically prepared state internal to the learner. Universal grammar is a set of specifications on the structure of language that is designed to fit within a learnability theory.

The two sets of theories concur in their assumption that language acquisition does not proceed through the intentional intervention and analysis by the learner. For both, language acquisition is governed by factors essentially outside the learner's control, whether they be biological or of an unconscious or automatic kind of cognition. Therefore, each type of theory will explain language differently, and perhaps explain the acquisition of different linguistic classes differently, but the nature of the explanation and what it contributes to an integrated explanation will be similar.

Connectionist theories

An important connectionist theory that has the additional virtue of having addressed problems in second language acquisition is the competition model (Bates and MacWhinney 1989). Like all connectionist theories, it is based on associations perceived in linguistic input. It is more functionalist than other models in that it also depends on competitions between form–function mappings in the underlying networks. As the competitions are resolved, a network emerges that strives for the most parsimonious and efficient solution to the form–function problem.

The underlying networks are built up through the perception of the distributional frequencies of particular forms in the language. Those networks are the grammar. Language acquisition, on this view, is a 'cue-driven distributional analysis'. The main factor in first language acquisition by children, second language acquisition by adults, or language acquisition by computers, is that the input delivers information that is translated into associative systems.

An explanation of language acquisition and language structure that relied strictly on environmental contingencies would have a difficult time accounting for the inherent similarity of all natural languages. In the competition model, these universal features of grammar that show up across languages are traced to universals of human cognition. The human mind, that is, creates languages that have particular characteristics. This outcome is inevitable, because all human minds contain the same set of processing universals. At this point, then, the competition model turns to biology to justify an inescapable fact of language structure—universality.

Learnability theories

Learnability theory takes as its premise that there is a pre-programmed acquisition device that is prepared to receive and uncover the structure of language through minimal input. Unlike the competition model, the universal device consists of linguistic principles, not cognitive ones. What emerges through the learning process is the target grammar.

The main linguistic description that is used to fit this learning account is Chomsky's theory of principles and parameters. The principles are features that govern all languages and the parameters are a set of optional features that can be set to indicate a limited range of specific values on certain dimensions. In this way, universal grammar describes the constraints on the learning device by documenting the general properties shared by all languages.

White (1989) identifies three facts of language acquisition that support the invocation of universal grammar. First, input to the language learner underdetermines the final grammar, so it is not clear how children could abstract all the relevant rules of the grammar. Second, the input is degenerate and so it is difficult to understand how the correct rule gets represented. Third, there is no negative evidence, so it is difficult to account for how children learn to exclude incorrect structures. The fact that children manage to construct an adult grammar in the context of these three deficiencies of the input suggests that a construct like universal grammar must be deployed during acquisition.

What role does universal grammar play in second language acquisition? Is it still available to adults? Does it function in the same way as it did for children in first language acquisition? Second language learners have already acquired a grammatical system and have constructed a representation of grammar that contains the parameter settings for the specific language they speak. At least some of these settings will be the same as those needed in the target language, and so it does not seem efficient to start from the beginning and reset all the switches.

The possibility of similar settings across languages has been the basis for an interesting conception of the role of transfer in second language learning. The learner begins the process of acquisition with the parameters fixed in the positions set by the first language. If the second language takes a different value on the parameters, such as allowing pro-drop where the first language did not, that setting is adjusted. What transfers, then, are not structures but parameter settings.

There are different views regarding the availability of the universal grammar (UG) to adults in second language acquisition. These range from admitting full access to UG for adult second language learners; admitting partial or indirect access, such as via the grammar of the first language; to denying further access past a biologically-specified critical period.

It seems reasonable that some synthesis of these views is needed to explain the role of UG in adult second language acquisition. Even if UG continues to be available throughout life, it undoubtedly changes in form. Felix (1986) proposes that UG emerges developmentally, making different linguistic principles available to older language learners than to younger ones. Using neurolinguistic evidence, Keane (1988) makes a similar argument. She claims that all biological structures, including UG, develop with age and experience. In this sense, UG is an emergent neurological property of development and not a fully specified system, and so could not possibly have the same role in second language acquisition as it did for first. The very experience of having learned a language changes the UG, and this, coupled with the cognitive maturity of adults, provides adult second language learners with a different set of resources to exploit.

There is considerable evidence that in some way universal grammar continues to operate during adult second language acquisition. But a more detailed description of what UG encompasses, how it changes, and which aspects of language structure it can explain or not explain, is necessary to understand its influence. White (1989) delineates the aspects of language that UG affects and those that it does not. The linguistic features that seem most controlled by UG are those relating to syntax, although even here it may be only a part of syntactic structure that is under UG control. Those aspects that appear to be outside of UG are lexicon, and possibly discourse and pragmatics.

The linguistic approach to the problem of second language acquisition appears to be most fruitful in offering explanations for the acquisition of syntax. Using learnability theory, the claim is that some aspects of the second language syntax are learned by means of the universal grammar that controlled first language acquisition and has remained accessible to adults for second language acquisition. Using connectionist theory, the claim is that structural features of the input produce a complex network of form–function relations that comprise the grammar of the language. Although the resulting network is different for each new language learned, the processes that generate these networks are the same.

What emerges most clearly is an explanation of how linguistic structure, especially syntax, is built up. The linguistic approach provides the best explanation for why acquisition proceeds in the direction it does, what influence other languages have on that acquisition, and what the stage sequence must be. This contribution is the same whether the universal mechanism responsible for constructing this grammar is considered to be a set of cognitive universals that uncover the structure of input or a set of linguistic universals that are wired into an acquisition device.

Irrespective of the particular linguistic theory adopted, there are other aspects of language that the devices proposed in these explanations do not control. Most notable among these is lexical semantics. This part of language must be learned by adults in some other way. This proposal fits particularly well with the claim that lexical acquisition cannot be the same for child first language learners and adult second language learners because the real lexical problem for children is a conceptual one. Adults only need to learn the names for things.

Psycholinguistic approach

The premise of psycholinguistic approaches is that features of the learner's mental processes, or changes in the processes that are available, are responsible for the acquisition of language. Here, the explanation is an internal description of cognitive resources.

There are two problems that psycholinguistic approaches to second language acquisition can address. The first is the relation between meaning and language and how these meanings are learned; the second is the nature of linguistic representation and the way in which two languages are related in such a representation.

Language and meaning

Recent work in first language acquisition has assigned an increasingly important role to conceptual development. In this, preverbal meaning is one of the foundations upon which language acquisition is built, as Bowerman (1987: 464) points out: 'Without certain assumptions about children's meaning representations, no theory [of language acquisition] can get off the ground'.

There are two issues to solve in explaining the role of meaning in children's language acquisition: the problem of the origin of meanings and the mapping problem.

(a)   Origin of meanings

Complex ideas can be built up out of simpler ones, but how do children learn the simpler ones? Jackendoff (1990) argues that the development of word meanings must be based on a combinatorial system built out of innate primitives. He refrains from being explicit about such matters as what the primitives are or how many there must be. His argument, rather, is a logical one in which he finds it inescapable to posit a set of meaning components as part of the innate conceptual apparatus that children bring to first language acquisition. In an important sense, then, meaning is innate.

(b)   The mapping problem

The mapping problem is the dilemma introduced by Quine (1960). How do language learners know what part of the perceived environment is the appropriate referent for a newly heard label? How do children know that 'ball' is the particular toy and not the shape; that 'apple' is a specific fruit and not any edible thing; that 'car' is the vehicle and not the action of movement? Markman (1990) argues that this problem could only be solved if children were biologically predisposed to direct their attention to some kinds of entities and not others when learning new words. If children were biased to attend to whole objects and not properties of objects, for example, there would be no mapping problem.

The mapping problem, however, is not solely determined by innate pre-dispositions. The context in which children learn their first language reduces the number of competing hypotheses children might construct about word meanings and ensures that correct deductions are made. Macnamara (1972) demonstrated long ago that children use context to understand such syn-tactically conflicting utterances as: 'in a box', 'in a hurry', and 'in a minute'. He argued that children understand meanings because they understand con-texts and that this pragmatic comprehension is at least as important as their more formal linguistic competence in promoting understanding.

(c)   Relation between meaning and mapping

What happens between children's earliest ideas about preverbal meanings and their labelling of these meanings with language is a less well-examined process. Mandler (1988), however, provides one particularly convincing account that is based on developmental research.

Concepts such as animacy include fairly sophisticated perceptual and conceptual information, and Mandler finds children using such concepts by about nine months of age. She argues that these concepts are built up out of children's early sensorimotor representations by being redescribed into a new format as image schemata. This development of abstract con-cepts out of earlier perceptual precursors avoids the problem of having to endow the child with innate primitives. Language can be mapped directly onto these image schemata, making their development the important precondition for children to learn language. A cognitive advance is a direct precursor to the child's first word.

There is some influence that goes in the opposite direction, of language structures influencing meaning representations. Bowerman (1989) has studied the development of spatial concepts by American and Korean children. The spatial lexicons in English and Korean make different kinds of distinctions and make different spatial relations relevant to changes in word meanings. For example, where English would use 'put in' for *apple in bowl* and *hand in glove*, Korean distinguishes these with different terms that express 'tightness of fit'. Putting on a hat takes a different term than putting on a ring. The studies show that American and Korean children build up different conceptions of spatial similarity, and that these different conceptions must be signalled by linguistic differences.

Empirical evidence and theoretical argument therefore seem to agree that children's acquisition of meaning in first language acquisition predates language acquisition *per se* and is to some extent biologically supported. Children's hypotheses about possible word meanings are constrained by innate assumptions. Still, these can be modified by the semantic structures expressed in the language about to be learned. Mapping words onto conceptual representations is dependent upon cognitive restructuring of perceptual representations.

Adult second language learners do not confront these problems of meaning. There is no mapping problem for adults, and the meaning primitives, whatever they are, have long ago been explicated. But since there is at least some influence in the opposite direction, second language learners may experience modifications to their conceptual system as they acquire a different linguistic system, specifically one in which different partitions of events are assumed. Moreover, Bowerman points out that lexical organization is not so systematic that it could be explained by innate or derivable rules alone. Cognition is inevitably involved. The problem of learning meanings, then, begins for young children with some innate constraints and quickly becomes a problem of cognition. Adult second language learners have only the cognitive resources with which to learn meanings in the new language.

Representation of two languages

Psycholinguistic approaches to second language acquisition also address the relation between two or more languages in a linguistic representation. Specifically, does the mental representation of multilingual speakers consist of a separate system for each known language or a single unified linguistic representation that contains the details of all the languages spoken by that person? These competing views lead to different interpretations of how the language was learned in the first place.

If two languages share a single representational system, then one would expect considerable transfer from the first to the second language. A speaker attempting to access information about one language may inadvertently retrieve the corresponding forms in the other language, unless the languages were somehow tagged or marked for their separateness within the same representational system. In contrast, if the two languages were represented in completely distinct systems, then a mechanism for interfacing them would need to be considered, since transfer and translation between languages are, if not easy, at least possible.

(a)   Distinct representations

Genesee (1989) argues that the existing evidence does not fit well with unitary representations. His claim is that children using two languages represented in a unitary system would be indiscriminate in selecting which language lexical items were drawn from. Conversely, if children were able to select languages as a function of such factors as context and interlocutor, then that would indicate that the child had separate access to the two linguistic systems, even if terms were sometimes borrowed. The critical cases would be those in which the child was required to use the weaker language. A unitary representation would imply more transfer from stronger to weaker language in this case than in the converse.

Although existing data have not been formally analysed in this way, those data that are available do not support the unitary view. Functionally, there seems to be some measure of differentiation from early on, and this separation of languages by context, purpose, and interlocutor is taken as evidence that the representation of the two languages must be distinct.

Genesee also reviews evidence to show that young infants, the youngest being four days, can discriminate between the sounds of two different languages to which they are exposed. In short, bilingual children, and of course adults, do not confuse the two languages.

The cross-linguistic borrowings characteristic of the speech of young bilingual children that have constituted the primary evidence for a unitary representation can be explained by reference to the strategies of overextension and underextension used in monolingual first language acquisition. In the absence of the exact word, children choose something that is close, but they recognize that it stands as a substitute for the correct term that they lack.

(b)   Unified representation

Cook (in press), in contrast, favours the view that the representation of multiple linguistic competence is unified. The main point of his argument is that neither the L1 nor the L2 of bilingual speakers, no matter how proficient they are, is exactly the same as either the L1 or L2 of the respective monolingual groups. He notes differences in both vocabulary and syntax. These differences, he argues, are best explained by a system in which the two languages share a common representation and therefore have the opportunity to influence each other. In distinctly represented systems, one would expect each language to stand as an independent structure, and the L1 at least to be the same as the L1 representation for a monolingual speaker of that language. But, he argues, transfer operates in both directions, and both languages are influenced by the presence of the other.

Cook also cites the frequency and context of code-switching. In spite of millisecond delays evident when speakers switch languages, distinct representations, he claims, could not be the basis for code-switching which happens in such contextually sensitive ways and with such ease and frequency.

Finally, evidence that bilingual children enjoy metalinguistic advantages over their monolingual peers offers further support to the argument that the two languages are in close contact and influence each other. Only a unified representation could achieve this.

(c) Resolution of the alternatives
In the earlier discussion, a reconciliation of competing views depended on adopting a more differentiated conception of language proficiency. Similarly, the different views for representation may best be envisaged as applying to different aspects of language. Different components of linguistic knowledge may be represented in different types of systems. An outline for such a system is shown in Figure 1. There is a central unified representation of 'language' as well as independent but related representations for the details of specific languages.

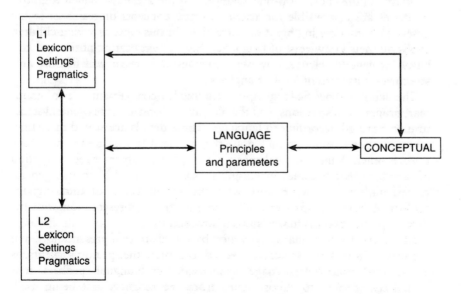

Figure 1 Mental representations of L1 and L2 knowledge

One problem in explaining second language acquisition has been how to account for learners' initial levels of competence in such areas as grammar. When adults begin to learn a second language, they already know something about language and about grammar. Consequently, they do not need to build up a completely new linguistic representation for syntax. In the unitary view, this is not a problem, as the new language becomes encoded in the same representational space as the first language. Hence, the new language can profit from the insights already gained from the first language. At the same time, details of the second language risk becoming confused with the prescriptive details of the first language. In the distinct representation view, it is more difficult to explain the advantages that adults bring to the task of second language acquisition.

In the present view, the unified system contains the representation of abstract linguistic knowledge that is common to all languages. This abstract knowledge is derived from a combination of the universal grammar that is available to all speakers, and the conceptual knowledge attached to this during first language acquisition that signals the way in which language refers: what things get labelled and what restrictions on labelling exist in language in general. This is the portion that is common across languages.

It is this abstract representation of language, derived from universals that have been innately prescribed, that gets 'analysed' (Bialystok 1991) during the course of language acquisition. Analysis is the process by which linguistic representations become more explicit, more structured, and more accessible to introspection. This cognitive restructuring of grammar is what Bowerman (1987) calls 'off-line' change. It is the means by which cognitive processes are responsible for altering mental concepts of grammar in the absence of any ongoing input or correction. In this way, as young children explicate their knowledge of language, they are explicating notions of language in general. Hence, any new language they learn will fit onto this structure at its current level of analysis.

The details of specific languages, including lexicon, certain rules of grammar, pragmatic restrictions, and the like, are appended to this general structure and tagged according to language. These details are stored in distinct representations, although they none the less need to maintain connections to each other. A monolingual speaker, then, has an abstract representation of language that becomes increasingly analysed. Attached to this general representation is another store with the specifications of the language spoken. A bilingual speaker has a single abstract representation with the details for the two languages spoken attached to it.

Language use is primarily governed by the abstract representation, and the specific words and structures needed to express the speaker's intentions are selected from the language being used. For bilingual speakers, it is sometimes efficient to choose items from the language not being used. Speakers may not have the proper entry to match the intention, the second language may have a more precise expression for the concept, or pragmatic or contextual factors may make the selection of the second language more effective.

The view in which the two languages are attached to the same abstract system is consistent with evidence from second language acquisition. In a system of distinct representations, the two linguistic representations would need to be separately analysed, but that is clearly not what happens. Adult second language learners do not need to relearn the basic categories of language; they need only learn the details.

In a strongly-determined universal grammar view, the main learning problem for syntax is to reset the parameters. Thus, it may be that only the principles are stored in the common abstract representation and the parameter settings are stored in the tagged representations for the specific language.

The principal implication of this model is that learners do not lose ground in the level of analysis they have achieved in one language when starting to learn a second. This is why there is a certain influence on children's metalinguistic abilities as a function of bilingualism and why adult learners of a second language do not need to begin from scratch learning about the grammar of the new language before learning the specific rules or differences that apply. Attaching the new tagged system, then, is essentially a cognitive problem. It is minimally governed by biological considerations, since the greatest impact of those has been in setting up the abstract representation. It is somewhat governed by universal grammar, in that the details of any language must fit within the constraints of universal grammar. Presumably, learners would find it difficult if not impossible to learn a language that did not conform to those specifications.

To summarize, there are two main areas in which psycholinguistic approaches have contributed insights into second language acquisition. The first is the problem of meaning and the way in which humans learn the meanings of specific languages. The second is representation of knowledge of language. Both of these areas contribute most directly to understanding the development of the semantic system, although they have implications for the learner's knowledge of syntax. None the less, these psycholinguistic proposals are essentially neutral with respect to the kinds of syntactic problems that are solved by linguistic approaches. It is the representation of syntax and not its development that is central to a psycholinguistic approach. Similarly, proposals from a neurolinguistic approach, especially regarding phonological acquisition, do not alter any of the psycholinguistic explanations.

Towards explanation

How do learners learn a second language? Three different approaches to this question have been reviewed to determine the contribution that each makes to answering this question. Although each approach contributes to an explanation of several aspects of language acquisition, each is uniquely suited to explain one aspect in a more satisfying way than either of the other two approaches.

The neurolinguistic approach provides the best account of how the phonological system is acquired. Children learning their first language and adults learning a second language both appear to be at the mercy of a biological timetable for acquiring the ability to perceive and produce the sounds of a given language with the competence of a native speaker.

The linguistic approach, specifically with the aid of a universal device for either discovering or constraining the universal grammar, provides the best account of how the syntactic system is acquired. Children learning their first language could not possibly arrive at the accurate and complete description of language structure that they do if they had to rely exclusively on input and experience. Some innate constraint that structures the input according to general rules that organize all languages is necessary to achieve native-like competence in syntax. Adults learning a second language remain influenced by the constraints of universal grammar, but their cognitive sophistication frees them to discover new rules and to modify their existing level of competence.

The psycholinguistic approach provides the best account of how the lexical system is acquired and represented. Children learning their first language begin with the cognitive problem of developing a conceptual system before they can even learn their first word. Labelling concepts is essentially a cognitive problem, not a linguistic one. Adult second language learners have well-elaborated conceptual systems. Their ability to learn the vocabulary, and to some extent grammar, of a second language is limited only by their ability to learn and organize new information. In this way, the psycholinguistic approach has a residual effect in explaining some aspects of syntactic development as well.

These three approaches do not constitute isolated explanations of different pieces of the problem. A computer analogy may make their interrelation clearer. If one wanted a complete explanation of how a particular computer program worked, it would be necessary to characterize at least three parts of the system. The explanation of how each of the three parts functioned would be based on a different type of theory or analysis. Principles of mechanics and electronics would be necessary to explain the functioning of the computer hardware (cf. neurolinguistic approach), structural and engineering principles would be needed to describe the nature of the data entered into the program (cf. linguistic approach), and logical and computational principles would guide the description of the software that ran it (cf. psycholinguistic approach). To take the analogy further, it would also be necessary to describe the environment in which the computer is functioning: what other kinds of devices it is connected to, and what kind of power supply it has. Descriptions of this sort would correspond to sociolinguistic analyses of second language learning.

Comparing first and second language acquisition

The division of labour implied in this conception of second language acquisition can be used to examine the relation between explanations of first and second language learning. In principle, each of the three approaches serves the same function in explaining both types. Children, too, are influenced by a critical period for phonology, a universal grammar to organize structure, and conceptual knowledge to establish and label the concepts. In this broad sense, then, second language learning is the same as first language acquisition.

The difference between the two cases emerges from closer consideration of how the effects of each of these approaches is realized. In each case, there are two possible means through which the processes can operate and serve to develop their respective aspect of linguistic competence. On the one hand, the process may be predominantly under the control of biological wiring, and would operate in fairly predictable and routinized ways. On the other hand, the process may by predominantly at the mercy of the cognitive intervention of the learner, and active involvement in the learning process could accelerate or modify the course of development.

It is the balance between these biological and cognitive influences on development that distinguishes between first and second language learning. For children learning their first language, most of the variance is left to the innate biological factors. The greatest need for cognitive intervention is in the development of semantics, but even here innate meaning components simplify the burden on intentionality. Similarly, some cognitive reorganization is necessary to represent the syntactic system, but a considerable part of that structure is under the influence of innate constructs. Very little, if any, cognitive effort is required for phonology. These relations are shown in Figure 2. The shaded portion indicates the degree to which that domain of linguistic competence is acquired through cognitive intervention. The unshaded portion is the extent to which language learning in each domain is governed by biological factors.

For adults learning a second language, there is more room for cognitive mediation. The influence of intentional learning is apparent in all three aspects of linguistic competence, although a decreasing proportion of each domain is left to such learning as one moves from the semantic through to the phonological domains. These relations are represented in Figure 3. Again, the shaded portion indicates the extent to which intentionality characterizes learning in each linguistic domain and the unshaded portion is the allotment under biological control.

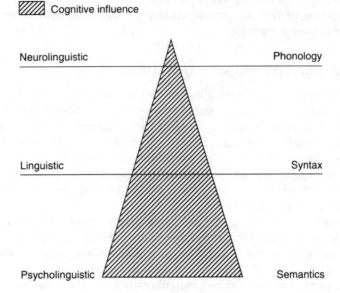

Figure 2   Cognitive and biological factors in L1 learning

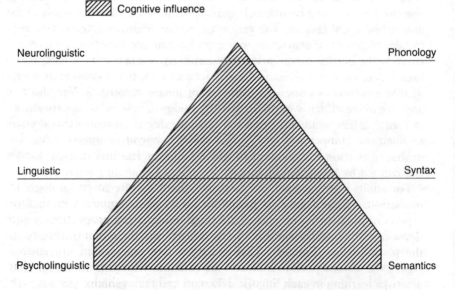

Figure 3   Cognitive and biological factors in L2 learning

In general, then, first and second language learning are the same process but have different expressions in development. Each group comes to the task with a different set of abilities, and therefore a different set of advantages. For this reason, first language acquisition and second language learning appear to be more different than they are: the stages and course of development can be quite different. For this reason, too, it is impossible to claim unequivocally that one group is privileged in the enterprise. Children enjoy certain biological advantages for some aspects of language but adults have an enormous cognitive advantage for others. Moreover, the role of social context has not even been dealt with in this discussion, but its importance in language acquisition is considerable. To the extent that children and adults carry out this activity under different contextual conditions, the two activities will appear different.

Common-sense views of second language acquisition

Let us return to the three popular intuitions about how learners learn a second language that were mentioned early on. In the present view, simplified input facilitates language learning because it makes it easier for the learner to focus on the relevant parts of the utterance. Only pertinent information is presented, so all the learner's processing resources can be recruited to interpret the utterance. The simplification further reduces the need for high levels of analysed knowledge of language by bringing the input into line with the learner's current level of analysis. Learners are in a better position to acquire new information from the input, as well as to demonstrate increased levels of comprehension and production.

Why does repeatedly naming objects work? It is a general learning principle that repetition of material presented in context helps it to be remembered, and this is just as true for language as for history and science. For language, however, there is a further benefit. Once some vocabulary has been mastered, the learner is able to begin producing comprehensible utterances, even in the absence of any grammatical knowledge. Foreign language phrase books have long been known to get travellers through countless awkward situations. If the Ll and L2 are similar, then the L2 lexicon can even be slotted into the grammatical frames of the first language, and this will go a long way in producing the illusion of competence. The real advantage, however, is that the second language learner can elicit input in the second language. This has its own special role in promoting learners' proficiency with the second language.

Why would listening to the second language work? As argued above, the universal grammar remains available in some measure to language learners throughout life. Input is essential if it is to sort out the settings needed for the target language. Simply listening, then, has its primary benefit in constructing hypotheses about the structure of the second language. These hypotheses can be represented in the language-specific system that is tagged onto the abstract representation of language. Although there may be some advantage to lexical and phonological acquisition, syntax would appear to be the main beneficiary of extensive listening to the target language.

There is precious little that we really know about *how* learners learn a second language. But each of the three disciplines I have discussed has something to contribute to the story. Minimally, it can be shown that each approach raises issues and questions that do not arise in the other approaches. The integration I have attempted in this paper is preliminary and schematic. In some cases I have simply listed some of the issues formulated by the various disciplines, and in others I have also assembled some of the evidence and theorizing that has been developed. In some sense, this framework constitutes a theoretical agenda through which research in second language acquisition will proceed. A general theory will be easier to construct when it becomes clear what all the parts are that need to be explained by that theory. First, we must name the parts.

Notes

1   Preparation of this paper was supported by grant A2559 from the Natural Sciences and Engineering Research Council, Canada, and a York University Research Leave Fellowship. The paper was written while I was a Visiting Scholar at the School of Education at Stanford University. I am grateful to Kenji Hakuta for providing both support and discussion in the preparation of this paper.

2   I wish to thank Jim Cummins for pointing out this difference and suggesting an explanation.

8 Comprehension testing, or can understanding be measured?

One of the facts of educational life is that students' learning must be assessed. Teachers themselves need feedback about their students' progress (or lack of it), and the world outside demands evidence of the teachers' success and of the students' readiness to take up places in work or further education. Given what we now know about understanding, how can we best measure it?

Bernard Spolsky's answer is uncompromising: we cannot. The very collocation of the two words *measurement* and *understanding* is unacceptable. Spolsky argues that misunderstanding is far more common than we normally assume, and that there can never be a single 'correct' understanding of any text. Like Brumfit, he sees the meaning of a text as being different for each reader/hearer in each different context. The seven-level scheme that he uses for classifying texts can be seen as an expansion of the four-level one described by G. Brown earlier in this volume; he then points out that the interpretation of a higher-level text is a creative process that operates at many levels simultaneously, and that involves interaction between the writer, the text and the reader/hearer's experience, interests, and intentions. In these circumstances, understanding must be viewed as a many-faceted, or multidimensional, concept. Yet measurement demands simplicity; it is a logical prerequisite of a measurement process that there be a trait (an ability or quality) that is unidimensional. We cannot measure someone's 'size', but only their height, or their weight, or some other unidimensional component of 'size'. Since understanding is far more complex than 'size', it follows that it cannot be measured. Spolsky argues that we should abandon the idea of measuring understanding and instead seek a means of describing it, for description is enriched by complexity, not impoverished.

The process of testing adds yet more layers of complexity to this problem, since testing is itself a communicative activity. In a test, the question-setter writes to the candidate, who reads this message and writes a response. A third person, the marker, then reads this message and judges it against some more or less implicit criteria. There is ample scope for misunderstanding here, even if we leave the text and author aside. Spolsky analyses this complex as a series of texts, each derived from the preceding ones, but each contributing, inevitably, some distortion or simplification. And the final text, a single number purporting to measure the understanding, must be the most distorted of all.

Yet the demand remains: we must measure students' comprehension. Is there any answer to Spolsky's pessimism? Perhaps we must learn to temper our ambition. Where measurement, rather than description, is necessary we may be able to narrow the concept rather as 'size' can be narrowed to 'height' in the selection of policemen. A useful consequence for foreign language assessment can be drawn from the distinction between 'achievement' and 'ability' testing. If our aim is to test how much of a foreign language a student has learned, rather than how well the student can read in that language, then our test could involve as much as possible what has been learned in the foreign language, and as little as possible any skills that were developed in the first language. This implies that comprehension questions would stay as close as possible to the simplest meaning of the text. It is on these grounds that de Jong and Glas (1987) argue that we should not try to test the ability to make inferences in foreign language listening comprehension tests.

The positive aspect of Spolsky's argument, that we should aim for description of understanding rather than measurement, should do much to shake the complacency of those who feel that testing reading and listening cannot be problematical because after all, we've been doing it for so long.

Comprehension testing, or can understanding be measured?

Bernard Spolsky
Department of English
Bar-Ilan University, Israel

Comprehension testing should be easy

On the face of it, tests of comprehension are so common that we should be safe in assuming that they set neither theoretical nor practical problems; after all, the very first modern language test (Handschin 1919) was a test of silent reading, that is, comprehension. Anyone planning a battery of language tests today would probably start by automatically assuming that the two principal parts will be tests of reading and listening comprehension. There will be little or no doubt about the necessity of these two sections and the ease of writing the items required, and the planning committee's time will be given to the more challenging task of testing writing and speaking proficiency.

None the less, I believe that there remain fundamental questions, as yet unresolved, about the theoretical feasibility of developing useful comprehension tests and about the appropriate interpretations to be made of the tests that do exist. To anticipate my argument in this paper, my point will be that understanding is a complex and multidimensional notion, one that calls for full description rather than for precise (and certainly not for unidimensional) measurement, and that the very process of testing leads to a new set of comprehension problems.

Understanding or misunderstanding

Perhaps a good entry to the problem of understanding is to recognize how common misunderstanding is. Think back on some recent conversations and communicative interactions. How often did you need to ask to have something repeated? How often did you read something through several times, each time getting a different or clearer reading? How often have you found on a later reading that new information you now have has led to a deeper or altered understanding? How often have you later realized that

142 *Language and Understanding*

you misunderstood what someone was telling you? And how often in an argument do we tell our opponent, 'You didn't understand what I was saying'? A good place to find evidence of misunderstanding and misreading is the correspondence column of a literary review magazine like the *Times Literary Supplement* or the discussion section of a journal. May I perhaps cite my own most recent example: a particularly obtuse reading by a reviewer of a recent paper I had submitted to a journal who took me to task for the ideas of a scholar that I was disagreeing with. The wide prevalence of misunderstanding signals the difficulty of understanding.

Levels of understanding

To carry the issue further, consider the question of what constitutes understanding; or rather, which of the many kinds and levels of understanding might be sufficient for a given purpose. Think about differences of text-types. Carton (1988) proposed seven different text-types:

non-propositional   – e.g. labels and signs
non-sentential   – e.g. menus and lists
truncated text acts – e.g. advertisements and bills
descriptions   – e.g. travel brochures, 'wanted' posters
narrations   – e.g. journalistic reports and fictional literature
complete text acts – e.g. directions and contracts
arguments   – e.g. essays and research proposals

There is a difference in what it means to understand each of these text-types. Take for instance narration. Let me cite one well-known story from the Bible:

> And the whole earth was of one language and of one speech. And it came to pass, as they journeyed from the east, that they found a plain in the land of Shin'ar; and they dwelt there. And they said to one another, Come let us make bricks and burn them thoroughly. And they had brick for stone and slime had they for mortar. And they said, Come, let us build a city and tower, whose top may reach to heaven; and let us make us a name, lest we be scattered upon the face of the whole earth. And the Lord came down to see the city and the tower, which the children of men were building. And the Lord said, Behold the people is one, and they all have one language, and this they begin to do; and now nothing will be withheld from them, which they have schemed to do. Come let us go down and there confound their language that they may not understand one another's speech. So the Lord scattered them abroad from there upon the face of the earth, and they ceased to build the city. Therefore is the name of it called Babel; because the Lord did there confound the language of all the earth; and from thence did the Lord scatter them abroad upon the face of the earth. (Genesis II:1–9)

The question that I would like to propound is what does it mean to understand this well-known story? Putting it more precisely, which of the various levels of understanding and interpretation that have been proposed constitutes the 'basic' or 'literal' level?

There is room in this paper for just a handful of the possible interpretations of this story. The medieval Jewish commentator, Rashi, using Talmudic sources, pointed out that the Lord did not need to come down to see, but that Scripture, by this exact form of expression, was teaching that judges should not condemn a defendant before they have seen the case and before they thoroughly understand it. For Rashi then, a scholar who considered his task as presenting the 'simplest' or 'literal' interpretation, the meaning of this unnecessarily anthropomorphic remark was the ethical lesson to be derived from it. Another medieval commentator, Abraham Ibn Ezra, proposed that the main purpose in building the Tower was to achieve fame. A third medieval commentator, Nachmanides, wrote that the point of the story was the purpose expressed in making themselves a 'name', to gain control of the power in the divine name (as any student of Kabala will understand, he concluded). The eighteenth-century Ladino commentator, Me'am Loez, understood that the Tower was built out of an erroneous belief that because the Flood had occurred in the year 1656, there would be another one every 1656 years, and though only 340 years had passed since the last one, the people of Babel felt they should be prepared. The nineteenth-century German Jewish scholar, Samson Raphael Hirsch, interpreted 'one language' to mean a single phonology and 'one speech' to mean a uniform lexicon and grammar 'resulting from attitudes shared in common toward things and their interrelationships'. 'In other words,' he continued, 'the human race was still united by complete harmony, physical and spiritual, for good and evil.' If there were space, I could easily go on for the rest of the paper multiplying these understandings of the text out of a single tradition; if I were to start on Christian, or archaeological, or linguistic, or historical, understandings, we could easily fill a volume trying to comprehend and explicate this single text.

Unfair, you might say; a sacred text calls for a special kind of interpretation, because it assumes a significant if hidden level of authorial intent, and because its externally derived value makes it worth detailed study. But note that a similar inherent worth justifies the constant striving for new and deeper interpretations of a great number of other texts, in literature, or philosophy, or science, or other scholarly areas. Indeed, one might want to argue that the goal of scholarship is to seek these new readings on the basis of the increased understanding of the old.

Other cases will help make the point. What is the difference between understanding a newspaper account of a crime and a similar account in a detective story? Where is the understanding that an account is fictional? Or how about understanding a poem? What is the level of understanding at which one would want to say that 'sufficient information has been conveyed'?

It is clear, I would argue, that even within a single text-type, there are multiple levels of comprehension: literal, metaphorical, poetic, rhetorical, instructional, moral, to name just a few. Now, you might want to reply, we do not usually test these in a comprehension test, where we are only concerned with the 'literal' or 'informational' level. But that is far from the case; it is normal in comprehension tests to ask for interpretation: what is the author's position . . .? would the author agree that . . .? which of these statements agrees with the author . . .? As Hemnon (1929) argued, reading should be tested at the paragraph rather than the word or sentence level, with the result that more interpretative questions are usually involved. Nor do I think that one is safe in assuming that these levels are easily rankable. It is often the non-literal meaning of an utterance that is (or should be) the most obvious.

You just don't understand me

Another approach to our problem might be to consider the kind of performance that is assumed to be evidence of understanding in everyday life. In ordinary face-to-face conversation, listeners are expected to give regular feedback to speakers to show that they have understood—nods, confirmatory exclamations, direct statements all serve this purpose—or to signal to the speaker when they do not understand—requests for repetition or explanation, offering of paraphrases. This kind of discourse process, true of all kinds of conversation, has also been studied in the special case of conversations between native and non-native speakers (Pica, Holliday, Lewis, and Morgenthaler 1989).

The process was succinctly analysed by Widdowson (1984: 81–5) who described the kind of negotiation of information exchange that takes place in normal conversations. Widdowson proposed that in such conversations, the speaker wishes to 'bring about some change or other by the transmission of information.' Whatever the speaker's ultimate purpose (instructing, persuading, deceiving, sharing, being sociable), its attainment depends on the passing of the information. But it will be clear that any shared information that precedes the exchange will be just as important a predictor of the ease and effectiveness of the communication as the words of the message themselves. The more familiar the topic, the easier it is to understand the message. In normal co-operative conversations, then, the listener generally plays an active part in the communication by signalling his or her level of understanding or the existence of a need for additional information. This is seldom allowed for in comprehension tests.

Active comprehension

What are the components of comprehension? First there are the actors: the creator of the text on the one hand and the understander of the text on the other. Each must be assumed to be an active participant: the creator is generally assumed to have consciously intended to communicate something, to have intentionally embedded meaning in the text. Mention of this intentionality reminds us that there usually is unconscious or unintended meaning in the text too: a speaker/writer can easily give away his or her hidden motives (as Freud taught us all), can reveal aspects of himself or herself (origin, education, attitude) that he or she did not know existed and did not intend to communicate. Thus, the speaker/writer is both conscious and unconscious creator of the text.

The activity of the understander is now much better understood, thanks to the work of reader-response criticism on the one hand (see e.g. E. Spolsky 1990) and top-down reading theories (e.g. Carrell 1991). The active reader comes to the text with intentions (to seek attitudes, to gain confirmatory information, to be entertained), that are based in part on previous knowledge and in part on genre-related expectations (Spolsky and Schauber 1986).

From the point of view of comprehension testing, many of these reader-related factors might be considered a source of interference or unreliability on the one hand, or provide facilitation on the other. One such feature is text-level rhetorical structure. Brown (1989) reported that in tasks calling on one subject to explain to another the content of short videos, both explanation and understanding are better when the narrator is given a title for the series. Similarly, Jonz (1989) showed that subjects did better on a cloze test that had a rhetorical structure than on one that did not, and Lee and Riley (1990) demonstrated that students did better on a free recall task when there was a structure.

A number of studies have taken up the relevance of previous knowledge. In a well-planned study, Hock (1990) gave three tests to 317 undergraduate students who were learning English as a second language: a test of general proficiency in English, a multiple-choice test in their field of expertise (medicine, law, or economics) written by subject-matter specialists, and a cloze test (assumed to measure reading ability) with passages related to the discipline. The results established that both language proficiency and prior knowledge predicted the cloze score; in each case, language proficiency appeared more important. In further analysis of the results, prior knowledge was found to be a weaker predictor of performance on texts in other fields. Further support for these findings was provided by the study by Flynn (1986), who argued that while production tests (elicited imitation) provided evidence of developing second language structural competence, comprehension tasks were less direct measures and were influenced by pragmatic context.

The question of what sources we have for information was raised in a study by Perkins and Brutten (1988). Information sources can be textual or non-textual, explicit in the text or implicit, and vary in frequency. With beginning and less qualified readers, still engaged presumably in bottom-up reading, the source made no difference; with readers on higher levels of ability, all three sources were important in accounting for scores on a reading comprehension test.

The reader then has nearly as much to contribute to the process of understanding as the writer.

Non-linguistic props for text comprehension

Assuming that comprehension of a foreign-language text depends not just on knowledge of the second language but also on prior knowledge of the topic or content, some studies have been concerned to look for evidence of bias. One of the most recent of such studies has been by Hale (1988) who was able to look at over 30,000 students taking TOEFL examinations. Hale selected twenty-one different reading passages, intended to be general, and divided them according to topic into biological/physical sciences and humanities/ social sciences. There was evidence of a statistically significant difference, so that subjects did better with a passage in their field, but the practical effect was slight: had all students been tested with passages in their own field, the difference would have been 3 points (the standard deviation of the test is normally about 65 points).

In a study that built on Hale, Henning (1990) looked at items in a UCLA English proficiency test to see if there was any bias according to the speciality of the topic of the item (in both reading and listening comprehension). No items in the listening, reading, and error detection subtests were found biased in favour of any specialization nor was evidence found of overall systematic bias. It must be borne in mind that the developers of these last two tests were aware of the practical problem of test bias, and were attempting (more or less successfully) to avoid it. A quite different approach is taken in the specialized field tests of English, such as the specific field modules of the IELTS (Westaway, Alderson, and Clapham 1990), where the texts are specially selected to be relevant to the various streams of candidates.

Assessing comprehension

We have so far considered three components: the speaker/writer, the comprehender, and the text. The obvious direct—see Clark (1978) but Bachman (1990) dislikes the term—testing equivalent might well be self-report or self-assessment (cf. Oscarson 1989, for a review). Assuming that the person taking the test has no special incentive to lie, and assuming the question is within his or her experience, (see Heilenman 1991; Blanche 1991) then such a question as 'Can you understand most of a news broadcast in the foreign language?' or 'Can you follow a lecture in your subject in the foreign language?' might be an appropriate way to proceed.

For those who have less confidence in the subject's own judgement, there are a wide range of techniques available to test comprehension. All basically consist of three parts: first, a written (or oral) text in the foreign language is presented to the subject; then a specific task is set; then the subject's response is scored and interpreted. The texts vary on a number of dimensions: channel, length, assumed difficulty, topic (absolutely and relative to the subject's assumed knowledge), and time allowed to read or times to hear the text. The tasks vary in the nature of the prompt (an instruction, or a question, or a blank, or a multiple-choice question); the channel (in speech or writing); the amount to be written (nothing, as in a multiple-choice question; a word, as in a cloze; a sentence or so, as in an open-ended question; a longer passage, as in a summary, or paraphrase, or translation); the language to be used (target or native). The scoring methods too vary, especially in the extent to which there is believed to be one correct answer, or to which the score depends on the examiner's explicit or implicit intuitive judgement. Finally, the interpretation of the scores varies in its own way.

Why testing adds complications

It is important to my central concern in this paper to draw attention to the extra components introduced in the whole process by testing. To a complex enough model of speaker/writer, text, and understander, we add several more critical parts: a tester who becomes speaker/writer and creator of a second text that sets tasks for the understander, a third text produced by that understander, a reader/interpreter of that new text (the tester or marker), and a fourth text, a mark or score or grade that awaits the interpretation of an additional participant, the test user. I cannot resist drawing a model of this (see Figure 1).

Speaker/writer 1	encodes information consciously and unconsciously in
Text 1	the text to be comprehended by
Reader 1	the candidate/test-taker who understands it according to previous knowledge, language ability, sense of purpose, etc.; and is then asked by
Speaker/writer 2	who has spoken/written
Text 2	the questions that make up the test to become
Speaker/writer 3	the test-taker answering questions who produces
Text 3	the answers which are read and marked by
Reader 2	the examiner, who becomes in turn
Speaker/writer 4	and produces
Text 4	the grade or score which must be interpreted by
Reader 3	the test-user. (And there may be turtles further down too.)

Figure 1

This helps us see some of the problems of language testing. Our original interest was in learning about Reader 1's understanding of Speaker/writer 1's text, text 1. To get to it, we need a tester, Speaker/writer 2, who produces text 2. Now text 2 is itself an interpretation of some limited set of the multitude of possible readings of text 1. As Statman (1992) has recently pointed out, this limitation means that we test in a comprehension test only those parts of the interpretation that we think important; it may well be that the reader/test-taker has come up with many more, and better points than the ones we included in the test. With a fully contextualized test, of course, there is more chance that the candidate will realize which interpretation the examiner is seeking.

What are the criteria for deciding the contents of text 2? At its best, it is the tester's own reading of the passage. But it may easily be confounded. For example, text 2 might be an instruction to fill in gaps left in text 1 (i.e. a cloze test). Or it may be a set of multiple-choice questions. And the criteria might not be the tester's own reading, but rather certain interesting statistical features of large numbers of text 3s, that is to say the psychometric properties of some specific marking (text 4) of a number of text 3s. Now it is not hard to recognize that the text 4 produced in this way may have only a partial relationship to our original concern, Reader 1's understanding of text 1, and is only remotely likely to bear the full weight of meaning that the test-user Reader 3 is likely to put on it.

Psychometric issues

A fundamental problem with text 4, the final score, is that it attempts to squeeze too much information into itself. There is a regrettable general craving, when testing, to arrive at a single score representing a measure. Psychometric theory holds that it is possible to measure human abilities in much the same way as measuring other characteristics such as height or weight. To do this with any reliability, one needs to have a theory of the nature of the ability, a method of eliciting a behaviour that represents the ability, and an explicit procedure for assigning a rating to that ability. Measurement theory, which is built on a fundamental axiom that the ability being measured is unidimensional (otherwise, it can be described but not reduced to a single measure), has been particularly concerned with controlling and excluding irrelevant sources of erroneous measurement that will make the test unreliable. For example, there is evidence that human judges vary among themselves and make different judgements at different times; the concern of psychometric techniques is to reduce this kind of random or identifiable source of error to the minimum.

The techniques are most highly developed for tests with a large number of multiple-choice items, where error can be identified by statistical techniques. Classical measurement theory aims to establish what proportion of the variation in observed scores on a test is to be attributed to non-relevant factors, assumed to be unsystematic or random variation in the scores. The most common approach is to look for evidence of internal consistency in the test itself by comparing the scores on randomly split halves of the test: the higher the correlation, the more the two parts of the test can be assumed to be measuring the same thing.

In the last few years, foreign-language testers have started to consider the implications of an alternative theory of measurement of human abilities called latent trait (or item response) theory. There are various analytical models in this theory, the one-parameter or Rasch model being strongly supported by some testers. These models provide a method of quantifying the probability of the patterns of responses of individual items and individual persons given the overall pattern of responses in an administration of a test. They make it possible to estimate the difficulty of an item and the ability of a test-taker. (For more detail on both classical and latent trait theories of reliability, see Henning (1987), or Bachman (1990).)

Comprehending comprehension scores

When the language behaviour has been scored reliably, the score needs interpretation. Some tests carry automatic interpretation: a mastery test, for instance, where each mistake shows something that needs to be relearned, or an assessment procedure using a guide-line where the assessment is already worded as an interpretation. In other cases, interpretation is needed to determine such points as pass and fail, levels of honours, or estimates of future language-related performance. Basic to interpreting the results of a test is an understanding of its validity.

Measurement theory has developed a large number of methods for judging the validity of the test score, that is for being confident that it represents the particular ability that has been postulated. No one approach establishes validity, which is rather the sum of a number of approaches.

Content or face validity refers to the extent to which the test appears to an observer or to the test-taker to be a representative sample of the ability it is supposed to be measuring. For example, an oral interview is likely to be considered a valid measure of spoken ability; a cloze or multiple-item test to be a questionable measure of writing ability. Its greatest importance is probably in making the test-taker willing to participate in an artificial task.

Concurrent validity is the extent to which a test correlates with other measures. In validating measures like the cloze and the multiple-item test of writing ability, their high correlation with essay tests was considered by some testers to justify their use.

Predictive validity, as the name suggests, is the extent to which the scores on a test correlate with some later criterion, such as how well entrance examinations correlate with results at the end of courses. In practice, this is hard to establish, both because there are many other factors that affect success in a course, and because the entrance examination has already been used to limit the candidates admitted to the course, thus reducing the spread of scores (and so the evidence of correlation).

Construct validity involves finding evidence that the various abilities (or constructs) that are assumed by the theory to exist can be shown empirically. One might for instance postulate that comprehension ability is made up of two separate constructs, vocabulary ability and grammatical ability, and the test should show the distinction. Following one approach to construct validity, a number of studies using the multitrait–multimethod procedure have attempted to explore the relationships between the traits or abilities being measured and the methods used to measure them. More recently, a number of studies have focused on the process of test-taking, asking candidates to report on the way in which they decided how to answer the questions; these studies have sometimes revealed that test-takers use strategies quite unlike the processes that are meant to be tested.

Construct validation of comprehension tests

The challenge that our analysis presents is the establishment of the construct validity of comprehension tests. It is not clear that this has been done. Fouly, Bachman, and Cziko (1990) tried a new approach in which 334 students were tested in ESL on ten tests. LISREL confirmatory factor analysis recognized three latent traits: an aural–oral construct, a structure–reading comprehension construct, and a discourse construct. The authors claim that there is no way of deciding between this model and another with a single higher-order ability construct.

A study with a related goal was reported by Buck (1989). Buck carried out two multitrait–multimethod studies. In the first, he used six measures: listening and reading picture recognition, listening and reading gap-filling, and listening and reading self-rating. The tests were taken by 220 Japanese college students. Various kinds of analysis failed to distinguish separate reading and listening traits. In a second study, the emphasis shifted to the nature of the texts. In contrast to those in the first study, the listening texts were unscripted, and delivered in a variety of accents, with all the hesitations and 'ungrammaticalities' of natural speech. Now he found good evidence of two different though closely related traits of language comprehension.

Levasseur and Pagé (1990) presented another claim for multiple components in text comprehension, defined as 'ability to construct a unified representation of the pieces of information given in the flow of successive sentences in a text' (ibid.: 98). Even in the first language, this was not fully developed by the age of fifteen. They presumed that there were five levels:

words, sentences, co-reference strings (sentences linked cohesively), paragraphs, and whole text. On free-recall tasks, older children did better.

Finally, a methodologically rigorous study by Davidson (1988) raises serious questions for all of these studies that purport to have recognized multiple factors. Davidson analysed twenty-one item-level data sets from nine different testing batteries. The various methods of statistical analysis that he attempted failed to produce any significant evidence of multiple factors accounting for the data. Davidson's study raises some very serious questions. One interpretation well worth exploring is that the potential factors are all suppressed by the presence of one dominating factor. The best candidate for such a blockbuster factor, the presence of which suppresses the variation in which we are interested, is reliability and its associated concept of unidimensionality. The tests that Davidson studied were psychometrically pure, highly reliable, with every trace of multidimensionality expunged. This interpretation finds support in a recent paper by Swain (1990) who reports on the development of tests for a major study she was involved in. A 'measure of internal consistency' was achieved in test development, she reports, 'largely by suppressing interesting differences . . .' In the 'pursuit of psychometric respectability, we ignored findings . . . that predict [that] variable performance will be the norm . . .'. In a recent paper, Henning (1992) has demonstrated that data artificially generated to include multidimensional factors can still meet the requirements of psychometric unidimensionality. This is reminiscent of the demonstration by Thomson (1939) that factorial analysis could not be used to demonstrate the existence of one or more factors claimed to underlie intelligence. Henning's paper would seem to suggest that we lack statistical methods to establish the uni- or multi-dimensionality of what we are measuring, something that is basic to establishing construct validity.

Conclusion

Thus, the pursuit of a suitable final interpretation (text 4), especially when we rely on a single measurement, leads us further and further from an accurate depiction of the complex set of properties involved in the task of accounting for the ability of the test-taker (Reader l) to arrive at an appropriate interpretation of the original passage (text 1).

This very distance sets us a serious challenge. If we are to arrive at any useful depiction of a student's ability to understand, then we must set very precise contextual constraints on the task, we must make clear to those who read the test results exactly what we—and the student—have done, and we must avoid as much as possible the temptation to over-generalize our interpretation of the student's performance. It follows from this that we will need to design and use a variety of reading assessment procedures (not only tests) to allow us to report on a variety of aspects of the student's ability to understand, and to establish some systematic way of reporting the results on all of them. The differences the student shows across this range of results will inform us at least as much as will the result of adding them together. However good our tests are, a single score will always mislead.

9 Sociolinguistics and second language learning

Lesley Milroy's paper focuses our attention on a different aspect of the relationship of language and understanding. Like the papers by K. Brown and Short (this volume), it is particularly concerned with the forms of language but, whereas they are concerned with how the forms contribute to our understanding of conceptual or cognitive meaning, Milroy is also concerned with how the choice of forms may contribute to our understanding of social meaning, of the social role which the speaker is choosing to play as a member of a particular speech community or peer group. However, she also points out that the potential for misunderstandings between members of different native-speaker speech communities is considerable, and may lead to states of cognitive uncertainty comparable to those encountered by advanced foreign-language speakers.

Her paper raises important issues for language teachers. The most obvious is the question of what sort of English to teach to foreign learners. The usual answer is 'Standard English', but, as Milroy points out in reviewing recent literature on this topic, even if we ignore other forms and just concentrate on British English it is by no means easy to determine what 'Standard English' is. All living languages are constantly, from day to day and hour by hour, evolving and adapting to changing speakers and changing circumstances, so that it is impossible to identify a particular set of forms as constituting 'current Standard English'. A recent study shows that experienced teachers of EFL were prepared to accept as 'correct' many written sentences which, a generation ago, had been condemned as 'ungrammatical' by an experienced EFL writer (Ahulu 1992). Many educated native speakers of English confess to being unsure in making a wide range of 'grammaticality' judgements, and as larger and larger corpora of English usage are analysed, we become increasingly aware of how remarkably variable 'acceptable' English is.

Milroy suggests that, rather than trying to refine this insubstantial notion of 'Standard English', a better approach would be to ask 'how successful is the standardization process' in speech or in writing, in pronunciation, in syntax or vocabulary, or in the language of a particular register?

Teachers have, for generations, quite readily found a satisfactory model for formal written English, because it is the most successfully standardized form. But considerable problems arise when they try to identify a satisfactory model for the spoken language because, as Milroy shows, it varies widely in pronunciation, morphology, syntax, and lexis in different parts of the country, among different social classes, and among different age-groups. This variability is so acute that the same individual, playing various social roles, may frequently display forms of standard and non-standard Englishes in different contexts. The teacher may be content to choose a rather limited production model of the spoken language, based largely on written English and spoken with the best local brand of English pronunciation. For many parts of the world, where students have little chance of encountering genuine native speakers, that is probably the most sensible decision. However, for those students, particularly advanced ones, who are likely to encounter live native English speakers, there is a much more formidable problem in deciding upon a model. Such students will need to understand spoken forms which bear little resemblance to written forms. They will want to understand a wide range of spoken varieties, and they will certainly find it helpful in establishing comfortable relationships with native speakers if they can understand the social allegiances expressed by a speaker choosing to use one set of forms rather than another.

The teacher may well be appalled at the difficulty of threading a way through such a maze. Here Milroy's paper offers a useful guide to specific areas of likely variability and difficulty.

Sociolinguistics and second language learning: understanding speakers from different speech communities

Lesley Milroy
University of Newcastle upon Tyne

Introduction

Sociolinguistics is that subdiscipline of linguistics which examines relationships between language and culture and language and society. In the case of monolingual societies, this frequently involves focusing on patterns of variation within languages, and trying to understand how this intralingual variation is used by native speakers.

I shall try in this paper to demonstrate the importance of this kind of 'understanding' of a language. It is not only the distinctive and sometimes opaque grammatical and phonological patterns of different dialects which are at issue here, but the way in which speakers use these patterns to symbolize social meanings such as intimacy or distance, solidarity or status. There are very many traditions of research encompassed within the term 'sociolinguistics', ranging from micro-level analysis of interactional phenomena (a convenient recent summary of this is provided by Brown and Levinson 1987) through to large-scale surveys of bilingualism and language choice (as reviewed by Fasold 1984). However, I think it is fair to say that most sociolinguists see themselves as trying at some level to provide an account of the contemporary language as it is actually used in everyday contexts. This involves a systematic and socially motivated description of how language encodes social meanings such as status, distance, solidarity, and intimacy. It also involves a departure from the idealized or literary models of monolithic standard languages which have formed the basis for much language teaching both to native speakers and second language learners.

Sociolinguists may focus on everyday speech for a range of theoretical reasons; for example, like Labov, to develop a dynamic and socially sensitive theory of linguistic change and of the nature of (variable) grammars (Labov 1981, 1990). He has consistently argued that this is possible only with the data of everyday spoken interaction rather than formally elicited language. J. Milroy, on the other hand, is particularly interested in developing a socially realistic account of the history of English, from the perspective of modern sociolinguistic theory (Milroy 1992), while Trudgill (1986) gives an account of dialect contact based on accommodation theory, which itself is subject to some revision (Giles and Coupland 1991). My own interests are in developing a theory of how language variation (in both monolingual and multilingual societies) relates to social structure (Milroy and Li 1991; Milroy and Milroy 1993). Although the theoretical focus of sociolinguists therefore varies, they typically agree on the need to avoid excessive idealization away from the diversified and variable data of everyday interaction.

Many teachers of English as a second language have become particularly aware of the extent of diversity within English, particularly perhaps British English. Sociolinguistics can offer a principled and socially sensitive account of this diversity, and also its converse—language standardization. Standard languages cannot rationally be viewed as static phenomena; in fact a totally standardized language is a written rather than a spoken language, a dead language. Later in this paper, I shall argue that standardization is better interpreted dynamically as a *sociolinguistic process* than as a label which can reliably be attached to a particular variety of English. While the term 'Standard English' is a convenient shorthand expression, it is important to be clear that it is no more than this.

In the following sections, we shall explore these various perspectives on the contemporary language offered by sociolinguistics. First, I shall offer syntactic and morphological evidence from the work of sociolinguists who have typically focused on regional urban (but sometimes rural) varieties of British English, to indicate the range of what might be considered normal contemporary English. The various interrelated extralinguistic variables— regional, social, stylistic—which provide the framework for interpreting observable patterns of linguistic variation will also be discussed.

Following this account of grammatical variation, we shall consider the effect of the same regional, social, and stylistic factors on phonological variation, for it is in this domain that the most advanced sociolinguistic frameworks have been developed, and the social values associated with particular linguistic choices most clearly demonstrated. The concluding section draws together some salient sociolinguistic issues, with a discussion of the notion of 'Standard English'.

Sociolinguistic perspectives on syntactic variation

Some important general points about syntactic variation are illustrated by the examples in (1) to (12) below, much of the information in this section deriving from chapters in Trudgill and Chambers (1991) and Milroy and Milroy (1993). Particularly prominent are examples taken from Beal (1993) on Tyneside English, and Miller (1993) on Scottish English. Although grammatical (particularly syntactic) variation is much more difficult to analyse quantitatively than phonological variation (see Chambers and Trudgill 1991; Milroy L. 1987: 158ff.), quantitative analysis is an important sociolinguistic tool for two reasons. First, it captures the fact that speakers do not always apply linguistic rules categorically, enabling a variable element to be described in terms of the relative extent of its use, rather than as categorical. The second major advantage of quantitative analysis is in allowing different levels of use of a linguistic element by subgroups in the population to be compared; males versus females, different social classes, different ethnic groups, or groups with different kinds of informal social structure. The language use of a particular group or individual in *different social contexts* may also be systematically compared. Although sociolinguistic analysis of grammatical variation in all languages so far studied is less well developed than analysis of phonological variation, such evidence as is available suggests that phonological and syntactic elements vary along similar dimensions.

The examples of syntactic variation in this section are discussed under three broad headings. (1) to (4) represent expressions which are regionally distinctive but socially neutral, insofar as their use does not appear to be associated with particular status groups. Non-standard syntactic forms are not always socially stigmatized, as sometimes seems to be assumed.

Examples (5) to (8), on the other hand, represent syntactic forms which to a greater or lesser extent are socially marked. Such social marking is shown in two main ways. First, levels of use vary systematically with speaker-type, sex, social class, and situational context being clearly observable dimensions of variation. Second, speakers can often be observed to correct themselves and even to comment overtly on socially marked features.

Finally, (9) to (13) represent a range of constructions which might be described as characteristic of informal spoken language (see Brown and Yule 1983: 4ff.). The extent to which this dimension of variation interacts with regional and social marking is difficult to determine.

(1)   **A:** Would you like a cup of tea?
      B: No thanks, I'm just after my dinner. (Northern Ireland)
      (Gloss: I have just finished dinner)

(2)   It would take you to get there early. (Northern Ireland)
      (Gloss: It is advisable to arrive early)

(3)   (i) She mustn't come into town at this time.
      (ii) The lift mustn't be working. (Tyneside)
      (Gloss: The evidence forces me to conclude that she doesn't come into town/that the lift is not working. (cf. Standard English 'The lift can't be working)')

(4)   You've not got to go into the bedroom. (Tyneside)
(Gloss: You are not allowed to go into the bedroom.) (cf. Standard English 'You are not obliged to go into the bedroom.'))

(5)   (i) I went to the doctor and he told us to take it easy.
(ii) They gave we a bottle of whisky and wor Christmas bonus. (Tyneside: see description of portion of personal pronoun system at (13) below)

(6)   I'll treat yous (*you* pl.) girls to a fish supper. (Northern Ireland)

(7)   (i) He went to the hospital but was never tret. ('treated': Tyneside)
(ii) Tell me what he done to you. (Northern Ireland)

(8)   (All Tyneside)

(i) I can't play on a Friday. I work late. I might can get it changed though.
(Gloss: I might be able to . . .)

(ii) He wouldn't could've worked even if you had asked him.
(Gloss: wouldn't have been able to . . .)

(iii) A good machine clipper would could do it in half a day.
(Gloss: would be able to)

(9)   She once asked me did it interfere with me.

(10)   In the morning will suit me better.

(11)   (i) My friend's got a brother used to be in the school.
(ii) The boy I was talking to last night—and he actually works in the yard—was saying it's going to be closed.
(iii) The girl that her eighteenth birthday was on that day was stoned. (intoxicated)

(12)   You know that new Asda? See I hate going in there.

Examples like (1) to (4) are not limited to a few old-fashioned rural or urban working-class speakers, but heard regularly amongst speakers of a wide range of social groups in Northern Ireland and Tyneside respectively. This apparently socially neutral variation may be linguistically quite subtle; for example, B's utterance in (1) needs to be understood in terms of the Irish English tense/aspect system which differs quite markedly from that of Standard English not only in its surface realization of underlying semantic distinctions, but in terms of the semantic distinctions which it actually encodes (Harris 1984). Any account of (3), on the other hand, involves an appreciation of the distinction between epistemic and deontic modality (Huddleston 1984: 166f): both examples illustrate a characteristically local pattern of negation for epistemic *must*. Similarly, the rather difficult area of modality and negation is implicated in (4) (see Huddleston 1984: 168; Beal 1993). Trudgill and Chambers (1991: 146) comment that such variation in tense and aspect expressions is very widespread.

Examples (5) to (8) illustrate certain other parts of the grammar which are also particularly prone to variation; these are pronoun system (5), (6), verb morphology (7), and the modal auxiliary verb system (8). However, as Cheshire (1982) shows, the *primary* auxiliary verb system is also subject to variation, along with associated functions such as full clause interrogatives, tag interrogatives, and negatives. Consider first a portion of the Tyneside pronoun system, with reference to (5) above:

(13)   *Nominative*, 1st and 2nd person: (*singular*) I, you (*plural*) us, yous
       Oblique, 1st person: (*singular*) us (*plural*) we
       Possessive: 1st person (*plural*) wor

Other common non-standard pronoun systems involve a distinction between second person singular and plural forms. In urban areas with large populations of Irish origin (such as Merseyside, Tyneside, Glasgow), it is common to find the second person plural pronoun realized as *yous*, as exemplified in (6). This form is generally avoided by educated speakers in careful styles, who may nevertheless use it variably according to situation (see J. Milroy 1992). For example, one Northern Irish postgraduate student was observed to address a class of undergraduates as *you* for the entire duration of a fifty-minute seminar, switching to *yous* as he left the room following the formal wind-up of the class. In some parts of England (for example both urban and rural South Yorkshire and Derbyshire), the old form *thee* is still used, apparently to mark social values such as solidarity and intimacy. *Thee* appears to function in much the same way as *T* pronoun expressions in other languages with a *TV* second person pronoun contrast (see Fasold 1990 for a recent discussion). Note, however, that these comments are based upon my own relatively unsystematic observations of a limited number of South Yorkshire speakers, and that the social values associated with the *thee/you* contrast have not been systematically studied.

Turning now to irregular verb forms, note that variation in past and perfect participle forms is very widespread, sometimes reflecting usages which at an earlier time were characteristic of educated written English. A small sample of such currently used non-standard forms from Tyneside is shown in (14) below:

(14) | Base | Past | Perfect participle |
|------|------|--------------------|
| get | got | getten |
| treat | tret | tret |
| put | put | putten |

There is one other point of general importance which we can illustrate with reference to socially marked irregular verb forms such as those shown in

(7): even where a set of variant forms is particularly socially marked in the sense that it is overtly stigmatized by some speakers, the *social range* of users is not always clear. Eisikovits (1991) makes this point with respect to irregular past and perfect participle verb forms in Australian English, which she analyses very thoroughly using several different quantitative and qualitative procedures. With respect to the British examples cited in this paper, we may note that (7ii) is the attested utterance of a highly educated and respected Belfast surgeon. This means that the question of the social values assigned to socially sensitive variant forms needs to be treated with some care, as these values may differ from community to community. They may in any case be quite ambiguous, particularly in high-status speakers, reflecting a conflict between 'outsider' values symbolized by legitimized standard languages and 'insider' values symbolized by localized languages or dialects. This kind of symbolic opposition between different linguistic variants seems to be quite general in both monolingual and bilingual urban communities (for a detailed discussion see Milroy and Milroy 1992).

Similar remarks apply to double modal expressions such as (8), which have been observed regularly in the informal spoken language of an elderly Tyneside female university graduate, and are also characteristic of Scottish and Northern Irish dialects. K. Brown (1991) offers a thorough analysis of double modals in Hawick, a Scottish border town about seventy-five miles north-west of Tyneside. Particularly valuable is his discussion of restrictions on the distribution of double modal forms. The urban Tyneside examples presented here are taken from Beal (1993), and such expressions are very common in the Tyneside city of Newcastle.

Examples (9) to (12) illustrate the difficulty of distinguishing between constructions which are common in the spoken language generally on the one hand (see further Crystal 1980; Milroy and Milroy 1991 and references therein), and on the other hand regionally and socially marked forms of the kind already discussed. This particular problem is discussed extensively by Miller (1993) with respect to Scottish English. For example, the indirect question construction with subject/auxiliary verb inversion and a zero complementizer exemplified in (9) was recorded in Belfast (cf. '. . . whether it interfered with me') but seems to be generally rather common. Both its social and regional distribution are unclear. Similar comments might be made about the temporal expression realized as a prepositional phrase functioning as sentence Subject, exemplified by (10). The examples under (11) represent various types of relative clause construction discussed by Miller (1993) which seem not to occur in formal spoken or in written English, but probably have a wide regional and social distribution in the spoken language. Again, we lack detailed knowledge of this distribution, and it is hard to see how it could be systematically investigated. The interface between syntax and discourse is represented by (12), one of several similar examples discussed by Miller. Expressions such as *you know* and *see* seem to function as discourse-organizing particles, indicating, for example, the interpersonal orientation of conversationalists (see Schiffrin 1987).

Some of the examples discussed in this section raise the question of how far native speakers with different dialect systems can understand each other. Two assumptions seem to underlie such little discussion as can be found in the mainstream literature, the first being that syntactic differences between dialects are relatively trivial and the second that *context* generally assists in resolving difficulties. In fact, neither of these is self-evidently true, since some differences are rather subtle and reach to core parts of the grammar. Let us conclude this section with a brief consideration of some relevant examples.

(15)   **A:** How long are yous here?
      B: Till after Easter.
      (2.00 seconds pause: **A** looks puzzled)
      C: We came on Sunday.
      A: Ah yous are here a while then.
      (Contextual note: **A** is a native of Donegal, Republic of Ireland; **B** and **C** are Standard English speakers resident in Ireland)

(16)   Mildred mustn't go out much.

(17)   (i) He hasn't got to drink so much beer.
      (ii) You haven't got to swim in the gala.

Example (15) hinges on a range of systematic differences between the Irish-English and Anglo-English tense/aspect systems (cf. (1) above); and A's first utterance can be interpreted as equivalent to either (i) or (ii) below:

(i) How long will you remain here? (Standard English interpretation)
(ii) How long have you been here? (Irish-English interpretation)

This sequence, discussed in detail by Milroy, L. (1984), shows that although context cannot always be relied on to resolve ambiguity, normal conversational repair mechanisms come into play, as evidenced by C's contribution after the disruptive two-second pause.

Smith (1987) investigated comprehension of some of the Tyneside expressions described above (see (3) and (4)). Groups of Tynesiders and Southern English speakers were presented, under controlled experimental conditions, with sets of ambiguous sentences like (16) and (17). In fact, both groups seemed to have access to both (Standard) deontic and (Tyneside) epistemic interpretations of *mustn't*, although Tynesiders preferred the epistemic interpretation. However, the groups differed significantly in the way they interpreted sentences like (17), with Tynesiders greatly preferring the local ('not allowed to') interpretation. The influence of context turned out to be interesting here, with sentences like (17i) being more prone to the local interpretation than (17ii). The probable reason for this is real world plausibility, since a person is more likely to be prohibited from drinking beer than swimming in a gala. However, southerners resident in Tyneside often report a general awareness of confusion around this modal area, which they cannot make explicit.

Work in the conversational analytic tradition is relevant to an understanding of how conversationalists operate with this kind of vague partial knowledge. Conversation analysts emphasize the collaborative negotiation of understanding by speakers, who accept ambiguity and vagueness on the assumption that they will eventually together evolve an understanding which is good enough for current communicative purposes. Herbert Clark and his associates have recently published some interesting work on the way contributors to a conversation work together to achieve mutual understanding, which is very suggestive for communicative situations where participants understand each other rather less than perfectly (Clark and Schaefer 1987, 1989; Clark and Wilkes-Gibbs 1986).

Social values and language variation: some examples from phonology

It was noted earlier that the social values associated with variation between standard and non-standard forms are most clearly evident in the level of phonology. Phonological variation is a familiar territory to sociolinguists, who have typically described the distribution of particular pronunciations throughout a population in terms of such social factors as age, ethnicity, sex, and social class of speaker, taking account of the influence of contextual style. Fasold (1990) provides an overview of this work. In this section, we shall consider some data which are representative of rather general patterns, concentrating on broader issues of sociolinguistic structure which emerge from quantitative analysis, rather than on the linguistic and phonetic details which underlie this analysis.

Figure 1 shows a typical pattern of *linguistic change in progress*, where variable vowel index scores of speakers from seven age groups are plotted on a *stylistic continuum*; the vowel is /e/ in the environment of a following /l/ in Norwich (as in *help*). Note that the 10–19 age group has radically increased their use of the centralized variants of (e), most noticeably in casual style.

This pattern of change can be contrasted with the pattern of apparently stable stylistic variation represented in Figure 2, which shows speakers' alternations between [n] and [ŋ] (as in *running, shooting*). Here, the styles are sharply differentiated even by younger speakers who, relative to their elders, show no sign of using particularly high levels of either variant.

Taken together, Figures 1 and 2 show how analysts may infer patterns of linguistic change, with reference to the variables of age and contextual style (see Chambers and Trudgill 1980: 93). Data such as these bear on

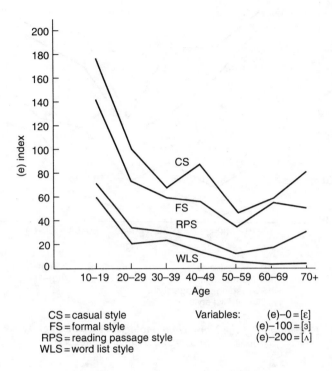

*Figure 1   Distribution of the Norwich phonological variable (e) by age and style
(source: Chambers and Trudgill 1980: 93)*

common conceptions of a relatively stable spoken standard variety, which we shall discuss in the final section of this paper.

Table 1 shows speaker scores for the same (ng) variable by sex, class, and style. Such patterns are typical of what is reported in the literature for male/female differences; in most cases where there is a difference (exceptions are ringed) male scores indicate a greater frequency of non-standard or low-prestige alveolar (ng).

The language/network and language/sex relationships in Ballymacarrett, Belfast, as shown in Figure 3 offer an interesting comparison with Table 1. This diagram, which shows patterns of optional deletion of the word-medial fricative in words such as *mother, brother, together,* is included because of the magnitude of the sex differences in language use which it reveals, even within a single social class. Also evident is the effect of the *social network* variable. While the social class variable gives some idea of

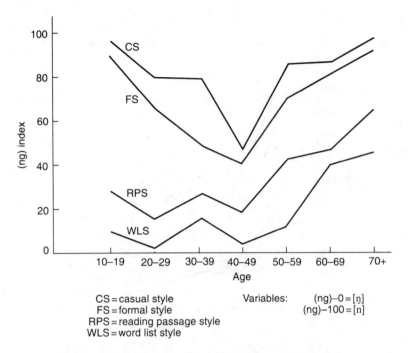

*Figure 2   Distribution of the Norwich phonological variable (ng) by age and style
(source: Chambers and Trudgill 1980: 91)*

the 'linguistic market' value of particular variants, the network variable reflects solidarity-based patterns of language variation. High network scores indicate high levels of social integration into a small-scale, community-level group, and are associated with high levels of use of non-standard variants. While Table 1 shows how variables of class, sex, and style underlie patterns of variation, Figure 3 shows how speakers use linguistic variables simultaneously to signal social identities associated with gender and social network structure. It is data such as these, and the solidarity-based values associated with the network concept in particular, which give us some idea of speakers' motives for maintaining non-standard forms.

All the data presented in this section show the extent to which so-called non-standard features are present in even high-status speech, to different extents in the different contextual styles of each of the sexes.

The social values associated with particular variant realizations can be inferred from a quantitative analysis; for example, in Table 1 we see that high levels of the velar (standard) variant of (ng) are associated with higher-status social groups, and with women. Such quantitative work as has been carried out on syntax (see L. Milroy 1987: 143ff., Eisikovits 1991) suggests

Class	Sex	Style WLS	RPS	FS	CS
MMC	M	000	000	004	031
	F	000	000	000	000
LMC	M	000	020	027	017
	F	000	000	003	067
UWC	M	000	018	081	095
	F	011	013	068	077
MWC	M	024	043	091	097
	F	020	046	081	088
LWC	M	066	100	100	100
	F	017	054	097	100

MMC = middle middle class   WLS = word list style
LMC = lower middle class   RPS = reading passage style
UWC = upper working class   FS = formal style
MWC = middle working class   CS = casual style
LWC = lower working class

Table 1: Norwich (ng) by class, style, and sex (from Trudgill 1983: 171)

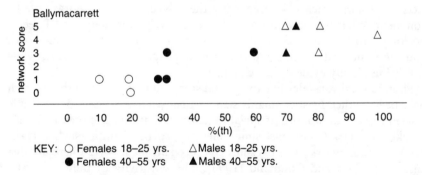

Ballymacarrett

KEY: ○ Females 18–25 yrs.   △ Males 18–25 yrs.
      ● Females 40–55 yrs   ▲ Males 40–55 yrs.

Figure 3   Percentage of zero realizations of (th) in intervocalic positions in a working-class area of Belfast.

a general pattern of distribution for syntactic variables of the type discussed in the previous section. However, the situation is a little more complicated than this, since patterns of variation are subject to change. This means that variants which at a particular point in time are associated with low-status groups may in their turn become preferred by higher-status groups. A recent example of this pattern of changing evaluation is provided by Mees's phonetically detailed work on realizations of /t/ by schoolchildren in Cardiff (Mees 1987).

Several investigators such as Macaulay (1977), Romaine (1975), and Trudgill (1974) have associated glottal or glottalized realizations of /t/ with urban working-class speech in different British cities. Sometimes, as Macaulay's work in particular shows, such realizations are quite overtly and strongly stigmatized. Mees's investigation shows a striking reversal of the social evaluation pattern reported by these investigators some ten years earlier, in that glottal realizations appear more frequently in the speech of middle-class than of working-class adolescents. This is a striking finding, since glottal realizations often seem to be perceived as stereotypical of low-status British English. However, Mees's research, which shows how quantitative sociolinguistic procedures can elucidate the social mechanisms by which social values associated with particular realizations actually change, is congruent with Wells's observation that glottal realizations, once characteristic of working-class speech, are now common in mainstream RP (Wells 1982: 106). We know that similar changes in social evaluation have taken place in the past; consider, for example, Labov's work on (r) in New York City (Labov 1972) and loss of historic /r/ in most dialects of British English (J. Milroy 1992: 143). The broader conclusion which we might draw is that the increase in glottal realizations is very much a 'change from below' (Labov 1972), reflecting the continuing democratization of accents and dialects in Britain which is so frequently the subject of contemporary public comment. What this amounts to is that a relatively homogeneous RP seems no longer to be required of educated speakers to the extent it once was, and the structural relationship between language and social status, while still being plainly evident, has changed.

Phonological variables like the glottal stop and many of the others which have been studied by sociolinguists and are shown in Figures 1–3 and Table 1 seem to have an important social function in that they are used by native speakers to mark (sometimes simultaneously) social identities such as class, gender, and network. The psychosocial mechanisms involved here are discussed by Giles and Coupland (1991). The sensitivity of these linguistic elements to stylistic formality suggests that in some sense they are under the control (albeit not quite conscious) of speakers. Bell (1984) has examined this dimension of variation and has argued that speakers seek to design their speech for audiences by drawing on the social connotations of particular variables. It is important to be aware of the extent to which this happens; consider, for example, the contrast in levels of use by different social groups shown in Table 1; such variation is more than a marginal phenomenon located at the fringes of a clearly identifiable standard.

Two issues are raised by sociolinguistically variable data which are of particular importance to second language learning. The first is the need for learners to cue themselves in to the sociocultural context which is encoded by these patterns of variation, to be aware of them, and try to interpret them. This seems to be one aspect of a larger listening and understanding task. Sociolinguistics attempts to describe the nature of the sociocultural context and the social meanings encoded by variants, and offers frameworks within which to describe and interpret them. The second important issue concerns the notion of a *standard*, which has already been touched on several times in this chapter. It is this question to which we now turn.

Sociolinguistics and second language learning: conclusion and implications

Melchers (1989) has recently commented critically on Quirk and Widdowson's (1985) recommendation that the learner should learn only 'a single monochrome standard which looks as good on paper as it sounds in speech', and on their associated suggestion that sociolinguistics 'undermin[es] belief in standard English' (Quirk and Widdowson 1985: 6). In fact, the view of Standard English and of language variation which underlies Quirk and Widdowson's comments is, for several reasons, very misleading. Most notable perhaps is a failure to acknowledge patterned variation as a ubiquitous characteristic of the contemporary language (and indeed of language generally) rather than merely a marginal phenomenon. To dismiss as subversive frameworks which are designed to describe and interpret such variation is surely unhelpful, although (as Melchers points out) such a stance might be comforting for the traditional language teacher. Further problems spring from Quirk and Widdowson's treatment of the standard as a static phenomenon. As we have seen, this is not so; the variety which we describe as 'Standard English' has in fact been created historically by a process which has over the centuries reduced the amount and kind of *socially permitted variation*. However, in view of our knowledge of variation in the contemporary language, I doubt if it could seriously be argued that the *overall amount of variation* in English has been progressively reduced by the standardization process.

Standardization of the language in respect of this imposition of uniformity is much like other kinds of standardization (e.g. of the coinage, or of electric plugs). However, unlike coins and electric plugs, language is inherently variable, and variant choices carry clear social meanings. If we want to consider seriously and dispassionately the nature of Standard English, the real question is not *what* it is (which is unanswerable), but *how successful is the standardization process* in different mediums (speech and writing) and at different linguistic levels. Currently, it is apparently less successful in the spoken language than it once was, perhaps particularly at the phonological level, in that change from below is clearly discernible and indeed subject to much contemporary comment. Standardization is a tendency towards uniformity which is socially very highly valued, but in fact never totally successful (see further Milroy and Milroy 1991).

Note that only a tiny proportion of the population of the United Kingdom can plausibly be described as RP speakers (as discussed by Trudgill 1983), and among younger speakers this variety is apparently becoming very much more blurred round the edges than it was once assumed to be. Furthermore, studies in the social psychological tradition have consistently revealed ambiguous attitudes to RP, and young people in particular may feel uncomfortable using it (see Giles and Coupland 1991 for a recent relevant discussion of such research). Brown (1990: 13) has commented on the desirability of expanding the concept of RP as a starting point for foreign learners, while Trudgill and Hannah (1985: 12) specifically suggest that the near-RP accents of Northern England be included. These scholars seem to be responding in a fairly sensible and cautious way to the changing sociolinguistic patterns in British English which I have tried to describe here. Melchers has also argued strongly for more liberal approaches to the facts of variation.

Certainly, it is important for learners to be aware of the various social, regional, and situational dimensions of variation, and above all to have understood the implications of the well-established sociolinguistic maxim that linguistic consistency is not normal and indeed would be dysfunctional in a language used in a real speech community (Weinreich, Labov, and Herzog 1968). Descriptive work of relevance to second language learners continues to emerge, such as that of Kerswill (1987); Bell and Holmes (1990); Cheshire (1991); Coupland (1990). All of these offer descriptions of variation in particular places, and frameworks within which to interpret it.

The relationship between social structure and language variation is, as we have seen, an important sociolinguistic concern. The widely studied language–class relationship can help learners to evaluate 'market value' and attitudinal factors relevant to contemporary spoken varieties of English (and indeed of other languages). The social network variable, on the other hand, can help learners understand that the types of interpersonal relationships holding between speakers can strongly affect their language choice. Indeed, the relationships contracted by the learner will affect language learning, a point made by Preston (1989). Sociolinguistics is therefore likely to be relevant to second language learning not only for its principled descriptions of variation, but also for its development of models which illuminate the social and situational context of language use in everyday situations.

10 Understanding texts: point of view

In interesting complementarity to the papers by Brumfit and Spolsky, Michael Short here focuses on those aspects of texts which may lead to *agreement* among native speakers about what the texts mean. These aspects are clearly equally important for the language learner striving towards a native-like understanding, and Short claims that the methods employed in teaching native speakers to make explicit linguistic statements about how they have arrived at their understandings of texts can be usefully considered by the foreign-language teacher.

He concentrates, in particular, on the topics of point of view and speech presentation. These phenomena have traditionally been studied with literary texts in mind, but Short's analyses demonstrate their prevalence in other genres as well. An awareness of how they are linguistically realized is therefore as important to learners of English in general as it is to literature specialists. Indeed, a second claim made by Short is that the descriptive systems initially developed to describe speech presentation in literature should be reformulated to take account of other genres.

From a pedagogical perspective, there is a clear advantage in introducing these notions to students in the context of short, simple texts before progressing to complex and demanding texts.

Short suggests that a particularly valuable technique for sensitizing students to these features is to allow them to focus on their own rewritings of texts from different points of view.

Understanding texts: point of view

Michael Short
Department of Linguistics and Modern English Language
Lancaster University

1 Introduction

In this paper, I want to explore how stylistic analysis (the linguistic analysis of (literary) texts) can be used to help us see how one aspect of textual understanding, point of view, is signalled in texts. Before I do that, however, some general remarks about my 'backdrop' assumptions will help to make the drift of my later discussion clear.

The main aim of stylistic analysis is to try to explain how, when we read, we get from the structure of the text in front of us to the meaning 'inside our heads'. As a consequence, I believe that stylistic analysis is an indispensable tool for mother-tongue and second/foreign language teachers. I do not mean to say by this that all students should be taught stylistic analysis. That sort of decision depends upon a detailed assessment of the needs and abilities of each particular group of students. But I do believe that all teachers of English would benefit from knowledge of stylistic analysis, as it would help them to show students how meanings get into texts and how to back up views they have about texts via close examination of them. This does not mean that teachers have, necessarily, to use the metalanguage and precision of advanced stylistics. Often that will be inappropriate. But detailed knowledge on the part of the teacher will help him or her to be able to explain things 'in layman's terms' to students. The argument, then, is much like one I would use concerning grammatical description. Students do not necessarily need explicit knowledge of grammatical description to be able to speak a language well. But such knowledge is very useful for the teacher when explaining things, perhaps in more simple terms, to the student. At more advanced levels, explicit knowledge of stylistic analysis (like grammar and other forms of linguistic description) will probably be useful, as it is difficult for students to discuss texts with any degree of precision without an adequate metalanguage and system of analysis. Evidence for this can be seen in Britain, where current English undergraduate students, who have little or no formal language training in school, find it relatively easy to talk about their feelings as a consequence of reading a story or poem, but difficult to talk sensibly about the text itself. Moreover, although anything associated with linguistics is often labelled by the literary community as 'hard', I suspect that stylistic analysis can be taught at lower levels than might presently be thought, precisely because it makes linguistic analysis relevant to the discussion of meanings and effects in texts. Until recently in Britain, stylistic analysis was thought of as a university subject. It is now being taught with considerable success and much student enthusiasm in many sixth forms, and we do not yet know where the 'lower limit' is. In some ways, stylistics, like most language analysis, is easier to teach to younger students, precisely because they have not yet learned that it is fashionable to scorn being analytical and precise.

Stylistic analysis is usually associated with the study of literary texts. This is mainly because literary texts are, by and large, the texts that our culture chooses to submit to detailed scrutiny. But stylistic analysis can be applied fruitfully to any kind of text, literary or non-literary, and, indeed, I will use both literary and non-literary examples during this paper. The reason that I think stylistic analysis can be applied interestingly to any kind of text is that, unlike the majority of university English teachers, I do not believe that literature is marked off from the rest of language by special linguistic properties (this is what I like to call the 'linguistic ingredients' or 'recipe' theory of literature) or by the need for special processing abilities (so-called 'literary competence') when it is read. I do not have the space to argue this view here, but it is important that I make this assumption explicit, as it is this that leads me to argue (a) that literary texts can legitimately be used in foreign language teaching, and (b) that stylistics, although originally developed to cope with literary texts, has a considerably wider range of application in language learning and language awareness programmes.

The last preliminary point I wish to make concerns the notion of *understanding*. Many literary theorists these days espouse the view that textual meaning is inherently variable. Texts mean different things to different people, and even to the same person on different occasions. For most stylisticians, however, this view is too extreme. Although it is clear that different people can arrive at different interpretations of the same text, because of the different assumptions which they bring along to it, I believe that this aspect of textual 'understanding' has been overplayed of late. Taken to the extreme which is presently fashionable in some circles, it is difficult to see how communication takes place at all. Although you may understand my text differently in some ways from its next reader, I believe that you will also share a much larger amount of understanding. Readers do bring variability of experience to a text, but they also bring considerable commonality in their understanding of the structure of the language in question and the strategies used to interpret language. This shared knowledge (which also includes considerable shared knowledge of the world too) is often overlooked in current literary theory, as is the interpretation-constraining role of the text. While acknowledging that meaning is never entirely fixed, stylistics concentrates on uncovering those aspects of textual meaning which are common among readers. Hence, the matters which I discuss below are of interest, I suggest, not because they chart my individual understanding of the extracts discussed, but precisely because the interpretations I uncover are very similar to those of others, and because examining how those interpretations come about is of value to teacher and student alike in their discussion of texts in the classroom.

2   Point of view: general introduction

The notion of point of view has been of central importance in twentieth-century criticism of the novel. Indeed, it is difficult to find modern discussions of the novel which do not discuss multiple viewpoints, changing viewpoints, interior and exterior views, stream of consciousness writing, and so on. Yet within literary criticism *per se*, there has been very little explication of the way in which the language of texts indicates point of view and exerts control over the attitudes we have to characters and events as we read stories. The stylisticians, on the other hand (e.g. Leech and Short 1981: Chapters 5, 8, and 10; Fowler 1986: Chapter 9; Toolan 1988: Chapters 3 and 4) have spent some time examining the language of point of view. Viewpoint can be controlled in an amazing variety of ways, but this paper will concentrate on two important and related aspects: (a) how viewpoint is controlled in narrative description, and (b) how it is controlled through the manipulation of the choices available to writers for the presentation of speech. These areas will be discussed in sections 3 and 4 below. Before we move to that discussion, some general aspects of point of view in relation to the participants involved in communication will be helpful.

In stereotypical spoken conversation one person speaks to another in some situational context, the addresser and addressee roles being swapped continually between the two participants (see Figure 1).

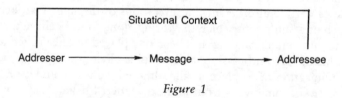

Figure 1

Not all speech situations are like this, of course. For example, in a lecture there is one addresser and many addressees, and the speech roles are not normally exchanged.

Figure 1's simple account of communication also accounts for the prototypical poem, where a poet (e.g. Wordsworth) tells each reader who reads the poem about some topic (e.g. daffodils) without the possibility of the reader talking back. The one essential difference between face-to-face inter-action and canonical poetry (and, indeed, most written communication and more speech than one might at first suppose—e.g. radio, television, and telephone conversations), is that the communication does not take place within a shared situational context. Of course, not all poems can be described in this simple way. So-called 'persona' poems (e.g. T. S. Eliot's 'The Love Song of J. Alfred Prufrock') have another addresser, who is distinct from the poet. But Figure 1 does, I believe, capture our prototypical assumptions about the discourse structure of poetry, which thus has two viewpoints to consider, those of the poet and the reader.

In fact, the three major literary genres can be distinguished one from another with respect to their general discourse structures. Prototypical drama needs two discourse levels to account for it properly. Character talks to character on the stage, that talk being dictated by the playwright and observed by the audience (see Figure 2).

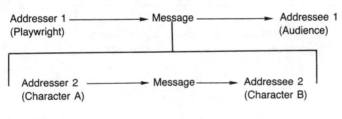

Figure 2

Discourse level 2 is embedded inside level 1, and, assuming two characters on stage, there are four viewpoints to consider. It is this 'doubled discourse' which accounts for so-called dramatic irony, where the viewpoint of the audience is different from that of some character(s); and in general terms we can see that the audience can infer what the playwright is telling them about the characters by noticing patterns and other features in their conver-sational interaction. The prototypical drama (which again has its excep-tions—e.g. the direct address of a character to the audience, or the use of a narrator intervening between the character and playwright–audience levels, as in Bolt's *A Man for All Seasons*), is thus more complex in terms of point of view than the prototypical poem.

Doubled discourses also occur in real life, in radio interviews, for example. Consider a programme like *Down Your Way*, where interviews usually begin with sentences like 'Hello, Mr Smith. You're a lathe operator who's worked with Jenkinson's for the last twenty years.' The interviewer and interviewee are obviously aware that the interviewee already knows what he is being told. Without consciously thinking about it, they are taking the listener's viewpoint into account: the interviewer is making sure that the listener has enough knowledge to be able to interpret the rest of the interview sensibly.

The novel is the most complex genre in terms of discourse structure, and so it is not surprising that it is the novel which has attracted the attention of viewpoint critics like Booth (1961) and Scholes and Kellogg (1966). The novel needs at least three discourse levels (see Figure 3).

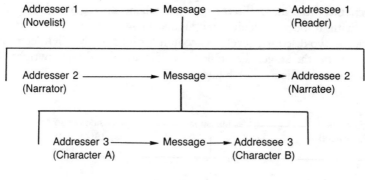

Figure 3

Arguably, even more levels may be needed, but this account will suffice for present purposes.

It is not just that the novel, in its canonical form, has more participants, and therefore viewpoints to consider than the other genres. Some novels have a large number of participants, and therefore many comparisons are needed among them for an understanding of the text. Faulkner's *As I Lay Dying* has fifteen different narrators, all of whom are also characters in the novel.

The last thing to notice is that although the three discourse levels need to be distinguished for a general account of the novel, in any particular novel, discourse levels can be 'collapsed' (and sometimes separated out again), leading to what I like to call different 'discourse architectures' for novels. Often, but not always, we can collapse levels 1 and 2 together in third-person narration novels. This is why many readers assume that the views of such narrators are identical with those of the novelist. This is not always true, of course, but it works well for many cases. In first-person narrations, on the other hand, the narrator is usually a character in the story, which explains (a) why we tend to sympathize with these characters, even when they do things we would not normally approve of (e.g. Alex in

A Clockwork Orange by Anthony Burgess), and (b) why it is first-person narrators, not third-person narrators who are most likely to be unreliable.

The 'collapsings' I have mentioned do not necessarily stay the same for a whole novel. In Dickens's *Bleak House* a first-person narration and a third-person narration are interwoven a chapter at a time. In Charlotte Brontë's *Jane Eyre*, the mature Jane is the narrator. Thus, levels 2 and 3 in Figure 3 collapse on the left-hand side, causing a conflation of narrator and character viewpoints. But this does not happen all through the novel. At the beginning, for example, when Jane's experiences as a child are described, we have a sort of halfway house in point-of-view terms, as the narrator (mature Jane looking back on her experiences when immature) both is and is not the character. At the end of the novel, on the other hand, levels 1 and 2 are explicitly collapsed together on the right-hand side of the diagram, when Jane says 'Reader, I married him.' This collapsing facility allows different points of view in the novel to be continually merged and separated, and helps to explain why viewpoint in the novel is such a complex matter. If students can understand how viewpoint works in the novel, they should be sensitive to its workings in practically any other text. And it is important to note that getting to grips with any text will involve sensitivity to point of view, which should thus be a matter of general concern in mother-tongue language awareness courses as well as for second or foreign language learners.

3   Point of view in narration

Below I present a check-sheet of features which indicate, or control, point of view in narration. I developed this check-sheet for my undergraduate students to help them be more systematic when examining point of view. The list is certainly not exhaustive, but it captures many of the important facets of the linguistics of point of view (see also Fowler 1986, Simpson 1990).

CHECKSHEET OF LINGUISTIC INDICATORS OF POINT OF VIEW
1   Given v. new information, e.g.
    (a) Definite/indefinite articles (*a/the*);
    (b) textually referring (anaphoric) pronouns (*you, it, they*, etc.).
2   Deictic (shifting) expressions related to place, e.g.
    (a) adverbials (*here/there*, etc., *to my left, in front of him*, etc.);
    (b) demonstrative pronouns (*this/that*, etc.);
    (c) verbs (*come/go*, etc.).
3   Deictic expressions relating to time, e.g.
    (a) adverbials (*now/then, today/that day, tomorrow, the following day*, etc.);
    (b) past and present tenses.

4   'Socially deictic' expressions, e.g.
   (a) personal and possessive pronouns (*I, you, he, mine, yours,* etc.);
   (b) variant socially relevant expressions for the same person, e.g.
       (i) the naming system: *Mick, Mr. Short, Dad*
       (ii) varying expressions in third person reference (sometimes called 'elegant variation'): *Bunter, the hapless owl, the fat ornament of the Remove, the grub raider of the Remove.*
5   **Indicators of the internal representation of a particular character's thoughts or perceptions, e.g.**
   (a) verbs of perception and cognition (*see, hear, imagine, think, believe*);
   (b) verbs related to factivity (cf. *I know that he was ill* v. *I think that he was ill* v. *He pretended to be ill*);
   (c) adverbs related to factivity (*actually, apparently*).
6   **Value-laden and ideologically slanted expressions, e.g.**
   I saw Mick Short v. *I saw that awful Mick Short;*
   He is a freedom fighter v. *He is a terrorist;*
   the Far East v. *South East Asia.*
7   **Event coding within and across sentences, e.g.**
   The man burst the door open v. *The door burst open;*
   Robin Hood ran past me v. *Someone ran past me. It was Robin Hood.*

Now, let us look at each category in turn, exploring what it tells us about point of view (the parts of the quotations discussed are italicized for ease of reference).

3.1   Given v. new information

Typically, definite reference by means of pronouns or the definite article indicates that the entity referred to is assumed to be known to the speaker. Indefinite reference indicates new information. Hence, in:

(1)   A figure appeared in the door.
      (John Fowles, *The Magus*, Chapter 62)

we assume that the person who has just appeared is not recognized by the first-person narrator.

   In theory, one might expect stories to begin with indefinite reference, as the referents in the story all remain to be introduced. And indeed, this is what we find in simple narrations like folk tales, fairy stories, and so on (e.g. 'There was *an* old woman who lived in *a* shoe'). But many stories begin with definite reference, giving the feeling that we are already involved in the scene and already know about the things referred to. We do not, of course. As sensitive readers we put ourselves in the appropriate position signalled by the text, pretending to ourselves that we are familiar with what is being described, close to the characters, and so on:

(2) *The* book was thick and black and covered with dust.[1]
(A. S. Byatt, *Possession*, Chapter 1)

The first sentence of this novel makes us pretend that we already know which book is being referred to, in spite of the fact that we do not, and that we must therefore be 'in the situation', wherever that is. Within a page, of course, the author will allow us to infer which book is being referred to. A much more extreme example is this opening sentence:

(3) They're out there.
(Ken Kesey, *One Flew Over the Cuckoo's Nest*)

Here, everything referred to is apparently assumed by the narrator as being known by us already. In fact, the novel is being narrated in the first-person by the inmate of a lunatic asylum, and a little later in our reading we will begin to wonder about the reasonableness of the way the narrator/character begins to talk to us. Is he making a point of getting us as close to his viewpoint as we can possibly be, or is he a defective narrator, not sufficiently taking into account that we need to be introduced properly to what he is talking about? This is the beginning of a two-way tug which takes place throughout the novel. We sympathize through the first-person narration with the narrator/character and his colleagues, who are apparently being oppressed by the nursing staff of the institution, but there is always a doubt in the back of our minds. If the narrator is in a lunatic asylum, how reasonable is his account of what happens?

With novels which begin with definite reference, we feel close up to the characters and events. Consequently, novels which begin with descriptions using indefinite reference tend to have an effect of distance:

(4) On *a* cold and starry Christmas-eve within living memory *a* man was passing up *a* lane towards Mellstock Cross . . .[1]
(Thomas Hardy, *Under the Greenwood Tree*, Chapter 1)

Here, only the reference to Mellstock Cross is definite, and it is almost as if we are seeing the man through a telescope.

3.2 Deictic (shifting) expressions related to place

Deictic expressions are good markers of viewpoint because they code whatever is referred to with respect to whether it is near to, or further from, the speaker or writer (e.g. '*this* chair' v. '*that* chair'), and so changes in viewpoint will often be signalled deictically. In fact, example (3) above has a deictic reference in the adverb *there*, which does not just indicate definite reference but also something referred to which is relatively remote from the narrator. Here is another example:

(5)   *Beyond the overgrown perimeter ditch of the airfield* was an old battle ground of 1937. *Here* the Chinese armies *had made* one of their futile stands in the attempt to halt the Japanese advance on Shanghai.[1]
(J. G. Ballard, *Empire of the Sun*, Chapter 2)

The most obvious deictic marker indicating that the third-person narrator (and therefore the reader as well) is sharing the spatial viewpoint of the main character, Jim, is the *here* at the beginning of the sentence, indicating closeness. But the initial adverbial phrase of the first sentence also marks place-relations in terms of the boy, who is a prisoner of war at the airfield. The airfield is closest, the perimeter ditch further away, and the old battle ground further away still.

In the following example, we can see that the third-person narrator is making us see things from the point of view of Mr Verloc (who is lying on the sofa, waiting for his wife to bring his evening meal) through the use of a deictic verb, which usually signals movement towards the speaker:

(6)   Mrs Verloc was *coming*.[1]
(Joseph Conrad, *The Secret Agent*, Chapter 11)

In fact, this is all part of a strategy of surprise on Conrad's part, in a novel which has a central theme of isolation and lack of communication between the characters. Mr Verloc, newsagent and undercover secret agent, has had a bad day. His wife, who does not know about his secret life, has forced him to take her simpleton brother, Stevie, with him on what, unbeknown to her, is an attempt to blow up the Greenwich Observatory. Stevie, primed by his sister to be helpful, insists on carrying Mr Verloc's case, which contains the bomb. The badgered Mr Verloc eventually, and unwillingly, agrees to let Stevie place the case in the observatory. Going across Green Park, Stevie trips over a tree root and blows himself to smithereens, and Mr Verloc has just told his wife an edited version of the sad tale. He thinks she is sympathetic and is bringing him his meal. Actually, she is about to kill him with the carving knife, to avenge her brother's death.

3.3   Deictic expressions relating to time

Clearly, the alternation between forms like *now* and *then*, *today*, and *that day*, signal close/far relations in terms of time, and so function in the same way as the examples we have examined in 3.2 above. Further examples are unnecessary to make the point, but it will be worth noting that tense is a deictic marker. So, in example (5), for example, the past tense is present time for Jim, and the pluperfect form *had made* represents what must be past time for the character (for a full account of tense in the novel, see Fleischman 1990).

3.4 Socially deictic expressions

The notion of deixis can also be extended to cover social relations, which have to do with closeness or remoteness in social or attitudinal terms. The naming and referring systems are thus good mechanisms for controlling our attitudes to characters and how close we feel towards them:

(7) There are four figures in the field, besides *Lewis* on the reaper-binder. *Mr Luscombe*: red-faced and crooked-grinning, one eye with a cast behind his steel-rimmed spectacles, a collarless shirt with a thin grey stripe, darned, the cuffs worn, cord trousers with peaks at the back for braces, but held up also by a thick leather belt. *Bill*, his younger son, nineteen, capped and massive, six inches taller than anyone else on the field, arms like hams, a slow giant, clumsy at all but his work ... but see him scythe, dwarf the distort handle and the blade, the swaling drive and unstopping rhythm, pure and princely force of craft. *Old Sam* in breeches, braces, boots and gaiters, his face forgotten, though not his limp; a collarless shirt also, a straw hat with the crown detached on one side ('let's in th'ole air a bit, doan'ee see') and a tuft of wilted heart's-ease tucked in the black band. And finally *a boy in his mid-teens, his clothes unsuited, a mere harvest helper*: cotton trousers, an apple-green Aertex shirt, old gym shoes.[1]
(John Fowles, *Daniel Martin*, Chapter 1)

The farmer is given the 'title plus last name' of respect, and so we will tend to feel distant from and maybe socially below him. Lewis gets last name only, and so we must be socially on a par or above him. Bill and old Sam get first names only, and so we feel closer to them. The only character who is not named is the boy at the end of the paragraph, who stands out as the only one accorded indefinite reference. He also occurs in the climactic position at the end of the paragraph and gets lots of descriptive attention. We thus feel rather remote from him, and yet he is also being signalled as being important in some way. In fact, we later learn that he is the Daniel Martin of the novel's title. There is no formal indication in this passage, but the description is through a first-person narrator, the older Daniel Martin, who is thus looking back on his childhood as if his former self was a stranger to him.

3.5 Indicators of the internal representation of a particular character's thoughts or perceptions

It almost goes without saying that if a character's thoughts or perceptions are represented we see things from that character's point of view, and sympathize with the character. Verbs of perception and cognition are clear markers:

(8)   Joe *watched* with glazed hopeless eyes. The horses were almost like his own body to him. He *felt* he was done for now.[1]
(D. H. Lawrence, *The Horse Dealer's Daughter*)

3.6   Value-laden and ideologically slanted expressions

Like 3.5, this is a category which students tend to spot without trouble. Essentially, it is easier for them to spot aspects of textual understanding that are controlled by lexical means than any other. In the following example, the story is told from the viewpoint of the character Fanny, and we are left in no doubt as to what we are meant to think of her old town when she comes back after many years' absence to marry Harry:

(9)   She opened the door of her *grimy* branch-line carriage, and began to get down her bags. The porter was nowhere, of course, but there was Harry . . . There, on the *sordid* little station under the furnaces, she stood, *tall* and *distinguished*, in her well-made coat and skirt and her broad grey velour hat.[1]
(D. H. Lawrence, *Fanny and Annie*)

These heavily evaluative adjectives are easy enough for students to spot. But because normal language use is transparent, other ideological codings can be more subtle (see Fowler 1986 and Fairclough 1989), and so require more careful attention.

3.7   Event coding within and across sentences

Example (1), which I used to illustrate the point-of-view effect of indefinite reference, can be seen, when it is placed next to the sentence which follows it, to be an example of event coding which indicates the psychological sequencing of a character's perceptions:

(10)   A figure appeared in the door. It was Conchis.
(John Fowles, *The Magus*, Chapter 62)

We can now see that the first-person narrator *did* know who the figure was. It is just that when he first saw him he did not recognize him. If, instead of (10), Fowles had written 'Conchis appeared in the door' the 'not-know–know' effect would have been lost. By moving away from what is the default style of representation, where physical perception and recognition are usually represented as instantaneous, Fowles gives us what we must interpret as the sequence of perceptions of the narrator/character, thus helping us to place ourselves within his viewpoint.

3.8   Point of view in non-literary texts

We have seen in our discussion of examples (1) to (10) that in novels we, as readers, are constantly 'positioned' in point-of-view terms through the use of a range of point-of-view techniques. But because we have concentrated on literary examples, we should not think that such positioning only happens in literary texts. Consider the following extract from an article on Cilla Black, the ex-singer who is now the presenter of a popular British TV programme called *Blind Date*. The article writer is describing things as if he, and we, are part of the audience about to watch the show:

(11)   Cilla is here. We have been warmed up by jolly Bill the Warm-Up Man, who has nudged us, winked at us, confided in us, asked us to clap in the right places, and told us to stand up, turn round, and shake hands with the person beside us. We all felt a bit silly then, but we have persuaded Bill we are a nice, lovely, happy lot, and now Cilla is here.

('Black Magic', *Independent Magazine*, 8 June 1991: 42–4)

Note the way in which at the beginning, like many novels, we are plunged *in medias res*, into the middle of what is happening. We have definite reference to Cilla, assuming we already know who she is, the present tense, indicating present time for us as well as the narrator, and the use of the near deictic *here*. We have been 'positioned' as part of the audience waiting for the show to begin. We feel close to the warm-up man, because he is referred to by his first name, and the narrator uses the pronoun *we*, which is ambiguous here between its inclusive and exclusive uses. After the present tense of the first sentence we move to the recent past with the present perfect in sentence 2, and then a more remote past at the beginning of sentence 3, only to be brought back, through a similar movement of tenses and a paragraph-final repetition of the first sentence, to our imagined presence as part of the expectant audience at the moment Cilla appears on stage. A reader who responds sensitively to this piece of journalistic prose has to be just as responsive to shifting point-of-view markers as the readers of most modern novels.

The next example is even more complex:

(12)   The neighbours said that Lorraine and Martin's fights happened mostly at weekends. Even above the blare of television you could hear the screams and sounds of crockery and glass being shattered, furniture crashing against the wall, the thud of bodies falling and sometimes, most distressing of all, a small child's plaintive cries of fear. Later, when all was quiet, a huddled figure in a blanket could be seen sitting motionless outside on a garden bench, head bowed. 'It was what I always did after being attacked. I'd go white as a sheet, ice cold and all trembly, and sit out there in a state of utter

confusion and despair, asking myself if she had hit me because of
something I'd done. Was it my fault after all? I was often struck by
how similar my reactions were to those described by battered wives.'
('Women Who Batter Men', *New Woman*, January 1991: 10–13)

Again, we begin *in medias res*, this time from the point of view of the
next-door neighbours, hearing a fight through the wall (note the use of the
modal *could*, and *screams* and *sounds*, which are imprecise words, indicating lack of precision in hearing (we do not know the content of what must
have been, at least in part, verbal exchanges), and also nouns derived from
verbs, helping us to infer that the neighbours could not work out who was
making which noise. Similar remarks can be made about other words and
phrases in this paragraph (e.g. *furniture, bodies, a small child*).

At the beginning of the next paragraph we are shifted to the neighbours'
perception, which must logically be some time later, of the vanquished
arguer sitting outside in next door's garden. From there, we move, through
the direct speech, to the perspective of the victim, sitting in the garden,
worrying about what has happened. In spite of the clear indication from
the title, when I read this piece for the first time I still assumed, because of
my stereotypical assumptions about marital arguments, that the figure in
the garden was the wife. Until I arrived at the end of the paragraph. Clearly
the *in medias res* beginning, with its absence of specified reference, is being
used by the writer, in alliance with our stereotypical frame assumptions
about the sort of situation evoked, for a very sophisticated surprise effect.
It is clear from these examples that teaching students about point-of-view
is not some esoteric activity for the literati. Any reader of glossy magazines
needs to be able to spot point of view markers in a sophisticated complex
of shifting viewpoints and related effects.

3.9   Teaching point of view

The most traditional way to teach point of view in stylistics courses is to
take some passage, much as I have just done, and examine it carefully in
class to uncover what is going on and how it is controlled. A favourite
passage for me is the fight scene at the beginning of the second section of
Chapter 59 of the first edition of *The Magus* by John Fowles. It is particularly good for what I have called 'event coding' and 'psychological sequencing'. But it is also possible to be more adventurous. When I introduce my
first-year English undergraduates to the study of viewpoint, I have, first, to
convince them that a few hours spent examining the linguistic minutiae of
viewpoint is worth their while. By and large, they do not want to have
their noses rubbed into the linguistic gravel of textual structure. They much
prefer to curl up by the fire with a good novel, be entertained, and then
have an unthreatening chat about it. So I 'soften them up' for point-of-view

work by getting them to rewrite passages from different viewpoints, so that we can then discuss their different versions in class. They tend to be more interested in the linguistic details of their own writing than that of others. I have, for example, given them diary entries describing some incident from *The Secret Diary of Adrian Mole* by Sue Townsend, and asked them to rewrite that entry from the point of view of some character other than Adrian. You have to frame your instructions carefully; otherwise some budding authors throw away the original text and start again, in which case you do not have two versions close enough to compare. But handled carefully, this kind of work does lead students into an interest in viewpoint markers.

4   Speech presentation categories and point of view

It will be clear from the discussion of example (12) above that the presentation of speech also has a role to play in the manipulation of point of view (indeed, the presentation of character thought is also of importance—see Leech and Short 1981, Chapter 10—but I do not have the space to discuss that here). In example (12), the writer uses direct speech without any introductory reporting clause as a mechanism to help delay as long as possible the identification of the victim as the husband. In order to be able to chart the ways in which speech presentation relate to point of view, we first need a taxonomy of speech presentation modes to relate to function and effect.

4.1   Direct and indirect speech

Most people come across the distinction between direct speech (DS) and indirect speech (IS) at school. Like the other children of my generation, I had to do exercises in class 'translating' direct speech into indirect speech and back again. Hence, it is well known that tenses have to be 'backshifted' and pronouns changed when we move from DS to IS:

(13)   She declared, 'I will marry you here and now.' (DS)

(14)   She declared that she would marry him there and then. (IS)

It can also be seen from these examples that deictic markers like *here* and *now* also have to be changed to *there* and *then*. In fact, once we have noted, as we already have in 3.3 above, that tense and pronouns are also markers of deictic position, we can see that, apart from the changes involving the inverted commas and the syntactic relation between the reporting and reported clauses, all of the 'translation' changes are deictic. They shift viewpoint, if we see the sentences as being in a novel, from the character's viewpoint (13) to the narrator's (14). As a consequence, the two examples make different claims with respect to what I have called 'faithfulness' (Leech and Short 1981, Chapter 10; Short 1982). In (14), we would normally assume that the narrator claims to represent faithfully the propositional content of what is said. In (13), however, we assume that an additional claim is made, namely that the words and structures reported are those that the character actually used (though note that in the novel there is no anterior speech: the novelist makes it all up).

4.2   The narrator's representation of speech acts

Stylisticians have shown over this century that, in order to account properly for the ways in which speech is represented, we need more speech presentation categories, and that DS and IS are not necessarily at the extremes of the scale of speech presentation. Firstly, it is possible to represent speech without even giving the propositional content of what was uttered, as in:

(15)   She declared her intentions.

Here, all we know is what speech act was involved and a rough topic for that speech act. For that reason, I have called this form of speech presentation the narrator's representation of speech acts (NRSA). It is the point at which speech presentation and the narration of actions and events overlap in the novel, precisely because speech acts are *actions* performed through speech. In fact, it is possible to represent speech even more minimally, merely indicating that speech occurred, without giving any explicit indication of the content. I recently received a memo from an administrator in my university which laid out in writing the substance of a conversation we had had, without any indication in the typed part of the memo that we had met. At the bottom, in longhand 'We spoke' was written. I wondered to myself whether she read John Le Carré. This particular formulation is a mannerism associated with the character Percy Alleline in Le Carré's spy novels, novels which experiment in interesting ways with viewpoint, including speech presentation.

4.3   Free direct speech

Stylisticians have assumed for some time that there is a category 'more direct' than direct speech, so-called free direct speech (FDS):

(16)   She declared I will marry you here and now. (FDS)

(17)   I will marry you here and now. (FDS)

What happens here is that the remaining markers of the narrator (quotation marks and the reporting clause) are removed, leaving the character 'completely on her own'. (I will suggest below, however, that it is better to see these formulations as variations within the direct speech category.)

4.4   Free indirect speech

Finally, there is a hybrid form, in between DS and IS, which in effect contains a mixture of the linguistic forms associated with DS and IS. This form is usually known as free indirect speech (FIS):

(18)   She would marry him here and now.

This sort of sentence, which many grammarians would claim is ungrammatical, often turns up in the novel. The third person pronouns and backshifted tense are typical of indirect speech, whereas the lack of a reporting clause/reported clause structure and the use of the near deixis is typical of direct speech. Example (18) is merely one of a large series of possibilities within this category. Any mix of direct and indirect speech features in a speech-report sentence is enough for it to be assigned to the free indirect category.

4.5   The scale of speech presentation and its functions

If we put all of these categories together on a scale of presentation, we arrive at the sort of diagram to be found in Leech and Short (1981: Chapter 10); see Figure 4.

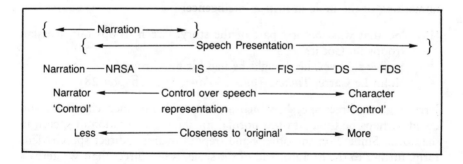

Figure 4

What this diagram attempts to represent is the sliding scale of viewpoint represented by the scale of speech presentation choices. At the left-hand side of the scale, we have the narrator's representation of a character's speech with minimal faithfulness claims (no propositional content, no words and structures used). At the other extreme, we apparently have character speech alone, with complete faithfulness to the 'original utterance' and no narrator involvement at all. Writers can vary the narrator/character 'mix' by choosing different points on the scale in their representation of character speech, and so affect point of view. Choices at the extreme right have the character apparently unmediated through a narrator. As we move leftwards on the scale, what is said is filtered more and more through the narrator, who 'intervenes' between us and the 'original' speech. This scale and its effects applies as much in non-literary speech reporting as it does in the novel.

The twentieth-century novel has made considerable use of the free indirect category, especially for the representation of character thought. Although I do not have the space to go into thought presentation here, it will be helpful to point out that the major reason for this is the fact that FIS represents a 'semantic halfway house' between the faithfulness claims of direct and indirect speech. It is difficult, often impossible, to work out whether the words and structures represented are those of the narrator or the character, and this semantic indeterminacy opens up myriad possibilities for the manipulation of point of view. It becomes possible, for example, for a writer to begin with narration and slide inside the thoughts of a character without the reader being fully aware of the viewpoint shift which is taking place, a useful strategy in getting the reader to sympathize with one character rather than another.

Speech presentation variation can be used to indicate characterization in the novel. Consider the following, from Le Carré's *Tinker, Tailor, Soldier, Spy*, where the bluff and good-hearted Jerry Westerby retells an incident in Czechoslovakia which contains an essential detail in George Smiley's final unmasking of the mole in British intelligence:

(19)   'So that was the first part of the story. Czech troops out, Russian troops in. Got it?'
       Smiley said yes, he thought he had his mind round it so far.
       (John Le Carré, *Tinker, Tailor, Soldier, Spy*, Chapter 28)

Jerry is given direct speech, which accords with his open character, and could perhaps be thought of as normal for the representation of speech in the novel. Smiley, on the other hand, replies in free indirect speech. This form, further to the narrator end of the scale, is less direct than Westerby's utterance, and can easily be interpreted as indicating that Smiley is being reserved at this point, not wanting to give anything away, even though the information Westerby has given him is vital.

The 'muting' effect of free indirect speech in the context of direct speech seen above can also be found in journalistic writing. Here is an extract from an interview that Peter Jenkins had with the artist, David Hockney. Hockney has just said that all good painters, when they get older, become more confident, and so 'looser':

(20)   Would it happen to Hockney? Did he have any vision of 'late Hockney'?
       'I do hope to get better,' was all he said.

Yes, but it was not just getting better, was it? As he had said, it was getting looser.
'When I said that, I pointed out, I think, that late Picasso is a kind of Cubism of the brush. Very interesting things began to happen. People never looked at them like that because they were much too busy looking at other things. Picasso didn't care, of course.'
('And Then What?', *Independent Weekend*, 29 February 1992)

Here, one of the foremost journalists of his generation consistently uses free indirect speech for his own speech and direct speech for Hockney, thus allowing Hockney's words to shine through in the recording of what appears to have been a genuine and earnest debate between the two men. Jenkins wants to represent his own views as well as Hockney's, and so he uses speech presentation variation to get the 'weighting' right.

4.6   Free direct speech revisited

It is my concern with integrating formal and functional accounts of speech presentation, allied to a wish to take stylistics outside literature, that has led me to change my views somewhat on the scale of presentation as I have outlined above. I now believe, for example, that it is not worth making a *category* distinction between direct and free direct speech. Rather, I think that these two modes which have been distinguished are really variations within one category, namely direct speech (note that each category has a scale of possibilities inside it). The reason for my change of heart is that although it is possible to make a DS/FDS distinction on *formal* grounds, I cannot find a *functional* reason for making the distinction. This became clear to me when I used my model of speech presentation to examine speech reports in newspapers (Short 1988). Consider the following headline:

(21)   Bring in Baker, Bush told
       (*Independent on Sunday*, 31 May 1992)

As far as I can see, putting inverted commas around the reported clause would not change the faithfulness claim in any way at all. It would merely make the status of the reported clause even clearer than it already is. The inverted commas are probably omitted for space reasons, the comma and the inversion of the reporting and reported clauses already giving enough indication of the direct speech status of 'Bring in Baker'. There are, of course, differences in effect to be gained by using what has been called free direct speech as opposed to direct speech, but I think that a more accurate functional account of those differences is to see them as relatively minor variations within the direct speech category. Hence Figure 4 above should be amended by removing the FDS category on the right-hand side.

4.7   Speech summary

My work in extending speech presentation analysis to cover newspaper language as well as the novel has led to other insights. In Short (1988), I also found that I had to deal with a phenomenon which I have labelled 'speech summary'. This feature becomes clearer in journalistic prose than in the novel precisely because there is a real anterior speech event which the reported speech reports. Consider the following report of an interview with Mrs Atkinson, the wife of the ex-Manchester United football manager, who lost his job after leaving his wife to live with another woman:

(22)   She also disclosed that her husband had been unfaithful 10 years ago
       when he was at Oxford United.
       (*Daily Express*, 11 June 1984)

It is difficult to believe that Mrs Atkinson uttered the sentence 'Ron was unfaithful 10 years ago when he was at Oxford United', or something very similar. Much more likely is that this sentence of the article represents a summary of a whole string of things she said. Here, speech summary turns up in indirect speech, but I have found examples of it in practically every other speech presentation mode. The discovery of this phenomenon in newspapers also opens the way for the re-analysis of some conversations in novels as including speech summary, with consequent changes in our ability to characterize the overall meaning and effects of such passages.

4.8   Direct speech revisited

Another result of my work on newspaper data ties up in an interesting way with a claim made by Tannen (1989). She suggests that there are many occasions in which direct speech is used in ordinary conversation, where it cannot plausibly be an exact representation of the words and structures used in the original speech event. People quite often use direct speech to report conversations they took part in many years before. It is difficult to believe that somebody could remember exactly what was said such a long time earlier. More likely, direct speech is being used in these cases for some kind of rhetorical effect, like increasing the vividness of the conversation portrayed.

A parallel example from Short (1988) is the *Sun*'s headline in its report of Mrs Thatcher's dissatisfaction with an official portrait of her:

(23)   UGH! GET RID OF MY SQUINT
       Premier Margaret Thatcher took one look at her new portrait and
       said: 'Get rid of that squint!' For the painting, which went on show
       yesterday in London's National Portrait Gallery, shows the Prime
       Minister with her gaze decidedly awry. And artist Rodrigo Moynihan
       admitted last night: 'Mrs Thatcher is not entirely happy with it.'

Mr Moynihan, 74, a former professor at the Royal College of Art, confessed to 'quite a lot of trouble' over Mrs Thatcher's eyes. And he added: 'I could be quite happy with one more sitting and I know she would be.' The problems began when Mrs Thatcher asked him to put more grey in the blue eyes in the portrait. 'She also noticed a squint—though she pointed it out fairly diplomatically,' Mr Moynihan said.

(*Sun*, 21 June 1984: 6)

From the evidence of the succeeding description, it looks unlikely that Mrs Thatcher ever uttered the words 'Ugh! Get rid of my squint'. Rather, the journalist has made the newspaper's presentation of what she said more lurid to catch the reader's attention, make the style of the paper more racy, and so on. Over the last few years, many readers have come, with good cause, to distrust what the tabloid press tells them. Direct speech presentations, particularly in newspaper headlines, are part of this more general phenomenon, one which, presumably, it makes good educational sense to teach explicitly to young readers, so that they are not so easily misled.

It should be noted, though, that even when reporters try their best to report accurately using direct speech, and have the technical means to do so, they may still have to change the quotation to some extent from the form of the original utterance. This is because they have to obey two sets of dictates, one relating to faithfulness to the original speech being reported, and one relating to their reporting situation (including the viewpoint of the reader/listener). Hence, if in the House of Commons an MP says 'My right honourable friend the member for Lancaster is right', the subject noun phrase, even in direct speech, may have to be changed to 'Elaine Kellett-Bowman, the MP for Lancaster', or some similar locution, in order to ensure that the reader will understand the reference. The issue thus becomes not whether or not some piece of direct speech should have used only the words originally spoken, but what sorts of changes are deemed reasonable and unreasonable to make.

5   Conclusion

In general terms, what all this shows is that the way we interpret the speech presentation modes may vary from one situation to another. The canonical set of assumptions, often explicitly taught in schools, whereby direct speech faithfully represents the words and structures used in the anterior speech event, but indirect speech represents faithfully the propositional content only, best fit academic writing, where one has to be particularly careful about acknowledging one's sources and representing others accurately. These assumptions are less likely to account well for speech report in extempore conversation, the written report of speech where there is no proper record, and written reports where there are proper records, but where other factors (like selling your newspaper) may be more important to the writer than strict reporting accuracy.

Accounts of speech presentation, like those of point of view in general, are becoming increasingly complex as they strive to fit the formal and interpretative facts while encompassing a wider and wider range of natural data. In this area, what we can see is that a series of stylistic techniques developed originally for the analysis of the novel are of relevance to anyone interested in understanding how we communicate with one another, and to teachers of English literature and English language, whether to native- or non-native-speaker students. Point of view control and speech presentation manipulation are factors in all language, not just the language of literature, and a sensitivity to their complexities is increasingly important as we encounter a wider and wider range of text-types and textual practices. Moreover, adapting stylistic descriptions to account adequately for a wider range of text-types in turn leads to changes in theory and descriptive apparatus, which help us to understand better the literary texts they were first developed to explain.

Notes

1   Emphasis added.

Bibliography

Ahulu, S. 1992. *English in Ghana*. Unpublished PhD thesis, Research Centre for English and Applied Linguistics, University of Cambridge.

Aitchison, J. 1987. *Words in the Mind: An Introduction to the Mental Lexicon*. Oxford: Basil Blackwell.

Aitchison, J. 1992. 'Good birds, better birds and amazing birds: The development of prototypes' in H. Béjoint and P. Arnaud (eds.) *Vocabulary and Applied Linguistics*. London: Macmillan: 71–84.

Albert, M.L. and **L.K. Obler.** 1978. *The Bilingual Brain: Neuropsychological and Neurolinguistic Aspects of Bilingualism*. New York: Academic Press.

Altmann, G.T.M., A. Garnham, and **Y. Dennis,** 1992. 'Avoiding the garden path: Eye movements in context'. *Journal of Memory and Language* 31: 685–712.

Altmann, G.T.M., A. Garnham, and **J.A. Henstra.** 1994. 'Effects of syntax in human sentence parsing: Evidence against a structure-based proposal mechanism'. *Journal of Experimental Psychology: Learning, Memory and Cognition* 20: 209–216.

Armstrong, S., L. Gleitman, and **H. Gleitman.** 1983. 'What some concepts might not be'. *Cognition* 13: 263–308.

Austin, J. 1962. *How To Do Things With Words*. Oxford: Clarendon Press.

Bachman, L.F. 1990. *Fundamental Considerations in Language Testing*. Oxford: Oxford University Press.

Baker, C.L. 1989. *English Syntax*. Cambridge, Mass.: MIT Press.

Barnes, D. 1976. *From Communication to Curriculum*. Harmondsworth: Penguin.

Barsalou, L.W. 1983. 'Ad hoc categories'. *Memory and Cognition,* 11: 211–27.

Bartlett, F.C. 1932. *Remembering*. Cambridge: Cambridge University Press.

Bates, E. and **B. MacWhinney.** 1989. 'Functionalism and the competition model' in B. MacWhinney and E. Bates (eds.) *The Crosslinguistic Study of Sentence Processing*. Cambridge: Cambridge University Press.

Beal, J. 1993. 'The grammar of Tyneside and Northumbrian English' in J. Milroy and L. Milroy 1993.

Bell, A. 1984. 'Language style as audience design'. *Language in Society* 13: 145–204.

Bell, A. and **J. Holmes** (eds.) 1990. *New Zealand Ways of Speaking English*. Clevedon, Avon: Multilingual Matters.

Beretta, A. 1991. 'Theory constructions in SLA: Complementarity and opposition'. *Studies in Second Language Acquisition* 13: 493–511.

Bialystok, E. 1991. 'Metalinguistic dimensions of bilingual language proficiency' in E. Bialystok (ed.) *Language Processing by Bilingual Children*. Cambridge: Cambridge University Press.

Blakemore, D. 1987. *Semantic Constraints on Relevance*. Oxford: Blackwell.

Blakemore, D. 1992. *Understanding Utterances*. Oxford: Blackwell.

Blanche, P. 1991. 'Using standardised achievement and oral proficiency tests for self-assessment purposes: the DLEFLC study'. *Language Testing* 7: 202–29.

Blass, R. 1990. *Relevance Relations in Discourse.* Cambridge: Cambridge University Press.

Bley-Vroman, R. 1989. 'What is the logical problem of foreign language learning?' in S. M. Gass and J. Schachter (eds.) *Linguistic Perspectives on Second Language Acquisition.* Cambridge: Cambridge University Press.

Booth, W. 1961. *The Rhetoric of Fiction.* Chicago: Chicago University Press.

Bowerman, M. 1987. 'Commentary: Mechanisms of language acquisition' in B. MacWhinney (ed.) *Mechanisms of Language Acquisition.* Hillsdale, NJ: Erlbaum.

Bowerman, M. 1989. 'Learning a semantic system: What role do cognitive presuppositions play?' in M. L. Rice and R. L. Schliefelbusch (eds.) *The Teachability of Language.* Baltimore: Brookes: 133–65.

Brown, G. 1986. 'Investigating listening comprehension in context'. *Applied Linguistics* 7: 284–303.

Brown, G. 1987. 'Modelling discourse participants' knowledge' in J. Monaghan (ed.) *Grammar in the Construction of Texts.* London: Frances Pinter: 90–99.

Brown, G. 1989. 'Making sense: The interaction of linguistic expression and contextual information'. *Applied Linguistics* 10: 97–108.

Brown, G. 1990. *Listening to Spoken English* (2nd edition). Longman: London.

Brown, G., A. Anderson, R. Shillcock, and **G. Yule.** 1984. *Teaching Talk.* Cambridge: Cambridge University Press.

Brown, G. and **G. Yule.** 1983. *Discourse Analysis.* Cambridge: Cambridge University Press.

Brown, K. 1991. 'Double modals in Hawick Scots' in P. Trudgill and J.K. Chambers (eds.) 1991: 74–104.

Brown, K. and **J. Miller.** 1980. *Syntax: A Linguistic Introduction to Sentence Structure.* London: Hutchinson. (2nd edition). 1991. London: HarperCollins.

Brown, P. and **S. Levinson.** 1987. *Politeness.* Cambridge: Cambridge University Press.

Brown, R. 1973. *A First Language: The Early Stages.* Cambridge, Mass.: Harvard University Press.

Brumfit, C.J. 1984. *Communicative Methodology in Language Teaching.* Cambridge: Cambridge University Press.

Bruner, J.S. 1986. *Actual Minds, Possible Worlds.* Cambridge, Mass.: Harvard University Press.

Buck, G. 1989. 'A construct validation study of listening and reading comprehension'. Paper read at the 11th Language Testing Research Colloquium.

Carrell, P. 1991. 'Second language reading: Reading ability or language proficiency'. *Applied Linguistics* 12: 159–79.

Carston, R. 1988. 'Implicature, explicature, and truth-theoretic semantics' in R.M. Kempson (ed.).

Carton, A.S. 1988. 'Categorising questions in respect to content and text structure'. Paper read at the 10th Language Testing Research Colloquium.

Chambers, J.K. and **P. Trudgill.** 1980. *Dialectology.* Cambridge: Cambridge University Press.

Chambers, J.K. and **P. Trudgill.** 1991. 'Dialect grammar: data and theory' in P. Trudgill and J.K. Chambers (eds.) 1991: 291–97.

Chandler, M. 1991. 'Alternative readings of the competence-performance relation' in M. Chandler and M. Chapman (eds.) *Criteria for Competence: Controversies in the Conceptualisation and Assessment of Children's Abilities.* Hillsdale, NJ: Erlbaum.

Cheshire, J. (ed.) 1991. *English Around the World: Sociolinguistic Perspectives.* Cambridge: Cambridge University Press.

Cheshire, J. 1982. *Variation in an English Dialect: A Sociolinguistic Study.* Cambridge: Cambridge University Press.

Chomsky, N. 1968. *Language and Mind*. New York: Harcourt, Brace and World, Inc.

Clark, J.L.D. (ed.) 1978. *Direct Testing of Speaking Proficiency: Theory and Application*. Princeton, NJ: Educational Testing Service.

Clark, H.H. and E.V. Clark. 1977. *Psychology and Language: An Introduction to Psycholinguistics*. New York: Harcourt Brace Jovanovich.

Clark, H.H. and E.F. Schaefer. 1987. 'Collaborating on contributions to conversation'. *Language and Cognitive Processes*, 2: 19–41.

Clark, H.H. and E.F. Schaefer. 1989b. 'Contributing to discourse'. *Cognitive Science*. 13: 259–94.

Clark, H.H. and D. Wilkes-Gibbs. 1986. 'Referring as a collaborative process'. *Cognition*, 22: 1–39.

Clark, J.L.D. (ed.) 1978. *Direct Testing of Speaking Proficiency: Theory and Application*. Princeton, NJ: Educational Testing Service.

Cole, R.A. and J. Jakimik 1980. 'A model of speech perception' in R.A. Cole (ed.) 1980. *Perception and Production of Fluent Speech*. Hillsdale, NJ: Lawrence Erlbaum Associates.

Collier, V.P. 1989. 'How long? A synthesis of research on academic achievement in a second language'. *TESOL Quarterly*, 23: 509–31.

Comrie, B. 1976. *Aspect*. Cambridge: Cambridge University Press.

Cook, V. 1992. 'Evidence for multi-competence'. *Language Learning* 42: 557–91.

Coupland, N. (ed.) 1990. *English in Wales: Diversity, Conflict and Change*. Clevedon, Avon: Multilingual Matters.

Crystal, D. 1980. 'Neglected grammatical features in conversational English' in S. Greenbaum, G. Leech, and J. Svartvik (eds.) 1980. *Studies in English Linguistics for Randolph Quirk*. London: Longman: 163–6.

Crystal, D. 1987. *The Cambridge Encyclopaedia of Language*. Cambridge: Cambridge University Press.

Cummins, J. 1981. 'Age on arrival and immigrant second language learning in Canada: A reassessment'. *Applied Linguistics* 2: 131–49.

Curtiss, S. 1977. *Genie: A Psycholinguistic Study of a Modern Day "Wild Child"*. New York: Academic Press.

Davidson, F. G. 1988. *An explanatory modeling survey of the trait structures of some existing language test datasets*. Unpublished PhD dissertation, UCLA.

Davis, S. (ed.) 1991. *Pragmatics: A Reader*. Oxford: Oxford University Press.

Day, R.S. 1968a. *Fusion in Dichotic Listening*. Unpublished doctoral dissertation, Stanford University.

Day, R.S. 1970. 'Temporal order judgements in speech: Are individuals language-bound or stimulus-bound?' *Haskins Laboratories Status Report* SR-21/22, 71–87.

Dickson, W.P. (ed.) 1981. *Children's Oral Communication Skills*. New York: Academic Press.

Dixon, R.M.W. 1991. *A New Approach to English Grammar, on Semantic Principles*. Oxford: Clarendon Press.

Dowty, D. 1991. 'Thematic proto-roles and argument selection'. *Language* 67: 547–619.

Dulay, H. and M. Burt. 1974. 'Natural sequences in child second language acquisition'. *Language Learning* 24: 37–53.

Edwards, D. and N. Mercer. 1987. *Common Knowledge*. London: Methuen.

Eimas, P.D., E.R Siqueland, P. Jusczyk, and J. Vigorito. 1971. 'Speech perception in infants'. *Science* 171: 303–6.

Eisikovits, E. 1991. 'Variation in the lexical verb in inner-Sydney English' in P. Trudgill and J.K. Chambers (eds.) 1991: 120–43.

Fairclough, N.L. 1989. *Language and Power*. London: Longman.
Fasold, R. 1984. *The Sociolinguistics of Society*. Oxford: Blackwell.
Fasold, R. 1990. *The Sociolinguistics of Language*. Oxford: Blackwell.
Felix, S.W. 1986. *Cognition and Language Growth*. Dordrecht, Netherlands: Foris Publications.
Fillmore, C.J. 1968. 'The case for case' in E. Bach and R.T. Harms (eds.) *Universals of Linguistic Theory*. New York: Holt Rinehart and Winston.
Fillmore, C.J. 1970. 'The grammar of hitting and breaking' in R. Jacobs and P. Rosenbaum (eds.) *Readings in English Transformational Grammar*. Waltham, Mass.: Ginn.
Fleischman, S. 1990. *Tense and Narrativity: From Medieval Performance to Modern Fiction*. London: Routledge.
Flynn, S. 1986. 'Production versus comprehension: differences in underlying competences'. *Studies in Second Language Acquisition* 8: 135–64.
Flynn, S. 1989. 'The role of the head-initial/head-final parameter in the acquisition of English relative clauses by adult Spanish and Japanese speakers' in S.M. Gass and J. Schachter (eds.) *Linguistic Perspectives on Second Language Acquisition*. Cambridge: Cambridge University Press.
Fodor, J.A. 1983. *The Modularity of Mind*. Cambridge, Mass.: MIT Press.
Fodor, J.A. and Z.W. Pylyshyn. 1988. 'Connectionism and cognitive architecture: A critical analysis'. *Cognition*, 28: 3–71.
Forster, E. M. 1927. *Aspects of the Novel*. Harmondsworth: Penguin.
Fouly, K.A., L.F. Bachman, and G.A. Cziko. 1990. 'The divisibility of language competence: a confirmatory approach'. *Language Learning*, 40: 1–12.
Fowler, R. 1986. *Linguistic Criticism*. Oxford: Oxford University Press.

Ganong, W.F. 1980. 'Phonetic categorization in auditory word perception'. *Journal of Experimental Psychology: Human Perception and Performance* 6: 110–25.
Garman, M. 1990. *Psycholinguistics*. Cambridge: Cambridge University Press.
Garnes, S. and Z.S. Bond. 1980. 'A slip of the ear: a snip of the ear? A slip of the year' in V.A. Fromkin (ed.) *Errors in Linguistic Performance: Slips of the Tongue, Ear, Pen and Hand*. New York: Academic Press.
Garnham, A. 1987. *Mental Models as Representations of Discourse and Text*. Chichester, Sussex: Ellis Horwood.
Garnham, A. and J.V. Oakhill. 1987. 'Interpreting elliptical verb phrases'. *Quarterly Journal of Experimental Psychology*, 39A: 611–27.
Garnham, A. and J.V. Oakhill. 1988. ' "Anaphoric islands" revisited'. *Quarterly Journal of Experimental Psychology*, 40A: 719–35.
Garnham, A. and J.V. Oakhill. 1989. 'The everyday use of anaphoric expressions: Implications for the "mental models" theory of text comprehension' in N.E. Sharkey (ed.) *Models of Cognition: A Review of Cognitive Science*. Norwood, NJ: Ablex.
Geeraerts, D. 1989. 'Introduction: Prospects and problems? Prototype theory'. *Linguistics* 27: 587–612.
Genesee, F. 1989. 'Early bilingual development: One language or two?' *Journal of Child Language* 16: 161–79.
Giles, H. and N. Coupland. 1991. *Language: Contexts and Consequences*. Milton Keynes: Open University Press.
Green, G.M. and J.L. Morgan. 1981. 'Pragmatics, grammar and discourse' in P. Cole (ed.) *Radical Pragmatics*. New York: Academic Press.

Grice, H.P. 1967. 'William James Lectures'. Reprinted in H.P. Grice 1989: *Studies in the Way of Words*. Cambridge, Mass.: Harvard University Press.

Grice, H. P. 1975. 'Logic and conversation' in P. Cole and J.L. Morgan (eds.) *Syntax and Semantics 3: Speech Acts*. New York: Academic Press.

Gutt, E.A. 1991. *Translation and Relevance: Cognition and Communication*. Oxford: Blackwell.

Hale, G. A. 1988. 'Student major field and text content: interactive effects on reading comprehension in the Test of English as a Foreign Language'. *Language Testing*, 5: 59–62.

Halliday, M.A.K. and R. Hasan. 1976. *Cohesion in English*. London: Longman.

Halliday, M.A.K. and R. Hasan. 1989. *Language, Context, and Text*. Oxford: Oxford University Press.

Halliday, M. A. K. 1985. *An Introduction to Functional Grammar*. London: Arnold.

Handschin, C.H. 1919. *Handschin Modern Language Tests: Test A*. Yonkers-on-Hudson, NY: World Book Company.

Hankamer, J. and I.A. Sag. 1976. 'Deep and surface anaphora'. *Linguistic Inquiry*, 7: 391–428.

Harris, J. 1984. 'Syntactic variation and dialect divergence'. *Journal of Linguistics*, 20: 303–27.

Heilenman, L.K. 1991. 'Self-assessment of second language ability: the role of response effects'. *Language Testing*, 7: 174–201.

Hemnon, V.A.C. 1929. *Achievement Tests in the Modern Foreign Languages*. New York: Macmillan.

Henning, G. 1987. *A Guide to Language Testing: Development Evaluation. Research*. Cambridge, Mass.: Newbury House.

Henning, G. 1990. 'National issues in individual assessment: the consideration of specialization bias in university language screening tests' in J.H.A.L. de Jong and D.K. Stevenson (eds.) 1990: 38–50.

Henning, G. 1992. 'Dimensionality and construct validity of language tests'. Paper read at the 14th Language Testing Research Colloquium.

Hirst, P. 1974. *Knowledge and the Curriculum*. London: Routledge.

Hock, T.S. 1990. 'The role of prior knowledge and language proficiency as predictors of reading comprehension among undergraduates' in J.H.A.L. de Jong and D.K. Stevenson (eds.) 1990: 214–24.

Hoey, M. 1983. *On the Surface of Discourse*. London: George Allen and Unwin.

Huddleston, R. 1984. *Introduction to the Grammar of English*. Cambridge: Cambridge University Press.

Hugly, P. and C. Sayward. 1979. 'A problem about conversational implicatures'. *Linguistics and Philosophy*, 3: 19–25.

Hymes, D. 1964. 'Towards ethnographies of communicative events'. Reprinted in P.P. Giglioli (ed.) 1972 *Language and Social Context*. Harmondsworth: Penguin.

Jackendoff, R. 1990. *Semantic Structures*. Cambridge, Mass.: MIT Press.

Jarvella, R. and J. Lubinsky. 1975. 'Deaf and hearing children's use of language describing temporal order among events'. *Journal of Speech and Hearing Research*, 16: 58–73.

Jespersen, O. 1927. *A Modern English Grammar on Historical Principles*. Copenhagen: Ejnar Munksgaard.

Johnson, J.S. and E.L. Newport. 1989. 'Critical period effects in second language learning: The influence of maturational state on the acquisition of English as a second language'. *Cognitive Psychology*, 21: 60–99.

Johnson, J.S. and E.L. Newport. 1991. 'Critical period effects on universal properties of language: The status of subjacency in the acquisition of a second language'. *Cognition* 39: 215–58.

Johnson-Laird, P.N. 1983. *Mental Models: Towards a Cognitive Science of Language, Inference and Consciousness.* Cambridge: Cambridge University Press.

de Jong, J.H.A.L. and D.K. Stevenson (eds) 1990. *Individualising the Assessment of Language Abilities.* Clevedon, Avon: Multilingual Matters.

de Jong, J.H.A.L. and C.A.W. Glas. 1987. 'Validation of listening comprehension tests'. *Language Testing* 4: 170–94.

Jonz, J. 1989. 'Textual sequence and second-language comprehension'. *Language Learning* 39: 207–49.

Katz, J. 1972. *Semantic Theory.* New York: Harper and Row.

Keane, M.L. 1988. 'The relation between linguistic theory and second language acquisition: A biological perspective' in J. Pankhurst, M. Sharwood Smith, and P. Van Buren (eds.) *Learnability and Second Languages.* Dordrecht, Holland: Foris Publications.

Kempson, R.M. (ed.). *Mental Representations: The Interface between Language and Reality.* Cambridge: Cambridge University Press.

Kerswill, P.E. 1987. 'Levels of linguistic variation in Durham'. *Journal of Linguistics,* 23: 25–49.

Kilby, D. 1984. *Descriptive Syntax and the English Verb.* London: Croom Helm.

Krashen, S.D. 1985. *The Input Hypothesis: Issues and Implications.* London and New York: Longman.

Labov, W. 1972. *Language in the Inner City.* Philadelphia: Philadelphia University Press.

Labov, W. 1973. 'The boundaries of words and their meanings' in C.-J.N. Bailey and R.W. Shuy (eds.) *New Ways of Analyzing Variation in English.* Washington, DC: Georgetown University Press.

Labov, W. 1981. 'Resolving the neo-grammarian controversy'. *Language* 57: 267–308.

Labov, W. 1990. 'The intersection of sex and social class in the course of linguistic change'. *Language Variation and Change* 2: 205–54.

Lado, R. 1957. *Linguistics across Cultures: Applied Linguistics for Language Teachers.* Ann Arbor: University of Michigan Press.

Lakoff, G. 1987. *Women, Fire and Dangerous Things.* Chicago: University of Chicago Press.

Lakoff, G. and M. Johnson. 1980. *Metaphors We Live By.* Chicago: University of Chicago Press.

Leather, J. and A. James. 1991. 'The acquisition of second language speech'. *Studies in Second Language Acquisition* 13: 305–41.

Lee, J.F. and G.L. Riley. 1990. 'The effect of prereading rhetorically-oriented frameworks on the recall of two structurally different expository texts'. *Studies in Second Language Acquisition* 12: 25–41.

Leech, G.N. and M.H. Short. 1981. *Style in Fiction.* London: Longman.

Lenneberg, E.H. 1967. *Biological Foundations of Language.* New York: Wiley.

Levasseur, D. and M. Pagé. 1990. 'Comprehension of sentences and of intersentential relations by 11- to 15-year-old pupils' in J.H.A.L. de Jong and D.K. Stevenson (eds.) 1990: 97–107.

Levinson, S. C. 1983. *Pragmatics.* Cambridge: Cambridge University Press.

Lyons, J. 1968. *Introduction to Theoretical Linguistics.* Cambridge: Cambridge University Press.

Macaulay, R.K.S. 1977. *Language, Social Class and Education: A Glasgow Study.* Edinburgh: Edinburgh University Press.

Macnamara, J. 1972. 'Cognitive basis of language learning in infants'. *Psychological Review* 79: 1–14.

Mandler, J. 1988. 'How to build a baby: On the development of an accessible representational system'. *Cognitive Development* 3: 113–36.

Markman, E. M. 1981. 'Comprehension monitoring' in W. P. Dickson (ed.) 1981: 61–82.

Markman, E.M. 1989. *Categorization and Naming in Children.* Cambridge, Mass.: MIT Press.

Markman, E.M. 1990. 'Constraints children place on word meanings'. *Cognitive Science* 14: 57–77. .

Marslen-Wilson, W. 1989. *Lexical Representation and Process.* Cambridge, Mass.: MIT Press.

McClelland, J.L. and J.L. Elman. 1986. 'The TRACE model of speech perception'. *Cognitive Psychology* 18: 1–86.

McClelland, J.L. and D.E. Rumelhart. 1981. 'An interactive activation model of context effects in letter perception: Part 1. An account of the basic findings'. *Psychological Review* 88: 375–407.

Mees, I. 1987. 'Glottal stop as a prestigious feature in Cardiff English'. *English World-Wide* 8: 25–39.

Mehan, H. 1979. *Learning Lessons: Social Organisation in the Classroom.* Cambridge Mass: Harvard University Press.

Melchers, G. 1989. 'Sociolinguistics and foreign language teaching' in B. Hamerberg, (ed.) *Scandinavian Working Papers in Bilingualism* 8. Department of English, University of Stockholm.

Miller, J. 1993. 'The grammar of Scottish English' in J. Milroy and L. Milroy (eds.) 1993.

Milroy, J. 1992. *Linguistic Variation and Change.* Oxford: Blackwell.

Milroy, J. and L. Milroy. (eds.) 1993. *The Grammar of English Dialects in the British Isles.* London: Longman.

Milroy, J. and L. Milroy. 1991. *Authority in Language.* (2nd edition). London: Longman.

Milroy, L. 1984. 'Comprehension and context: successful communication and communicative breakdown' in P. Trudgill (ed.) *Applied Sociolinguistics.* London: Academic Press: 7–31.

Milroy, L. 1987. *Observing and Analysing Natural Language.* Oxford: Blackwell.

Milroy, L. and W. Li. 1991 'A social network perspective on code-switching and language choice: the example of the Tyneside Chinese community' in *Codeswitching in Bilingual Studies: Theory, Significance and Perspectives.* European Science Foundation, Strasbourg: 233–52.

Milroy, L. and J. Milroy. 1992. 'Social network and social class; towards an integrated sociolinguistic model'. *Language in Society* 21: 1–26.

Newport, E.L. 1990. 'Maturational constraints on language learning'. *Cognitive Science* 14: 11–28.

Norris, D. 1991. 'The constraints on connectionism'. *The Psychologist* 4: 293–96.

Oakden, E. C. and M. Sturt. 1922. 'Development of the knowledge of time in children'. *British Journal of Psychology* 12: 309–66.

Oscarson, M. 1989. 'Self-assessment of language proficiency: rationale and applications'. *Language Testing* 6: 1–13.

Overton, W.F. 1991. 'Competence, procedures, and hardware: Conceptual and empirical considerations' in M. Chandler and M. Chapman (eds.) *Criteria for Competence: Controversies in the Conceptualisation and Assessment of Children's Abilities.* Hillsdale, NJ: Erlbaum.

Painter, C. 1985. *Learning the Mother Tongue.* Oxford: Oxford University Press.
Perfetti, C.A. 1985. *Reading Ability.* Oxford: Oxford University Press.
Perkins, K. and S.R. Brutten. 1988. 'Using a facet design to assess the effects of the form, source, and the frequency of information necessary to answer ESL reading comprehension questions'. *Language Learning,* 38: 171–85.
Peters, R.S. (ed.) 1973. *The Philosophy of Education.* Oxford: Oxford University Press.
Piaget, J. 1926. *The Language and Thought of the Child.* New York: Harcourt Brace.
Pica, T., L. Holliday, N. Lewis, and L. Morgenthaler. 1989. 'Comprehensible output as an outcome of the linguistic demands on the listener'. *Studies in Second Language Acquisition* 2: 63–90.
Pinker, S. 1984. *Language Learnability and Language Development.* Cambridge, Mass.: Harvard University Press.
Pinker, S. and A. Prince. 1988. 'On language and connectionism: Analysis of a parallel distributed processing model of language acquisition'. *Cognition,* 28: 73–193.
Preston, D. 1989. *Sociolinguistics and Second Language Acquisition.* Oxford: Blackwell.

Quine, W.V.O. 1960. *Word and Object.* Cambridge, Mass.: MIT Press.
Quirk, R. and H.G. Widdowson. (eds.) 1985. *English in the World: Teaching and Learning the Language and Literatures.* Cambridge: Cambridge University Press.

Reddy, M. 1979. 'The conduit metaphor' in A. Ortony (ed.) *Metaphor and Thought.* Cambridge: Cambridge University Press: 284–325.
Romaine, S. 1975 *Linguistic variability in the speech of some Edinburgh schoolchildren.* Unpublished M.Litt. thesis, University of Edinburgh.
Rosch, E. 1975. 'Cognitive representation of semantic categories'. *Journal of Experimental Psychology: General,* 104: 192–233.
Rosch, E. and B.B. Lloyd. 1978. *Cognition and Categorization.* Hillsdale, NJ: Lawrence Erlbaum Associates.
Rumelhart, D.E. and J.L. McClelland. 1986. 'On learning the past tense of English verbs' in J.L. McClelland and D.E. Rumelhart (eds.) *Parallel Distributed Processing: Explorations in the Microstructure of Cognition. Volume 2. Psychological and Biological Models.* Cambridge, Mass.: MIT Press.
Ryle, G. 1949. *The Concept of Mind.* Harmondsworth: Penguin.

Sacks, O. 1985. *The Man Who Mistook His Wife For a Hat.* London: Duckworth.
Sag, I.A. and J. Hankamer. 1984. 'Toward a theory of anaphoric processing'. *Linguistics and Philosophy,* 7: 325–45.
Sanford, A. J. and S.C. Garrod. 1981. *Understanding Written Language.* Chichester: John Wiley.
de Saussure, F. 1960. *A Course in General Linguistics.* Baskin, W. (trans). London: Peter Owen.
Schiffrin, D. 1987. *Discourse Markers.* Cambridge: Cambridge University Press.
Scholes, R. and R. Kellogg. 1966. *The Nature of Narrative.* Oxford: Oxford University Press.

Scovel, T. 1988. *A Time to Speak: A Psycholinguistic Inquiry into the Critical Period for Human Speech*. Cambridge, Mass.: Newbury House.

Seidenberg, M.S. and J.L. McClelland. 1989. 'A distributed, developmental model of word recognition and naming'. *Psychological Review*, 96: 523–68.

Seidenberg, M.S., K.K. Tanenhaus, J.M. Leiman, and M. Bienkowski. 1982. 'Automatic access of meanings of ambiguous words in context: some limitations of knowledge-based processing'. *Cognitive Psychology*, 14: 489–537.

Sejnowski, T. and C. Rosenberg. 1986. *NETtalk: A Parallel Network That Learns to Read Aloud*. The Johns Hopkins University Electrical Engineering and Computer Science Technical Report JHU/EECS – 86/01.

Short, M. 1982. 'Stylistics and the Teaching of Literature: with an example from James Joyce's *Portrait of the Artist as a Young Man*'. In R. Carter (ed.) *Language and Literature: An Introductory Reader in Stylistics*. London: George Allen and Unwin.

Short, M. 1988. 'Speech presentation, the novel and the press' in W. van Peer (ed.) *The Taming of the Text*. London: Routledge: 61–81.

Simpson, P. 1990. 'Towards a modal grammar of point of view' *Liverpool Papers in Language and Discourse* 3: 38–73.

Smith, K. 1987. *Non-standard grammar and syntactic comprehension*. Unpublished BSc (Speech and Psychology) dissertation, Department of Speech, University of Newcastle upon Tyne.

Smith, N.V. and D. Wilson. 1979. *Modern Linguistics*. London: Penguin.

Smith, N.V. (ed.) 1982. *Mutual Knowledge*. London: Academic Press.

Sperber, D. and D. Wilson, 1985/6. 'Loose talk'. *Proceedings of the Aristotelian Society*, NS LXXXVI: 15371. Reprinted in Davis, 1991.

Sperber, D. and D. Wilson. 1986. *Relevance: Communication and Cognition*. Oxford: Blackwell.

Sperber, D. and D. Wilson. 1987. 'Presumptions of relevance'. *Behavioural and Brain Sciences*, 10: 73–54.

Sperber, D. and D. Wilson. 1990. 'Rhetoric and relevance' in D. Wellbery and J. Bender (eds.) *The Ends of Rhetoric: History, Theory, Practice*. Stanford: Stanford University Press: 140–55.

Spolsky, B. 1988. 'Bridging the gap: A general theory of second language learning'. *TESOL Quarterly*, 22: 377–96.

Spolsky, E. (ed.) 1990. *The Uses of Adversity: Failure and Accommodation in Reader Response*. Lewisburg; London, and Toronto: Bucknell University Press; Associated University Presses.

Spolsky, E. and E. Schauber. 1986. *The Bounds of Interpretation: Linguistic Theory and Literary Text*. Stanford: Stanford University Press.

Statman, S. 1992. 'Convergent examinations and the divergent student'. *System*, 20: 2.

Swain, M. 1990. 'Second language testing and second language acquisition: Is there a conflict with traditional psychometrics?' in J.E. Alatis (ed.) *Georgetown University Roundtable on Languages and Linguistics 1990*. Washington, DC.: Georgetown University Press: 401–12.

Swales, J. 1990. *Genre Analysis: English in Academic and Research Settings*. Cambridge: Cambridge University Press.

Swinney, D. 1979. 'Lexical access during sentence comprehension: a reconsideration of context effects'. *Journal of Verbal Learning and Verbal Behavior* 18: 645–59.

Tanenhaus, M.K., J.M. Leiman, and M.S. Seidenberg. 1979. 'Evidence for multiple stages in the processing of ambiguous words in syntactic contexts'. *Journal of Verbal Learning and Verbal Behavior*, 18: 427–41.

Tannen, D. 1989. *Talking Voices: Repetition, Dialogue and Imagery in Conversational Discourse.* Cambridge: Cambridge University Press.

Taylor, T.J. and D. Cameron. 1987. *Analysing Conversation.* Oxford: Pergamon.

Thomson, G.H. 1939. *The Factorial Analysis of Human Ability.* London: University of London Press.

Toolan, M. 1988. *Narrative: A Critical Linguistic Introduction.* London and New York: Routledge.

Trudgill, P. 1974. *The Social Differentiation of English in Norwich.* Cambridge: Cambridge University Press.

Trudgill, P. 1983. *On Dialect.* Oxford: Blackwell.

Trudgill, P. 1986. *Dialects in Contact.* Oxford: Blackwell.

Trudgill, P. and J.K. Chambers (eds.) 1991. *Dialects of English: Studies in Grammatical variation.* London: Longman.

Trudgill, P. and J. Hannah. 1985. *International English.* (2nd edition) London: Arnold.

Vendler, Z. 1967. *Linguistics and Philosophy.* Ithaca, NY: Cornell University Press.

Warren, R.M. 1970. 'Perceptual restoration of missing speech sounds'. *Science,* 167: 393–5.

Weinreich, U., W. Labov, and M. Herzog. 1968. 'Empirical foundations for a theory of language change' in W.P. Lehmann (ed.) *Directions for Historical Linguistics.* Austin: University of Texas Press.

Wells, J.C. 1982. *Accents of English.* (3 vols) Cambridge: Cambridge University Press.

Westaway, G., J.C. Alderson, and C. Clapham. 1990. 'Directions in testing for specific purposes' in J.H.A.L. de Jong and D.K. Stevenson (eds.) 1990: 239–56.

White, L. 1989. *Universal Grammar and Second Language Acquisition.* Amsterdam/Philadelphia: John Benjamins.

Widdowson, H.G. 1978. *Teaching Language as Communication.* Oxford: Oxford University Press.

Widdowson, H.G. 1983. *Learning Purpose and Language Use.* Oxford: Oxford University Press.

Widdowson, H.G. 1984. *Explorations in Applied Linguistics 2.* Oxford: Oxford University Press.

Wierzbicka, A. 1985. *Lexicography and Conceptual Analysis.* Ann Arbor, MI: Karoma.

Wierzbicka, A. 1990. ' "Prototypes save": on the uses and abuses of the notion of "prototype" in linguistics and related fields' in S. Tsohatsidis (ed.) *Meanings and Prototypes: Studies in Linguistic Categorization.* London: Routledge.

Wilson, D. and D. Sperber. 1988. 'Representation and relevance' in Kempson, 1988: 133–53.

Wilson, D. and D. Sperber. 1992. 'On verbal irony'. *Lingua,* 87: 53–76.

Wilson, D. and D. Sperber. forthcoming. 'Linguistic form and relevance'. *Lingua* 90: 1–25.

Wittgenstein, L. 1958. *Philosophical Investigations.* Translated by G.E.M. Anscombe. (2nd edition). Oxford: Basil Blackwell.

Author index

Subject index